Mayan Dolls Don't Die

Mayan Dolls Don't Die

Frank Barham

Bridgeview Press
Philadelphia

Copyright 2017 by Frank Barham
All rights reserved according to U.S. Copyright Law
ISBN- 978-0999135334
Contact: Bridgeview Press
920 South Street, Suite 8, Philadelphia, PA 19147

Prologue

IN 1956, the Mexican government granted archeologist Doctor Wyllys Andrews, of Tulane University, New Orleans, Louisiana, permission to excavate Dzibilchaltun, an ancient Mayan site located twelve miles north of Merida, Yucatan, Mexico. The name Dzibilchaltun means place with writing on stones. The importance of this site, which served as home to 40,000 inhabitants, is not well understood. The cultural and economic importance of Dzibilchaltun is still being investigated.

In the base of a temple ruin in the heart of this ancient city, Doctor Andrews found a small room with a shallow well that contained seven humanoid figures made of unfired clay. They ranged from three to seven inches in height. His assistants called these artifacts "dolls." They were possibly dedicated to different gods. However, their true purpose is unknown. Ever since their discovery, the temple ruin, in which they were found, has been called the Temple of the Seven Dolls.

The ruin is only one of several temples in this ritual and administrative center. The important buildings were situated around an expansive plaza in the middle of a jungle clearing spanning hundreds of acres. Among the mix of stone buildings was the king's pyramidal palace and smaller palaces of priests and noblemen. Most of these buildings were stucco-covered and painted multiple colors. Some displayed images of Mayan gods.

Common people lived in oval shaped pole, reed, and palm leaf covered houses in villages scattered around the ritual center.

Why this ancient culture disappeared is not clear. Some experts believe the culture failed because of tribal wars. Others believe the Maya's deforestation of the jungle for wood to burn limestone may have caused climate change. This resulted in droughts and the inability to grow maize, a major dietary staple. Hunger may have led to wars for food and fertile lands.

When priests and rulers could no longer dupe themselves, or their people, into believing leaders were needed to "persuade" the gods to send rain or make crops grow, the priests and kings were no longer needed. Hence, city-state governments fell.

This novel provides a fictional answer for the purpose of the dolls and a look into the lives of the Mayan people who lived in ancient Dzibilchaltun.

The seven dolls are now on display in the Dzibilchaltun museum.

Acknowledgements

I want to thank Yucatan resident Joanne Wyllys, widow of archeologist Doctor Wyllys Andrews, for her personal assistance and the use of Doctor Wyllys' library. I also wish to thank Michael Lindlau for his assistance in preparing the manuscript.

Chapter 1

Dzibilchaltun, Yuca, 1511 AD
(Present Yucatan, Mexico)

Three men and one boy sat quietly in a special room in the Mayan king's palace. The small room's walls contained many life-size images of Mayan gods painted with vivid reds, greens, and blues. The gods' presence rendered the space sacred.

Sitting near the king, the tremulous boy, Hakum, muttered "I'm eleven today. I have to stay. I have to."

The Mayan king squirmed on a Jaguar-skin-covered floor cushion. Over and over, he adjusted his loincloth as the queen's high pitched scream shattered the night and echoed throughout the palace. Trying hard to hide his uneasiness, the king intermittently stared across the room to Larsek, Hakum's father and apprentice master.

Larsek, the first-born male of his family, served as the personal servant to the king. Hakum, the son of Larsek, had trained to serve the king's first son, a prince destined to become the king when the current ruler died.

The flickering flame of an incense torch, which hung near the high priest's feather crown, cast long shadows resembling jumping jungle animals on the stone floor.

Occasionally, the elderly high priest elbowed Hakum and said, "Stay alert, boy."

Preparing for a special ritual, the crossed legged high priest nodded as he prayed, "May it please the gods to send our king a son—a prince."

Due to the potential importance of the impending royal birth, the adults wore authority necklaces of silver and jade nuggets denoting their social and political rank. The priest's necklace contained several gold amulets signifying his exalted status.

Each man wiped rivers of sweat from their faces and bodies.

Responding to the priest's request, Hakum handed him a leather bag then listened as the weathered priest chanted ancient prayers.

Hakum flinched on hearing another distant scream. His eyes widened as he wiped his brow and watched the priest's ritual preparations unfold.

The priest looked at him. "Soon, we will have a new member of the royal family. Let us pray for a prince. The king doesn't need another daughter."

Hakum nodded.

The priest continued, "You should pray the mother does well so she can care for the baby."

"Maybe I will soon begin the privilege for which I have prepared," Hakum said. "I will be the personal servant to a future king."

A prolonged, piercing scream filled the room. With eyelids squeezed shut, Hakum shrugged as if trying to muffle the screams by covering his ears with his shoulders. He shivered with nervousness.

The priest took a handful of dry clay from a leather pouch then crumbled it into a stone bowl painted with figures of lightning bolts. Using a stone pestle, he ground the clay to dust. With a crooked finger, he smoothed the clay, muttered a prayer, and then placed bowl on the floor near his right knee.

Another scream caused Hakum to cover his ears with his hands. Then, the room filled with silence. Hakum held his breath.

Suddenly, echoes of distant shouts filled the palace.

A midwife ran to the waiting males yelling, "It's a prince!"

"The gods have heard my prayers," the king shouted.

Hakum winced as the priest squeezed his shoulder. "Hakum, your ward has arrived. I'll need more clay."

The priest added clay to the bowl. He ground and mixed it in with the first batch until all were a fine powder. He tossed a pinch of it into the air. "See how it floats? It's ready."

Hakum smiled. "What do we do now?"

"We wait."

The king paced along one wall, intermittently staring down a hall to see if his son was being brought to him.

Moments later, the sounds of footsteps echoed from the hall connecting the queen's delivery room to the ritual space where the king waited. A midwife entered, carrying a wiggling bundle in a white blanket stained with blood.

Hakum smiled at the sight of the prince.

The king reached for the prince, but the midwife held the baby toward the priest.

Larsek and the priest bowed at the waist. "Bow

to our king and new prince," the priest said, pushing Hakum's bowed head farther toward the floor. "Thank the gods I have lived to see the birth of a prince. Now, our king has an heir, and the doll ceremony can continue.

The midwife placed the bundled prince onto the floor in front of the priest.

With his head bowed low, Hakum looked sideways at the squirming bundle on the floor. Pushing a corner of the blanket from the baby's face, the prince's tiny fist escaped to grip the air.

Hakum asked, "Will he look like that when he grows up?

The king laughed then said, "No, but he is beautiful."

"All rise," the king said, waving his hands toward the ceiling. "This is an auspicious day. I have a son, and you have a prince." The king fingered his authority necklace, assembled from the authority necklaces of king's who preceded him. "My father would be proud."

Hakum kept his head bowed until the priest sat upright and said, "Sit up, Hakum."

The priest pulled back the flaps of the prince's blanket. For a moment, the odor of warm blood replaced the aroma of the sage torches used to mask the room's smell of mildew and drive away evil spirits.

"How is our queen?" the priest asked the midwife.

"She is resting. As you might imagine, she is tired, but she is well."

"Thank the gods," the priest said then smiled. "She will be able to suckle and care for him."

The king nodded and then knelt. His gold-toed

sandal and long authority necklace scraped the stone floor as he picked up his wailing son to expose the prince's silvery-blue umbilical cord.

The priest held the bowl of powdered clay toward the king who positioned the cord over the bowl. The priest murmured ancient incantations.

"Hakum, hold the bowl," the priest said, placing the bowl in Hakum's trembling hands. "Steady, boy."

The priest grasped the cord and squeezed blood from the cut end where, drop by drop, it fell into the bowl, raising a small puff of dust. "Now place the bowl beside me," the priest said.

The priest removed a stone knife from another leather bag, lifted the blade into the air, and then uttered a prayer in unison with the Most Holy One. The priest cut free the cord, leaving the ligature and stubby end of the cord attached to the baby's belly.

"Hakum," the priest said, "hold out the empty bowl." The priest dropped the severed cord inside then set the bowl on the floor. "The cord will be a future offering to the gods. "Now, give me the bowl of powder."

Hakum held out the bowl along with a thin rod of stone.

The priest mixed the clay powder and blood into a thick brown paste then asked Hakum for the bark book. It contained magic symbols and prayers asking the gods to protect the prince from evil and permit the clay doll, about to be made, to receive the prince's spirit. Holding the bowl between his hands, the priest said a prayer of blessing and then placed it and the book on the floor between him and the king.

"Hakum," the priest said, "we must look for birthmarks, defects, or malformed parts of the prince."

With the eye of a jungle hawk, Hakum and the king scanned the prince's body. The priest asked, "Hakum, what did you find?"

"The prince is missing the fifth toe on the left foot."

The king nodded.

"Correct," the priest said, scooping clay paste from the bowl then modeling it into an anthropomorphic shape resembling the baby's body.

"I'm glad evil spirits stole no more of him," the king said, examining the spot where the toe should be.

"As am I," the priest said, nearing the completion of his molding the clay into a spirit doll. When completed, the priest held up the image so the king could inspect it. He nodded his approval. The priest pinched a bit of clay from the area of the left fifth toe. Nodding to the king, the priest said, "The prince's doll is now as Prince Hiayalael is. He shall forever be known by this name."

The priest placed the doll on the open book then moved close to Hakum and looked him in the eye. "You are to care for this doll as if you were caring for the prince himself. Do you understand? As soon as the air and blood has hardened the clay, you are to take the prince's doll to the temple. There, other priests will perform the sacred spirit rites.

"Yes, High Priest. I understand. I've heard this many times from my father."

The priest asked, "Most Holy One, do you have beads for the prince's authority necklace?"

"I do," the king said as a midwife handed him a leather pouch. From it, the king removed a necklace of braided deer leather. He gave it to the priest who squeezed the last drops of blood from the umbilical cord onto the necklace. He rubbed the blood into the leather and blessed it with an ancient prayer ending with the words, "Never let the prince's authority necklace be questioned or usurped, for he will lose his powers, position, and identity."

The king removed three jade beads, two gold beads and one purple clam shell from the pouch. The priest blessed each item with a prayer then threaded them onto the necklace. He then held the whimpering prince upright so the king could place the too long necklace around the baby's neck.

"My prince," the priest said, "forever wear this necklace as a symbol of your authority."

The priest touched the clay doll with the tip of a crooked finger. "Hakum, it is dry. Take it to the temple."

The Most Holy One picked up the book on which the doll rested and said, "Hakum, entrusting this doll to your care bestows on you a sacred responsibility. Once the priests have completed their ritual, this doll will become one with Prince Hiayalael's spirit. The spirit contained in his blood is forever a part of this doll. The doll is the prince and he is the doll. As long as it is intact, his spirit lives. Do you know how important it is to care for it?"

"Yes, Most Holy One. My father has taught me my duties just as he has performed them for you."

"Good. Take the doll to the temple and then return it to the palace after it has been spiritualized. Keep it safe and let no other person touch it."

Hakum stood and bowed to the king and prince.

Getting the king's attention by coughing, Larsek approached him and bowed. "Most Holy One, with your permission, Hakum and I will deliver the doll to the temple together."

"Then go."

Hakum cradled the book, bearing the doll, in his outstretched hands. He bowed then, taking small, measured steps, he and his father headed for the main temple where a cadre of priests awaited the doll's arrival.

Chapter 2

The jungle surrounds of Dzibilchaltun, Yuca
1530 AD

Near the marketplace, Citu, a seven-year-old orphaned Mayan boy, squinted at the midday sun. *Is this what dying feels like?* He stumbled from tree to tree, feeling weaker and weaker.

Since the day Citu's mother and father were killed by a raiding tribe, he had been fearful of crowds. With only his infirmed *epa*, an aged grandfather to care for him, he had to avoid being taken as a slave or worse—sacrificed.

He whimpered, gripped at the clawing agony in his belly, and then slumped against a Ceiba tree while struggling to stay awake. Crying, he slid down the trunk then fell face first onto the sand, doubled over with pain.

"Mommy," he cried, barely above a whisper. "I don't want to die. I have to help *epa*. I can't let him die." Citu sat up. Stiffened with resolve, he exhaled a long sigh. His head fell backwards against the tree trunk as he gripped his belly. *Oh, to have some of mother's waah bread.*

Hot winds blew through the dying Yucatecan jungle, adding to his misery. The fetid air smothered him and intensified the odors of fish and sweaty men in the nearby marketplace. *I've got to get up. There's food in there.*

Citu forced himself to his feet. Holding onto the Ceiba tree for support, he waited for his head to stop spinning and then staggered toward a fishmonger's stall three hundred paces away. There, men from far inland bartered papayas and mameys for fish.

Citu crept to within a few feet of the stall. Licking his lips, he stared at the brown skinned mameys sticking over the edge of a basket. With a dirty finger in his mouth, he made eye contact with the merchant. "Mister, can I have a mamey?" Staring at the fruit, Citu mumbled, "I'm hungry."

"What?" the scowling merchant asked, barely noticing him. "Speak up, boy."

Citu pointed at the fruit and swallowed hard. "Can I have that little mamey?"

"Got anything to barter?"

"No," Citu said, his gaze dropping to the ground,

"Then go away."

"But—"

"I said go away." The man waved in a shooing motion.

A tear of pain rolled down Citu's cheek as he forced himself toward the next stall. There a man exchanged a papaya for dried fish, which he stuffed into a low hanging shoulder pouch. A piece of one fish tail fell to the ground unnoticed by the man.

Barely avoiding being stepped on by a distracted shopper, Citu crawled past men's ignoring legs, plucked the morsel from the sand and put it in his mouth.

"Out of my way, boy!" a shopper shouted.

Citu cowered, waiting to be kicked, but the man stepped over him and moved on.

Citu used his tongue to separate the fishtail from grit and spat out the sand. He chewed and then swallowed the fragment. *It's salty but tasty,* he said to himself as he watched a fishmonger rearrange his fish while speaking to a salt merchant.

"By the gods," the fisherman said, "I should stay home and eat my fish instead of wasting time here. I have to row farther and farther out to sea to catch anything for bartering. It isn't worth the effort."

Coveting a dried fish, Citu moaned and gripped his belly, but the pressure failed to relieve his pain. He swallowed hard, but the pain continued. *I wish I had just one fish to share with epa.* "Ohhhhhh." Citu groaned in pain as he fought exhaustion.

The salt vendor faced Citu. "What did you say?"

Citu looked away without answering.

Letting a handful of salt run through his fingers, the salt vendor continued to talk to the fish monger. "You're lucky. You can eat your fish." Looking at the cloudless sky, the salt vendor said, "Not since the burial of the sixth king's doll have so few merchants had so little meat or fruits to barter."

Citu stopped in front of another stall displaying mameys. On tiptoes to better see the fruit, his gaze darted from one mamey to another. A small one had been cut, revealing its orange fruit meat. Mustering his courage, he pointed to the cut piece. "Mister, can I have that little piece? My *epa* is sick and needs something to eat."

The merchant ignored Citu, except to shoo him away and continue his conversation.

Wiping his nose with his forearm, Citu said, "Please, can I have some mamey?"

"Go away!" the merchant yelled, backhanding the boy's face.

Citu fell backwards. "You nasty old man!"

Citu collected himself and crawled away.

Two stalls away, a boisterous, dust-covered fishmonger called to a salt vendor. The monger rubbed a craggy mole on his chin as he spoke. Citu crept closer, but the monger saw him and pounded his table. "Get away, boy! You stink." The vendor kicked at Citu.

Using his arms to protect his head, Citu gathered himself and left, shouting over his shoulder, "Your *fish* stink. They're rotten!"

In a half-conscious state of delirium, Citu remembered home and the time when his mother gave him a loincloth for his fourth birthday. He wrapped the garment in place, kissed a thank you on her cheek then watched her make *waah* bread. She handed him a small ball of wet maize and showed him how to pat it flat. She smiled, watching him pat it thinner and thinner. Each time he moved it from one hand to the other his transfers improved. She nodded, indicating the *waah* had reached the proper thinness then pointed to where he should place it on the cooking rock. He could still feel the stone's heat on his hand as he dropped the *waah* onto the hot surface. He remembered smoke blowing in his face. He coughed as he watched bubbles erupt from the top of the *waah*. His mother smiled and hugged him. He watched as her grin spread into a smile on seeing he had cooked his first meal.

Hunger pain brought him back to reality. *I have to try again.* He crept behind an unused stall and scanned several stalls holding barter goods, hoping one would go unattended. One vendor walked to a neighboring stall to talk. This gave Citu his chance to get some food.

Suddenly, the marketplace filled with shouts.

"Stop him! Stop that boy!" An old man yelled and shook his fist at Citu. "He stole my mameys!"

Citu gripped a stolen mamey in each dirty hand. Forcing himself to run, he snaked and bumped his way through small groups of men as he ran toward a path that led into the jungle.

Sensing the old man's legs were weak, Citu felt he could escape. He wearily wove his way between several men then passed the last stall. He felt the eyes of several merchants follow him, but the men did nothing to stop him. He chuckled while his bare feet threw up clouds of reddish dust that caused nearby men to cough and turn away.

For a split second, Citu glanced over his shoulder. The old man struggled to continue his pursuit when his sandal strap broke. Walking backwards, Citu saw the old man hobble and then fall face first to the ground, lost in a cloud of dust.

Citu chuckled when he saw the old man stare at him through the clearing dust.

Citu resumed his run, his long hair and ragged cotton loincloth flapping behind him. Unsure if he had gone far enough to make his getaway, he forced his cramping legs to carry him into the dying jungle. Between panting breaths, he bit into one of the two mameys. Hmmmm. *I'll save the other for epa.*

For a moment, Citu savored the cool, sweet taste of the fruit. He licked his lips while juice dripped from his chin. He stopped chewing long enough to glance over his shoulder. "Good, the old man isn't chasing me anymore." *I need to rest.*

Suddenly, Citu and the mameys flew through the air. "What the—?" He fell hard onto a pile of dry leaves. The fall knocked the wind from his lungs, leaving him gasping. For a moment, a dust cloud surrounded him, momentarily blocking his view of everything. Dizzy, he pushed himself off the ground then spied the shriveled leg of a wrinkled old man sitting in the shade of a nearby rock. The man pulled his walking stick from between Citu's crossed ankles then jabbed it in Citu's side.

"Why did you do that?" Citu asked, rising to his knees.

The man's leathery face yielded a single, brownish upper tooth smile that seemed to say, 'I got you.' The man called to two passersby, "Hold this thief. Don't let him get away."

The men pinned Citu to the ground, making it difficult for him to breathe.

"Let me go," Citu mumbled through tears, wondering if he would be whipped, staked, burned, or stoned as often happened to thieves.

Panting, the elderly mamey owner stumbled onto the scene, carrying his broken sandal. He sat down on a rock and caught his breath. He pointed at Citu and said, "Tie him up. I'm taking him before the king."

"Let me go!" Citu yelled between sobs and weak struggles to escape. "Let me go!"

"Silence!" the old man yelled. "I've seen you sneaking around the market. I know you steal. Everyone knows but not anymore. Not after the king finishes with you."

The men collected tree vines and stripped them of their few leaves.

They're going to tie me up and kill me. I've got to get away. "Let me go," Citu yelled while weakly kicking and squirming. "I'm hungry. Hungry!"

Breathing easier, the mamey owner hobbled to Citu and kicked him in the side. "You're a no good thief. That's what you are."

The men checked the strength of the vines binding Citu's wrists. "You'll not get out of these," one man said.

"On your feet, boy" the mamey owner said, pulling Citu's hair. "You have a meeting with the king."

The old man and the two villagers pulled Citu to his feet. He grunted, struggled, and attempted to kick his captors, but his small size and weakness prevented his escape.

The old man led the way as the assisting men dragged the restive boy toward The Center.

The tops of Citu's toes were raw from being dragged over coarse sand and the white stucco on the mile-long, sacred *sacbe* avenue leading to The Center's palace plaza.

"Let me walk!" Citu cried, trying to get his feet under himself. "You're hurting my feet. Let me walk."

The men dragged the bound boy across Dzibilchaltun's hot, expansive whitewashed plaza and then stopped at the foot of a building the height of which equaled that of twenty men.

"Uh oh," Citu muttered, scanning the area. A large brownish-red blotch, several paces away, stained the plaza's white-washed floor. *This is the place where they'll kill me.*

A few feet ahead, two guards held a bound,

slumped, and frightened looking man.

A fierce looking man at the top of the building bellowed to the guards holding the man. "Bring him here."

The guards dragged the whimpering man up the pyramid's steps to the first terrace then forced him to his knees.

Citu gasped on seeing how roughly the guards treated the man.

The shouting official at the top of the building pointed to the kneeling prisoner then called to villagers gathered at the foot of the pyramid, "This man has been found guilty of theft and lying to the elders." The official then addressed the king who stood nearby. "This prisoner asks for mercy."

The king walked close to the edge of the top terrace. He faced the prisoner and yelled, "I grant your request for mercy. You will not die, thief. Guards, cut out his tongue and sew his lips shut for lying. Then, cut off his hands for stealing. He is then free to go."

Citu caught his breath then whimpered, "That's what they're going to do to me."

The old man holding Citu raised his hand to protect his eyes from sunlight reflected from nearby whitewashed buildings. He looked toward the upper terrace of the pyramid and called to the king's official. "Hakum, honorable servant to our king!"

Wearing a small crown of yellow feathers and a green loincloth, Hakum's oiled chest muscles shined as he walked to the edge of the pyramid's upper terrace. He stared down at the old man.

He must be important, Citu thought. *He's the one who is going to kill me.*

"What is your need?" Hakum asked, striking his chest with both fists and extending his elbows at right angles to his body.

"Who is he?" Citu asked the old man while trying to free himself.

"Quiet, boy!" The old man said, shaking Citu. "Can't you see he holds his elbows out from his side? He's the king's personal servant. Treat him with respect."

"We beg council with the king," the old man yelled then bowed his head while smoothing his shabby leather loincloth lifted by a gust of hot wind. *Wish I hadn't lost my sandal. This plaza burns my feet.*

Hakum yelled, "What matter do you bring before the Most Holy One, old man?"

The old man pushed Citu to his knees. "I seek judgment on this thief. He stole my goods."

"Wait there," Hakum shouted. "I will inquire of The Most Holy One."

Hakum spoke to the man who wore a white loincloth with shiny pieces of gold. His crown made from long, turquoise colored *quetzal* feathers made him appear to be as tall as two men. His square face glowed like gold in the light reflected from a broad gold disc on his necklace.

The two men guarding Citu bowed on seeing the man with the gold face.

"Bow," the old man said, shaking Citu. "That's the king—the Most Holy One."

He's the one who will kill me, Citu thought, fear shaking its way through his limbs, leaving him visibly trembling.

"Who are you? What do you want, old man?"

the king yelled.

Head bowed, the old man yelled, "I am Maku, Most Holy One, a fisherman turned farmer. This boy stole two mameys, Most Holy One. They were my family's only food."

The king faced the growing crowd on the plaza then yelled, "Boy. What is your name?"

"Citu," the boy yelled, holding his chin high. Maku slapped Citu's head.

"Ouch!" Citu said, staring Maku in the eye and jerking at his bindings. "Why did you do that?"

"You should say *Most Holy One* when you speak to the king."

"Citu is my name, *Most Holy One*."

"Where is your family?"

"Dead, Most Holy One."

"Then why are you no one's slave?"

"I always stay close my *epa*. He lives near here. Before mother died, she said I needed to look after him. He's old and blind. He says he's dying."

Maku twisted Citu's ear as the boy yelled, "Most Holy One! Sorry."

The king spoke to Hakum who then entered the palace.

The king pointed at Citu. "Hunger grants no right to another man's goods. You have confessed your guilt, and guilt calls for penalties. Men have died for less serious crimes." The king shook his finger at Citu.

That's it, Citu thought. *He's going to kill me.* Citu prepared himself to hear his sentence. He slumped, wondering if he would be stoned, stabbed, strangled, or thrown into a hole to starve. *Will I die slow or fast? I hope fast like when father cut that monkeys' throat for food.*

Hakum returned with a shiny bow and a long arrow. He handed both to the king.

Citu thought, *He's going to kill me with an arrow.*

The king raised the bow, pulled the arrow and string into the ready position, and then sighted along the arrow pointed at Citu.

Citu stared at the arrowhead and tried to swallow, but it felt like swallowing cotton.

"Maku, pull the boy upright," the king yelled as he sighted along the arrow.

Using Citu's matted hair, Maku pulled the boy upright.

Citu took a deep breath, held it, and squeezed his eyelids shut. Suddenly, fear overtook his crumbling courage. He cried out, "Please don't kill me." He burst into tears, crying, "Mommy!"

A swooshing sound filled the air and instantly everything went quiet.

Citu thought he had gone to the gods, for he felt no pain. Waiting a moment, he opened his eyes and looked down to see blood running from below the arrow sticking from his chest, but there was no arrow. No blood. He suddenly became aware of a fading vibrating sound that came from a narrow strip of earth in front of him. The spent arrow had half-buried itself in the ground. For a moment, Citu stared at the juddering arrow. With little courage to muster, he slumped against the strength of the vines held by Maku and wept, shaking with relief.

"Let this be a lesson!" the king yelled. "Do not be brought before me again. This day, I order you to labor for Maku for two days in payment for his mameys."

Maku released Citu's hair.

Citu sighed then smiled. *They're not going to kill me.*

"Maku," the king yelled, "where are the fruits?"

"Most Holy One, they are half-eaten and lie where they fell when a justice-seeking villager tripped this thief."

For a moment, the king stood silently. "Maku, the mameys are now the property of Citu, in exchange for his labor."

"But Most Holy One, I have no work for this thief. My farm is dead."

"Find him work!" the king yelled. "I order it!"

Maku shook Citu and mumbled under his breath. "Get away from me you useless . . ." Sneering, Maku revealed his toothless gums as he flicked his unkempt pony tail from his face and turned toward the assisting villagers. "Untie him."

Freed, Citu ran from the plaza as fast as his weak legs would carry him.

He's a good king, Citu thought. *Someday, I will honor him, but where are those mameys? I've got to get one to epa.*

Shaking his head, the king returned to the coolness of his stonewalled library. *Unbelievable. Children stealing because of hunger. How could I not know of such a drought?* He walked to a window then looked out over the plaza. For as far as he could see there were stucco covered temples and palaces. *We are too low to see jungle.*

A servant had just slid one of the king's books into a niche holding other sacred documents.

"Careful with that, you idiot!" the king yelled and

walked to the niche. "There," he said, aligning the book's end with other books. "Bark books are fragile."

The queen put down the book she read and stared at her husband with her permanently crossed eyes. A descendant of the Olmec, she had a nose broader and flatter than the hooked nose of the Maya. "Bulek, why are you so upset? It's just a book."

"It's a sacred book," he said. "The book of prophesy."

The king picked up his favorite floor cushion bearing the image of the feathered god-man, Quetzalcoatl. After fluffing it, he placed the pillow beside the queen and sat down.

He caught Hakum's gaze. "Tell me about this shortage of food mentioned by that boy."

Taking small steps toward the king, Hakum bowed his head and spoke softly, "Most Holy One, this discussion is not for your ears."

"The truth," the king said, his face twisted with curiosity as he stared at Hakum. "I know I am isolated from many things, but I want the truth. Spare me nothing. I need to know the problems of the kingdom. Do my people go hungry?"

Hakum glanced at the floor for a moment then whispered, "Most Holy One, we have spoken of the lack of rain."

"Speak up, Hakum! I can't hear you. Is there a drought?"

Hakum raised his head and cleared his throat. "Yes, Most Holy One. The scant rainfall of this year's hot rainy season has dwindled as it has in previous years, but more so this year. Animals, dependent on the jungle's vegetation, moved south into more verdant areas of Yuca. Their migration costs the Maya a major food source. Crops wither and die. There are few fruits or animals in our jungle. The people eat only fish, but even they are scarce during this phase of the moon and calendar date."

"Why have I not heard of this?" The king yelled. "Do you or my people believe me too weak or unconcerned to hear of their need or act on their behalf? Don't they know I do more than appease the gods, so they will send the morning sun and favor our crops?"

Hakum crept closer to his master's side and looked into his face. "The people do not want you or the royal family to hear of this. It is our duty to care for the royals—not burden them."

The king stared out a doorway, sighed, and wiped at a thin thread of sweat that had washed away some of his golden makeup. "Their love is great, but I can't help them if their problems are kept from me."

"But, Most Holy One, neither you nor the queen can order the skies to rain," Hakum said defensively as he walked to the door and pointed at the cloudless sky.

"You speak truth," the king said, waving, "but the gods can ordain rain. I must speak with them." Arms behind his back, he paced and then stopped to face Hakum. "Plan with the high priest. Make preparations when the signs are right. Then I'll travel to speak with the gods."

"Bulek, careful what you say," the queen said. "That kind of trip is more than a simple finger prick for a drop of blood. It involves serious bloodletting."

Hakum looked perplexed as he turned his palms toward the ceiling. "Most Holy One, you should not speak so lightly of such a trip."

"The trip is not one I wish to make, but it is one I must take. It is my duty. Only I can appease the rain gods." The king waved his hand toward the door. "Go, Hakum. Make the plans." *Don't the gods know I have prayed and performed the daily rituals in their temples? Did they not hear me? Have they ignored me?*

The king took a few seeds from a basket and took them to a reed cage where he kept multicolored jungle birds as pets. "Here, my beautiful friends." He dropped the seeds into the cage. "Sing for me. I need your soothing song."

The king knew the pain and danger he would soon endure. He wanted to flee but fell onto his pillows, emitting a long sigh as the birds sang and the queen caressed his head.

Chapter 3

"What?" the king asked.

"Most Holy One," Hakum whispered. "Wake up. Your most humble servant informs his king that Ah Kinchil, the supreme sun god, rises. It is time for your trip."

Hakum tied open the twelve cotton door-panels covering the doorways to the king's private quarters. For luck, each cloth had a painted image of a Mayan god such as: Chac, the rain god; Ah Mun, god of maize and vegetation, Itzamná; chief of all gods, Ixchel, god of fertility; Kinich Ahau, sun god, and Kukulcan, god of learning.

After stretching his arms, the naked king rubbed sleep from his eyes then stood. "Get my hair binder and authority necklace."

The king yawned then said, "Does the queen still sleep?"

"She sleeps with the children, Most Holy One. Should I awaken her?"

"No. She avoids worry when she sleeps."

"Your announcement about the sun is comforting," the king said, noting the first rays of sunlight entering his bedroom. "The gods have blessed us with another day. Make everything ready for my offering."

The treasures strung on the king's necklace sparkled in the sunlight as Hakum placed it around the king's neck then centered the largest and rarest purple clam shell in Yuca on the king's chest.

"Most Holy One, the ritual bath is ready. Chekar prepared it with the sacred waters from Lake Xlacah."

Hakum handed the king his crown. The king placed it on his head and prayed. *Gods give me courage to do what I must for my people and you. Give us rain.* "Hakum, tie my loin cloth."

The king visited Dzibilchaltun's calendar building before starting his trip. The Mayan long count calendar, carved in a circular stone, read 11.15.12.0.18 (1532 AD). The king asked the scribes who maintained the stone if the date was favorable for his blood sacrifice.

"It is Most Holy One. The gods will bless you."

The king returned to his palace then prepared himself for a major ritual to honor Chaac, god of water, and propitiate the peoples' need for rain and ask *Yum Kax,* god of corn, to bless the people with new crops.

"Hakum," the king called and pointed to a niche containing a richly embroidered leather bag. "Clothe my spirit doll for a day of sacrifice then take it to the temple and place it on its pedestal. I want the people to see it and know my spirit is with them while I travel."

The king walked onto his terrace and watched the brilliant red morning sun creep over the temples along the eastern boundary of the plaza. Between two distant buildings, he could see several white gourds, which had once hung from leafy tree limbs to collect dew. Locals had poured this water on their gardens to promote growth. Unfortunately, the drought had left few leaves on which dew could form.

The high priest, waiting at the foot of the palace, bowed on seeing the king standing on his terrace.

The king thought, *Let me be strong before this priest.*

Dressed in full regalia, the king descended the palace steps, gripping the wide gold clasps at the neck of his robe. The clasps held prized sea shells and gold images of the corn god. Hakum carried the robe's train so it would not be dragged down ninety steps.

"The Most Holy One approaches," the high priest announced to his entourage who bowed and chanted a prayer.

Heading into the jungle, the king prayed in concert with the low murmurings of the richly robed high priest and acolytes. As the troupe made its way toward the Cave of the Underworld, their incantations rose skyward along with sandal-stirred dust.

With palms toward the sky, the high priest waved his wand and prayed, "Oh gods of the sky, jungle, and underworld, banish evil from our path. Bless our king who travels this day. Accept his holy offering. Grant us, and our people, your holy blessings."

The Most Holy One walked behind the priests praying, *Gods, give me strength to stay this course and courage to make my sacrifice.*

The group trod a path worn smooth by thousands of commoners' bare feet and noblemen's leather sandals. It wound its way through dense, dry underbrush and around rocks long ago exposed by harsh winter winds.

An elderly chanting shaman wore a jaguar skin and carried a clay smoke-pot containing embers for burning sacred plants. He swung the pot, creating a thin trail of sweet smelling, prayer imbued, smoke that spiraled skyward to the home of gods.

Rounding a tall outcrop of rocks, the group encountered several in-land farm boys carrying back-baskets of fruits to be bartered in Dzibilchaltun. The boys placed their baskets on the ground and knelt, faces in the dust. One boy held up a mamey for the king. Hakum broke rank, took the fruit, and thanked the boy. The boys then rose and went on their way.

The king thought, *I think I've seen that boy before. Citu?*

The king repeatedly said to himself, *Gods get me through this ceremony. Help me do it with honor.* With his face to the sky, the king chanted, "We acknowledge the spirits who protect this entourage. In supplication, we approach the Cave of the Underworld, the sacred place of sacrifice with humility."

The king felt shocked on seeing the cave. *Why must the gods withhold drink to even this sacred area?*

The edges of the cave's mouth had once been a sight of floral beauty, but now it displayed only withered vines, exposed roots and two green leafs. A semi-circular stone terrace marked the ceremonial area in front of the opening. The shape of the terrace mirrored the cave's opening. Viewed together, they mimicked a toothy open mouth.

The priests dropped offerings of seeds while the retinue cooled themselves with fans. They stood in a semicircle along the edge of the terrace, shifting their weight under the blazing sun.

In reaction to the groups' presence, the twits, howls, and grunts of the jungle's remaining inhabitants reached a crescendo and then hushed.

Smoke pot in hand, the high priest raised it to the cardinal directions. "Gods, banish evil spirits that obstruct our way to the Cave of the Underworld and there accept the offering of our Most Holy One. May the heavens send rain to nourish our lands."

Hakum handed the king a gourd of water to quench his thirst. With hands shaking with fear, he drank more than half its contents. *My mouth is as dry as the jungle.*

The priests chanted, "Holy cave, permit us to pass into your sacred belly, the wellspring of your sacred stream and path to the underworld. May it carry my offering to the sky gods ruling rain.

The high priest lighted four torches. He made a tall smoke circle then stepped through it like an animal stepping over a tree limb. The king followed. Torchbearers passed on either side of the king and stood in two parallel lines, creating a living channel through which the dignitaries would pass to enter the cave.

Two forward torchbearers illuminated the dark, narrow path while other torch bearers were dispersed among the group.

Thank the gods. It's cool inside, the king thought.

The group pushed their way through long tree roots, dangling from the cave's vault. Ancient prayers and chants rumbled through the fetid cave, reverberated, and returned as mournful echoes. Irritated by the pervasive smell of mildew, nostrils ached for fresh air.

Inching over narrow passages with low ceilings and slippery stones, the group reached the Holy of

Holies and its pool. The entourage removed their sandals under the flickering light of torches reflected in the sacred pool. From the distant depth of the cave came the roar of a sacred underground waterfall. Legends say it falls the height of one hundred men then disappears into an underground river that flows to the after world. The home of the gods.

"Listen to the gods' roar," the king said. "They bid us welcome."

The king prostrated himself on the damp floor. With arms extended alongside his head, he recited ritual prayers. His thoughts turned to his father and his father's father who had lain on this floor during their reign. *Had they been as filled with fear as me? Did they wish to flee as I do?*

Four priests assisted him to stand then led him to the edge of the pool. They bowed to him then each other. The king held his arms away from his sides, allowing the high priest to undress him. The priest murmured a prayer over each item ritually removed then handed to an acolyte.

A shiver of anxiety moved through the king's limbs as he glimpsed his nude, sweating body glistening in the torchlight and reflected in the forty-foot-pool. He took a deep breath then placed each foot onto one of two flat stones in the shallow end of the pool.

The high priest made a smoke offering to the gods then said, "Bring the sacred leaf."

The king stiffened his legs and said to himself, *I must do this.*

The shaman held out a banana leaf for the high priest to unfold. He removed a thin, obsidian knife two hand widths in length. He held it for everyone to see then placed it in the king's right hand.

The king fingered the blade's sharp, knapped and shiny edge then turned it over in his hand, assessing its surface. After repositioning his grip on the blade several times, he found a spot where its handle felt comfortable in his hand.

With his left hand, he grasped the upper and lower sections of his foreskin. Forcing them together, he stretched the skin away from his penis. Steeled for pain, the king placed the knifepoint against the top layer of foreskin and took a deep breath. With a single, rapid thrust, he pushed the blade through both layers of skin. The searing pain felt like a burning torch had been pushed into his groin. His only thought was to remove the knife to stop the pain, but as his shaking hand withdrew the blade, the horrific pain returned, leaving a finger width slit in each side of his foreskin.

The king's sacred blood fell into the pool, dispersing into a large blood-stained area of sanctified water. He panted as he struggled to keep the punctures aligned. Squatting, he rinsed the knife, stood, and then handed the blade to the high priest. The priest replaced the knife in its leaf.

The shaman presented another folded leaf to the high priest who unfolded it and removed the *kij,* a sacred rope containing three knots spaced six finger breadths apart. The priest presented the rope to the king as another ritual prayer was muttered.

Shaking, the king grasped one end of the forearm-length-rope and raised it toward the ceiling. *Gods, help me.* Murmuring an incantation, he forced a short length of the bees' waxed end of the rope though the foreskin holes then paused to allow the pain to subside. He gritted his teeth, held his breath, and then moaned as the bleeding increased.

Stiffening his legs, he curled his toes as if clawing the stones on which he stood. Through clenched teeth, he sucked air, making a loud slurping sound. He grasped each end of the bloody rope and drew it back and forth through his stretched foreskin. Dissolving tendrils of blood colored the sacred pool. As each knot passed through the slits, he moaned and trembled.

As the circle of crimson water grew in size, the priests chanted until the requisite blood had flowed.

The king thought, *Gods help me do my duty.*

Suddenly, a strong, disquieting gush of wind rushed from the depths of the cave, extinguishing all the torches.

Shocked, the king shouted, "What?" *I have never felt such darkness. Are the gods displeased? Have I offended them?* Forgetting his pain for a moment, he called out. "Oh gods, make us not blind by taking our light! Be not displeased with my offering!"

The high priest and assistants chanted as someone lit a torch from the embers in the smoke pot. Soon, all the torches were relit.

All eyes fell on the king.

He wondered what the group expected of him. Perplexed, he looked to his entourage for reassurance and guidance. *Do they and the gods want more blood?*

The king pulled the rope through his foreskin with great vigor. As he bled, he held his breath and scrunched his face. The holes grew larger. After a few minutes, he uttered a thunderous roar of pain and pulled the bloody rope from his foreskin. His knees shook from pain and fear—fear the gods were not satisfied.

He felt dizzy as he knelt to wash the rope and

his hands in the sacred pool. He shivered as he handed the rope to the high priest. Suddenly, he slumped forward, almost falling into the pool but forced himself upright and took a deep breath. He saw the high priest's hands shaking with what the king thought to be worry for his king. Another wave of dizziness struck him, forcing him to place his wet hand on the high priest's shoulder to steady himself. *Oh gods, do not take my day. My people must not see me fall. Do not leave me in the dark of death's sleep in this holy place.*

"Bring the *Ek' Balam* tree resin," the high priest shouted. "I need it to stop his bleeding."

Recovered, the king grasped his foreskin and applied pressure to the wounds. He rubbed the foul smelling brown salve on the holes then forced the salve inside. Only he could perform this act. Not even the high priest should come in contact with the king's sacrificial blood. To do so would deny the gods the offering.

"Hummmm," the king murmured then arched backwards on seeing his bleeding had stopped.

From his crown, he pulled a feather then dropped it into the bloody pool while uttering a prayer. "Float like a boat upon the waters. Carry this offering to the gods below and above."

The feather, a sign of subservience, bobbed gently on the slow moving water, flowing toward the incessant roar of the distant waterfall.

Making their way to The Center, the king's group sang songs of thanksgiving.

Periodically, the high priest prayed the gods would accept the offering made by the Most Holy One and send rain.

The high priest stepped aside, letting other men pass until the shaman approached.

The priest pulled the shaman aside then whispered, "I pray the gods are not displeased. I fear the breath that extinguished our torches carried a grave message. I'm afraid our king has lost the favor of the gods.

"Are you suggesting we need a new king?"

"No, but I pray Chaac accepts the king's second offering."

"High priest, I hear your concern and join your prayer. I still feel that cold, foreboding wind on my skin. I hope the gods did not blow their wrath."

"What if they did?"

Chapter 4

The king entered the plaza and surveyed the encircling temples, his palace and those of the noblemen. *How beautiful the buildings are today.* He headed toward the Temple of the Six Dolls. Climbing the western steps, his head swirled, and he felt faint. He paused and leaned forward to support himself on an outstretched arm. *Gods, don't strike me with sleep here.*

Startled by the sudden recurrence of the strange dizziness, he recovered then made his way to the temple's upper terrace. He walked inside the small square room in the middle of the terrace. With trembling hands, he removed his spirit doll from its pedestal then handed it to the high priest who had followed him up the steps. "Send my doll to the palace." Shaking, he said, "High Priest, I need your help."

"You shake. Are you alright, My King?"

"I am … with the god's help. I must tell the people of my sacrifice."

The high priest called to the conch men, "Call the villagers."

Out of respect, the people on the plaza turned their back as the king removed his clothes and walked, nude, to the temple's eastern terrace. There he would perform a ritual bath facing the morning home of the sun god. The sacred water would be poured over his head and body with the assistance of acolytes and the high priest.

As more villagers gathered on the western plaza, the king completed the bath but felt weak. *That feeling of dizziness hovers over me.* The king grasped the priest's arm to steady himself.

The acolytes dried him then dressed him in a leather loincloth covered with gold images of the gods. He donned his authority necklace and feathered robe. The high priest set the quetzal-feather crown on the king's head. The priests placed gold bracelets on each of the king's outstretched arms. Hakum placed the king's sandals on his feet then wrapped their laces around his legs and tied them below the knee.

The king and the high priest returned to the western side of the temple where the priest addressed the crowd. "The Most Holy One has performed the sacred sacrifice. Holy waters carry his blood offering on the sacred river to the gods."

The crowd slapped their thighs in appreciation and roared their gratitude. For a moment, the plaza buzzed with comments like, "Now, we'll have rain."

The king called to his people, "May my sacrifice please the gods and bring benefit to our people. Go home. Complete my ritual with your offering of a fish to the earth gods. Let each family sacrifice so the earth is prepared for Chac's offering of rain. Prepare and wait."

The crowd shouted, slapped their thighs, and then raised their arms in adoration. They uttered a ritual prayer then dispersed to make the required sacrifice of fish.

Two moon cycles had passed since the king's sacrifice. Despite his calm outward appearance, he worried over his ability to cause the sun god to rise each morning or persuade the gods to send sky water. He wondered if he had done too little to coax rain from the ancients and fretted over what more he could do. He read holy books of prophesy and prayed several times a day, asking the gods for guidance. His family and culture depended on the successful execution of his ritual duties.

Now he luxuriated in the coolness of the palace's thick walled dining hall while waiting for the high sun meal. One corner of the fifteen-pace-long rectangular dining hall served as a performance space for the soft music of a flute player. His instrument, carved by his long dead father, provided lilting sounds that soothed the king's troubled mind.

The room echoed with the sounds of conversation among waiting royals and nobles. The sweet fragrance of incense, wafted about by warm breezes, added to the festive atmosphere under a vaulted ceiling long ago painted with colorful images of the gods.

Only certain people were invited to attend the king's communal meal: Queen Ix Tzutz Nik, *known* for her beauty and crossed eyes; Princess Sac-Nicte (the first born child) age six, mature beyond her years, and the family clown; Princess Sazilakab (the second princess) age five and strangely distant; Prince Hiayalael (the firstborn son and King-in-Waiting), age four, the most physically active of the children. Prince Itzamná (second son), barely one year old, was physically disabled.

"Where is my prince, my beloved Hiayalael,"

the king asked, his gold bracelets rattling as he extended his arms in anticipation of his son's arrival.

Prince Hiayalael ran into the king's arms. He still wore skull-flattening boards tied to his shaved head. They had already produced a demonstrable amount of skull elongation and would be removed after another full sun cycle.

The queen, nursing her younger son, conversed with the high priest who sat beside her and picked at red berries in a basket. He often shared the high sun meal with the family, sitting beside the king and providing political advice. He received his position through inheritance and the blessing of the Most Holy One.

The king overheard the queen ask the high priest, "Did the gods send any signals of their intention following the king's sacrifice?"

"Yes, My Queen, the gods accepted the king's offering." The comment caused the king to smile. The priest dropped a berry in his mouth then said, "We will soon be blessed with rain. I expect nothing less in exchange for such a great sacrifice. I am also happy to hear the heat, swelling, and pain have left the king's wounds."

"Yes, his healing is nearly complete," the queen said, watching her oldest son dart about the dining room. He ran giggling, wanting to play with anyone who would toss him his rubber ball.

"Look how he runs," the high priest said, smiling and pointing at the boy whose bare feet sounded like appreciative slapping of thighs as he ran. "Youth is such a wonderful thing."

"I'm sorry he makes such a distraction," the king said. "Prince Hiayalael, sit with me and be quiet.

Allow us to talk."

"Don't worry for me," the high priest said.

The queen rubbed her youngest son's clubbed left foot. "I wish my second son could run with his brother. They could have so much fun."

"I'm sure you and the king are disappointed Hakum's wife's recent delivery produced another daughter. Our prince has no servant to care for him as Hakum cares for the king."

The king smiled then said, "Next time."

The second prince, Itzamná, rested quietly in his mother's lap. The king remembered what the high priest said at the boy's birth. "The prince's club foot was caused by evil spirits that surrounded our queen during her pregnancy. The presence of only one deformity is a sign evil spirits penetrated only a short distance into her womb before being kicked out by the prince's other foot."

"You are lucky to have such beautiful daughters," the high priest said to the king while nodding toward the oldest princess who fingered her long hair and sat quietly beside her mother.

"If our first child had to be a daughter, we could not have asked for a greater gift than Sac-Nicte," the king said. "She will make some nobleman a great wife and mother to his many children."

"Yes," the high priest said. "Her mother has served as a great example."

"Mayan culture provides a queen only minor roles in governance," the king said, "but I confide in my queen and often ask her opinion. She is my confidant and only wife—even though I could have many."

"My King. My Queen. Each of you is lucky to have the other," the priest said, "as you are to have

Princess Sac-Nicte."

The king looked upon Princess Sac-Nicte as a special gift from the gods. She made the king and queen laugh. At the age of nine months, she walked and spoke. At the age of twenty-seven months, she helped care for her year old sister.

To the high priest, the queen repeated the story of how Princess Sac-Nicte had burst into the room where her mother awaited Sazilakab's delivery. "Appearing perplexed, Sac-Nicte grabbed her father's hand as I cried out with each contraction. He picked her up and hugged her. Staring into his eyes, she asked, 'Daddy, why is mommy crying?' Bulek told her, 'Mommy is going to have a baby. Soon, you will have a new brother or sister.' I remember Sac-Nicte seemed lost in thought for a moment and then started to squirm. She said. 'Put me down, Daddy.' Bulek must have thought she wanted to leave the room, so he shook his head in surprise on seeing her walk to my side and take my hand. 'Don't cry, mommy. We'll send it back if you don't want it.'"

The king and high priest shared a hearty laugh on rehearing story.

The king nudged the high priest. "Look upon my queen. Is she not the most beautiful and loving woman in Dzibilchaltun?"

"Bulek," the high priest said, "you are blessed with such a striking queen and children. The gods be praised."

"Yes, the gods be praised . . . save for Sazilakab," the king said, a note of sadness in his voice. "She never expresses emotion and prefers solitude. All day, she sits quietly playing with that smooth stone. She dislikes textured things, never laughs and often bursts into screaming tantrums." Pointing to a wooden doll, the king said, "She seems overly attached to that toy—carries it everywhere. I wish things were different with her."

Princess Sazilakab wore an eye-crossing-bead that swung from a quill held in place by a head band. The bead dangled in front of her large nose to help her develop crossed eyes, a condition the Maya considered beautiful.

"How is your family?" the queen asked the high priest, his authority necklace rattling against the floor as he reached for a berry. "I hear your wife expects another child."

"Yes, the gods are giving. The child arrives in four moons."

The priest had one son, three daughters, and a male lover who lived with the family.

Looking toward a doorway, the king said, "I think I hear the servants."

Kitchen servants, carrying bamboo trays of food, waited outside a dining room door. Hakum brought the food inside and served the king, and then the Prime Prince.

Hakum said, "Most Holy One, today you drink your favorite maize-mush, sweetened with honey, and you eat a fish, a chick, and fruits from distant jungles."

"Perhaps we should have let this chick live," the king chuckled. "With time, it might have fed four guests."

The king took a bite of seared chick smeared with fruit pulp then addressed an elderly nobleman. "Meno, tell me about the sale of salt."

The slightly deaf Meno needed the question repeated. He then informed the king about excess salt stores.

"Too bad," the king said. "Is smoking now used to preserve meat instead of salt?"

"No, Most Holy One. There is no meat."

The king thought, *I don't want to hear any more about this drought and no food for animals. Did the gods not hear my plea? Accept my blood?*

Turning to nobleman Amus, the king asked, "How goes our trade with Ticul?"

"Most Holy One, we do some trade, but even their crops are poor. Their fruits are small. They need rain as much as we."

The king looked at the mamey in his hand, took a bite, and said, "Hmmm. It's tasty but small. Is it from Ticul?"

"Yes, Most Holy One," Amus said apologetically, "It's the best we can barter."

"Most Holy One, the drought has also affected our cotton," nobleman Xium said. "There is little of it, and it's quality is poor."

"Fear not," the king said, swirling his gold cup of mush. "Rain is on the way." He looked around. Most of the diners had finished eating. "Listen all. I have news."

The king clapped and pointed toward a doorway. All eyes watched as Hakum held back its cloth door. In stepped the king's doctor.

"High Priest," the Most Holy One said, "come kneel before me."

The room filled with chatter.

Appearing surprised, the high priest obeyed, kneeling on a cushion covered with images of the feathered god.

The king raised his hands for silence. "Today our high priest celebrates his fifty-fifth year. Twenty-two sun cycles ago, he was a young priest. He officiated at the spiritualization of my doll. He has well served his king. This day, the priest's service is honored by the Most Holy One with these gifts." *But I wish his prayers had been more fervent so I didn't have to make that sacrifice.*

From the doctor, the king accepted a bundle and from it removed two dark-green jade earplugs, three fingerbreadths in diameter. Holding them high, the king said, "If they were any larger, they would be for a king, and I'd have to surrender my throne." As the group laughed, the king continued, "I have asked the doctor to enlarge the high priest's ear holes so he can wear these new plugs."

The king lifted the priest's bowed head then pushed from his ear lobes the old plugs.

While the doctor cut and stretched the priest's earlobes, the quietly wincing priest gripped the painted pillow on which he knelt. The doctor then forced the new plugs into the enlarged and bleeding holes.

The priest hummed a song of thanksgiving, apparently to cover his pain.

"The stretch of skin over the new plugs will stop your bleeding," the doctor said, blotting blood from the priest's left ear.

After the plugs were in place, the king grabbed the high priest's shoulders. "Stand so all may see my recognition."

The diners slapped their thighs as the high priest walked past each guest and bowed, so they could see the gift. The priest, pursued by Hakum trying to blot a drop of blood from the priest's left ear, returned to the king's position and bowed.

"Thank you, My King, for this great tribute. You

have honored not only me but my family."

The king raised his hand. "Speak no more of this."

"Bring more mush for everyone," the king said to Hakum.

The celebration stopped as Hakum ran back to the dining room yelling. "Most Holy One, a runner from Chalmuch has arrived. He has run for three days and nights to bring news of a battle and great losses!"

The diners gasped.

The king leaped to his feet wounded by the news. "No. This can't be. Their king is our friend." The Most Holy One shook his head and said, "Give the runner drink then bring him before me. I'm anxious to hear his message. Bring him."

A small, dark-skinned man, covered with dust and sweating profusely, staggered into the room then collapsed at the feet of the king.

The diners were shocked into silence at seeing the exhausted man.

With head bowed, the runner delivered his message between gasps for breath and gulps of water offered by Hakum. "Most Holy One . . . King Makuk bids you . . . great fortune . . . and asks your assistance." The runner slurped more water and swallowed hard. "Our village has been attacked . . . and burned by King Slubkah. Many villagers have been killed and our food stores stolen."

"What sacrilege!" the Most Holy One said.

Catching his breath, the runner said, "Our survivors will die without those stores. King Makuk asks you to join him in retrieving the food. He will share it and any plunder in equal portions. Most Holy One, will you help us?"

"You may sit," the king said. "When did this

happen?"

The runner pushed himself upright. "Four sunrises before today, Most Holy One, while we slept. King Makuk and his queen escaped the palace at first light. They, and a few villagers, have taken shelter in the jungle."

"How many men attacked you?"

"King Makuk believed they numbered 150 or more, Most Holy One."

"King Slubkah is known for his acquisitiveness and willingness to kill anyone who obstructs his greed," the Most Holy One said. "We have fought him in the past. He is an evil ruler."

"How many men are with King Makuk?"

"Forty-three, Most Holy One."

"Where is King Slubkah now?"

"One of our guards saw his men traveling south—toward his village."

"What of your village women and children?"

"Most are dead," the runner said and then sobbed.

"Some . . . my wife and first daughter were taken, Most Holy One."

The high priest gasped.

Hakum said, "Most Holy One, with your permission, I will summon the village chiefs to the palace."

"Do it!" the king said, striking his palm with his fist. "Let the conch summon them then see to the runner's needs. Bathe and feed him. Have him wait for the reply of my council."

The high priest left the dining room trying to adjust the king's gifted ear plugs and thinking, *Was he trying to embarrass me with this gift? Does he think they will negate the ill will between us? If I wasn't afraid of bleeding, I would return them now.*

Chapter 5

The dying sun hung low in the purple sky when the elderly Chief Sukok of Sukok Village presented himself at the king's palace. Several hours later, three more chiefs arrived from Dzibilchaltun's distant villages.

Hakum escorted the chiefs to the council room where they sat on pillows painted with images of jaguars, the personal god of the king. Flickering yellow torch flames changed the color of the chiefs' face paint to various shades of grey—the color of funerals.

The chiefs discussed the information provided by King Makuk's runner. After deliberating, they would present recommendations to the Most Holy One about joining Makuk's revenge battle.

Hakum listened as Village Chief Cekmuk proposed men from Dzibilchaltun's four tribes join King Makuk in fighting the rebel king. "We must help King Makuk," Cekmuk stuttered, "but I fear King Slubkah's village will need more food, and he will come for ours, so we must make them fear us."

Village Chief Dzilmak paced as he spoke. "Cemuk, we can defend *our* stores. Why risk losing men in a battle because of King Makuk's weakness and lack of vigilance?"

"Chiefs," Hakum said, "you must focus on the question. Can we . . . should we . . . assist King Makuk? We need to advise the Most Holy One soon."

"Perhaps King Makuk isn't weak," Village Chief Xcanmut said, slapping the air. "Less than vigilant perhaps, but his village suffered defeat because of a surprise attack in the night."

Village Chief Xcanmut, permanently bent at the waist, stood and stared into the faces of the seated chiefs then Hakum. "King Makuk is our friend and ally. He has helped us in the past. We must do for him the thing he needs and asks of us. What else is there to consider?"

Chief Xcanmut sat down and waited for others' input.

Rubbing his chin while in thought, the more senior Chief Sukok, pondered the other chiefs' suggestions. He drank some water, rose, and then said, "We must aid him. Not to do so is to appear cowardly and to condone an evil against the peoples of Yuca." Sukok glanced at each chief then said, "Unless *you* cower, I will present this decision to the Most Holy One and ask him to lead us in battle."

The room fell quiet.

Hakum said, "I will tell the Most Holy One you have reached a decision.

Hakum left and, within minutes, returned to inform Chief Sukok the king waited for him in the palace hall.

Hakum ran ahead. He pushed aside a cloth door so Chief Sukok could enter the dimly lighted hall which smelled of sage smoke. Hakum then stood to the right of the king.

Four guards, holding torches, stood at the corners of the king's jaguar-shaped throne. Torch-flame shadows made the king appear ten feet tall. The once white ceiling above the throne had been blackened by eons of similar torch-lighted meetings. Jaguar paintings covered the walls. The images on the lower walls were partially worn away due to men leaning against them over centuries of such meetings.

"Most Holy One," the chief said, holding his simple crown of three green quetzal feathers at his waist as he bowed. "Our friend, our ally, our neighbor has suffered at the hands of evil men. They brought harm to King Makuk and his people and stole their food stores." Sukok's voice reached a crescendo. "Makuk and his people cry out to you and our people for assistance in their revenge." Sukok's words, like ancient pleas, echoed against the walls. He fingered his authority necklace and paced before the king. "The village chiefs have counseled and send these words." The chief stopped pacing and faced the king. "If it pleases you, Most Holy One, lead us on the path of revenge and recovery. Fear must not imprison us."

"Chief Sukok," the king said then paced before his throne. "My ears are not shut to your words or the plea of King Makuk. Inform the village chiefs we will join the fight. Male villagers between fifteen and thirty-five are to gather in The Center in two dawns." The king whispered to Chief Sukok, "We have not fought for many years. I dread the death of any man, but that is a risk we must take."

"I share your concerns, Most Holy One, but if you need your father's inspiration, may I suggest you read his books. Learn how he faced battle. Now, with your permission, I will gather our warriors."

"Go! Make the preparations."

Hakum said, "Most Holy One, I will tell the high priest of your decision."

On hearing the Most Holy One and his lieutenants prepared to battle King Slubkah, the high priest readied a sacrifice. As the sun god awakened, his rays tinted the morning sky with shades of red and orange. The high priest, standing on the temple terrace, waited for the sky to brighten then shouted, "Bring the animal."

Four men carried a screeching deer to the altar in the temple used for animal sacrifice. The deer, and a few other animals, were kept in a special corral for purposes of sacrifice never to be used as a source of food.

Four older assistant priests, called *chacs,* struggled to hold the kicking animal on the stone altar. While praying over the deer, the high priest plunged an obsidian knife into its belly. For a split second, the deer screeched and stiffened. Through a ten-inch abdominal slit, the priest cut through the deer's diaphragm. His hand then entered the animal's chest where the knife freed the beating heart. The animal went limp.

Torrents of blood spurted from the contracting heart held high over the priest's head. The four *chacs,* seeking a blessing, walked under the spurting blood.

Watching from the plaza floor, The Center's warriors chanted, "Victory for our allies and our king."

Sacrificed animals would normally be eaten by priests, but the king had sent word to the high priest that only a small portion of the deer was to be eaten by priests. The largest portion was to be reserved for the warriors who left for battle.

The Most Holy One joined the priests on the

temple terrace. He faced the warriors gathered on the plaza then said, "We fight for our ally and honor." The men, wearing loincloths and blue war paint, shouted their agreement as they were divided into four groups of sixty men. Each man provided his own weapon—most commonly a bow and arrows, but spears, knifes, axes, or clubs were also seen.

The queen worried for the king's safety. As he met with the warriors, she went to the Temple of the Six Dolls. There she pricked her finger and collected a few drops of blood on a piece of paper then burned it in a sacred vessel. "Spirit of the Most Holy One's fathers, gods of rain, corn and war, accept this, my royal blood, in exchange for the safe return of our king and our warriors. Our people await your rain and victory in the approaching battle."

A roar from the plaza interrupted the queen's prayer. Warriors shouted battle cries as the king yelled, "We run to join King Makuk and avenge his loss."

The queen walked to the temple doorway and watched King Makuk's messenger lead the Most Holy One and his warriors toward Makuk's location.

Determined warriors ran a full day through barren jungle, taking only occasional rest periods. The sounds of feet-crunched leaves sounded like multiple bursts of distant thunder. As the time of the god's sleep approached, the king ordered his men to camp and cook six monkeys killed along the way. The king ordered small, scattered fires to prevent smoke from being seen by the enemy should they be close by. Despite small portions, the men enjoyed the meat.

Before sleeping, the Most Holy One removed a

red-clay plate and incense from a pouch. He burned the sweet smelling mixture and asked Ek-chuah, god of war, for victory and a safe return home. The prayer had to be rushed because the gods would soon be asleep and unable to hear the prayer after nightfall.

Staring at the stars, the king thought of home, his queen, and children. *Will I return to my family? Will my warriors be safe? I wish I were more confident, but I will do all I can to make it so.*

At the time of the god's awakening, the men resumed their trek. The early start allowed the group to avoid much of the day's heat.

The king sent a messenger ahead to alert King Makuk of the approach of the Most Holy One and his warriors.

Excited to see his old friend, The Most Holy One called for his ceremonial war crown as he neared King Makuk's camp.

Elderly King Makuk hobbled forward to greet his royal guest. The kings removed their crowns out of respect, bowed to each other, and then shared a forearm grip in greeting.

"Welcome, Most Holy One, friend of many years," King Makuk said, revealing only two upper teeth between his smiling lips. "May the gods bless us and our undertaking? Come share our meal. We have made a place of shade."

For shade, the host had hung several prized painted cloth doors salvaged from his palace. In their shade, the two leaders sat on stones arranged as temporary thrones. Water and berries were first served to the leaders and then village chiefs who sat a short distance away. Once fed, the kings discussed the tragedy which had befallen King Makuk.

Later, the Most Holy One's village chiefs and King Makuk's representatives met. They were to create a battle plan.

Their discussions took longer than anticipated, allowing the kings to discuss war strategies of the Most Holy One's father and the fact he had once vied for King Makuk's wife.

After much debate, the council reached a battle plan to present to the kings.

After discussing the plan with King Makuk, the Most Holy One announced, "The plan is accepted, with one change." King Makuk nodded his agreement. The Most Holy One said, "Our army will march at the hour of the god's sleep to avoid the day's heat. It is our intent to strike Slubkah's village within three days march and strike before the god's awakening on the fourth day. We chose the night, so the enemy could not call upon their sleeping gods for assistance. This strategy favored us at the time of our last battle with the tribes to the west. Our decision to strike at night has been made with great consideration because we too will be unable to call on our gods." For a moment, the warriors became deadly quiet. "What say you village chiefs?" the Most Holy One asked.

The village chiefs took a moment to discuss the kings' addition to their plan.

With everyone in agreement, the kings ordered a mid-day nap so the warriors would be rested for the night march.

The sky dimmed. Just before sunset, a flash of red filled the sky.

"Red is not a good color," a warrior said within earshot of the Most Holy One.

"Fear not, soldier," the Most Holy One said.

The jungle quieted, except for hushed murmurings about the impending battle, home, death, and the unknown.

The Most Holy One watched as village chiefs shook their men from sleep. "Wake up, warriors. Don't forget sound travels in the night jungle. Let no man utter a sound or break a twig. Commit no acts to excite evil or announce our presence."

The Most Holy One suggested King Makuk send four of his swiftest runners ahead. "Have them scout the village and find where they store provisions. We'll need that information so food stores are protected from fire. Don't let the enemy escape with the food stores. Above all, keep the stores safe. Beware of village guards and scouts. They are to be killed, but in doing so, don't let their *ik* be carried to the enemies' ears."

Village Chief Sukok bowed to the Most Holy One then raised his hands to stop murmuring among the warriors. Sukok said, "On my signal—a birdcall—the four divisions will enter the village. You are to move like a field mouse stealing grain." Sukok raised his fist and tightened his lip. "Men, light your torches from village fires then burn the village—all of it! But let *not one* spark touch the food hut."

King Makuk and the Most Holy One stepped forward. Makuk said, "Spare no man, no woman, and no child. We have come to repay a blood debt and retake our food stores. Let the evil doers become food for jungle scavengers."

The Most Holy One raised his hand to indicate

the men should stop. They neared the enemy's village border. Watching the warriors nervously shift their weight, the king wiped sweat from under his crown as many of his men appeared to pray with silently moving lips.

"I sense our warrior's fatigue," the Most Holy One said to King Makuk and Chief Sukok. "We should rest here."

A short time later, a runner-scout returned to the kings' war council. "Smoke from the village is on the wind and not far away. The enemy is near."

The Most Holy One ordered a rested scout to travel ahead. "Scout the area. Bring news of the distance to the village, the number of campfires, and the number of guards posted.

Gathering his warriors, the Most Holy One extended his hands and patted the air. "Shhh." For a moment, only the sounds of insects and a few distant birds were heard. The king pushed concern for himself aside as he gathered his thoughts. He then spoke softly, "Men, we must move with the stealth of the jaguar. Break no twigs. Neither pant nor cough. Speak no words."

King Makuk nodded to the Most Holy One and addressed the warriors. "Silence must rule our way. We can avenge our harm only through stealth."

The warriors had traveled for a short time when the advance scout returned. Panting, he reported to the kings and chiefs. "The enemy is a short run away. One guard stands at the periphery of each of the village's four cardinal directions. The guards stand four-hundred steps from the central pyramid, and I counted fourteen fires

"Hmmmm," Chief Sukok said, appearing

thoughtful about the news. "Most Holy One, I sense something strange. We must be careful."

The Most Holy One thought, *My spirit brings thoughts of doubt. I too have anxiety and fear.* He paced for a moment. *Fourteen fires require a lot of wood. Why so many for a sleeping village? I wonder if fourteen fires are intended to frighten us. Do they know we are here?* The Most Holy One stopped pacing and rubbed his forehead. *Dried firewood is not plentiful for so many campfires. I think they are false indicators of the number of people who sleep in the village. I fear the enemy waits in the jungle and hopes to frighten us away from their empty village.*

Joining the pacing, Chief Sukok rubbed his hands. "Perhaps, Most Holy One, these fires are intended to dissuade us. Experience leads me to believe the village has fewer men than we think. If so, then we have won the battle. Our numbers are stronger."

"Unfortunately, we cannot call upon our sleeping gods for guidance," the Most Holy One said. "I suggest great caution from everyone. With your permission, King Makuk, I will address the warriors.

The chiefs gathered the warriors to hear the Most Holy One. "The four men chosen to dispatch the lookouts will be first to enter the village," he said. "Let their hands do what they do with the stealth of the Black Panther. Take care and all return to me safe."

The four divisions separated and stole their way to the staging areas for striking their designated sides of the village. The warriors' anxiety became palpable in the unbroken quiet of the jungle as sharp flints, sticking from fighting clubs, caught the glint of village fires. Sweat streaked war paint became more fearsome in the fires' glow and flickering shadows.

The Most Holy One and King Makuk stood nearby where they discussed their contingent plan, should surprises arise.

The Most Holy One beckoned senior Village Chief Sukok. "Give the birdcall to launch the raid."

Chief Sukok raised his shaking, cupped hands to his lips and called, "Keeeeeah. Keeeeeah."

The bird-like sound floated through the jungle, sending the warriors on the move toward the village.

Stirred by the call, the revenging kings moved to the village's edge. The Most Holy One watched the designated lookouts locate and creep toward the unsuspecting village guards. Holding their breath to prevent being heard, the lookouts clasped a hand over each guard's mouth and slashed their throats. The bloody bodies were then dragged into the shadows.

The guards' dispatch paved the way for avenging warriors to enter the central plaza. Like most Mayan centers, it had a surrounding ring of stone temples, pyramids, and palaces for its king, priests, and noblemen. An outer ring of thatch huts housed lesser officials and common villagers along with elevated huts for food storage.

With Jaguar stealth, the warriors crept to the campfires where they lit torches. When all were lit, the warriors spread out screeching and whooping. They threw flaming torches onto palm thatched roofs of huts and reed buildings most of which were located close together on the south side of the plaza. The warriors carefully avoided burning food-storage buildings.

The village became an inferno, with sky-reaching flames whose brightness rivaled sunlight. The Most Holy One could feel the inferno's heat as he and King Makuk watched from the edge of the plaza. Reed structures on three pyramid terraces and two palaces crumbled in flames. One hut after the other slumped into a pile of flaming debris while thick clouds of smoke rose from burned reed buildings.

The Most Holy One smiled, nodded, and moved about as if ready to dance with happiness on seeing the objectives of his battle plan achieved. Suddenly, he realized he heard no screaming women, saw no children or fleeing elderly villagers. He heard not a single human sound from the village.

The warriors' battle cries had died away when King Makuk turned to the Most Holy One and asked, "Where is everyone . . . the enemy?"

The Most Holy One shook his head. "Have we sprung a trap on *ourselves*?"

Suddenly, the jungle rattled with war cries. Enemy soldiers ran from every temple and pyramid along the periphery of the plaza, corralling the avenging warriors.

The enemy's surprise attack shocked the Most Holy One. His jaw dropped as he stared in horror. *Is this another sign of the gods' disapproval of me?*

Chaos engulfed the avenging warriors. Each man suddenly faced several local fighters who tried to separate and surround small groups of the avenging kings' warriors.

The Most Holy One did a cursory appraisal of the enemy's numbers then shook his fist at the sky. "Makuk, our warriors are outnumbered. We must join them . . . be seen leading this battle, so our warriors will continue to fight."

Grabbing axes and knives, the Most Holy One ran, yelling, toward the village center. He immediately became engaged in bloody, hand-to-hand fighting. He handled himself with great skill while dispatching several enemy warriors. His bodyguard took a spear in the back while attempting to protect him.

On seeing his bodyguard fall dead, The Most Holy one protectively backed up against King Makuk. "I want neither of us to take a spear in the back."

Fighting back-to-back, the kings moved along the edge of the plaza. Having dispatched several of the enemy, the Most Holy One watched the battle rage around him.

Arrows from both armies found targets—some intended and some not. Men's screams echoed across the plaza as warriors from both sides shouted terrifying war cries. The thuds of war clubs against war clubs were imprinted on the Most Holy One's memory, knowing one club owner would soon die. Spears made slurping sounds as they found their way into backs, chests, and abdomens. Many spears were pulled free and thrust again and again as men from both sides moved from fighter to fighter, hoping to live to fight again. Obsidian blades slashed throats, stabbed chests, and sliced arms leaving rivers of blood on the plaza's white-stucco floor. Blades, wielded in life-and-death struggles, more often than not found their targets, freeing streams of blood and cries of death.

The hollow sounds of skulls crushed by stone hammers echoed around the Most Holy One. Several hammer-heads escaped their handles and became missiles. Some struck members of the kings' tribe—some struck the enemy.

Men from both armies, their oiled ponytails in flames, ran from the fight. One such ally ran past the Most Holy One who tripped the warrior as he screamed and pulled at his burning hair. "Stay still!" the Most

Holy one yelled, while dumping handfuls of dirt on the flames. "You are saved. Now, join the fight with me and your brothers!"

Swinging a club, a screaming enemy chieftain ran toward the Most Holy One's back, momentarily exposed, as King Makuk fought in hand-to-hand combat. One of The Center's spearmen, standing slightly ahead of the Most Holy One, saw the advancing chieftain and swung his spear shaft against the oncoming man's throat, crushing his voice box. The gasping chieftain fell at the Most Holy One's feet, clutching his throat and writhing in pain. The spearman stomped on the fallen man's throat then stomped the man's grappling hand. From it rose the sound of bones breaking. The king's spearman then thrust his spear into the chieftain's chest.

The Most Holy One breathed a sigh of relief as blood gushed from the chieftain's wound. The dying man stared at his wound as he gasped and with his free hand endeavored to stem his hemorrhage. His face, silhouetted by the flames of the burning village, turned toward the night sky and in a weak, low guttural sound cried, "Nooooo."

In a short, brief bow toward the Most Holy One, the spearman yelled, "The Most Holy One's blood will not fall on this battlefield."

The king nodded. "Great warrior, stay by my side. I am indebted to you."

The battle raged for thirty minutes, leaving the plaza littered with bodies from both armies. Everywhere the Most Holy One looked, he saw death, dying, and destruction. The moans and groans of the wounded and dying shrouded the village. He scanned the plaza noting scattered pools of blood coalesce into lakes then spread along the plaza's uneven stucco floor. Some drained into underground cisterns used to store drinking water.

The Most Holy One watched night, made day by the inferno, give way to daybreak and the awakening of the sun god. Dawn revealed hundreds of soaring vultures whose outstretched wings darkened the smoke filled sky.

Smoke blew across the Most Holy One's location making it difficult for him to breathe. "We cannot fight in this smoke," he said, coughing repeatedly. "King Makuk, we must move. It's obvious the superior numbers of the enemy, and their element of surprise, has favored them. They're winning."

Looking disappointed, King Makuk pulled his spear from an enemy's abdomen and said, "I agree. We can't win."

"Conch man!" The Most Holy One yelled, "Blow retreat. We must consider another strategy."

As the conch sounded retreat, the Most Holy One waved and shouted, "Warriors. Go to the jungle on the north side of the plaza." Feather crown held over his head, the Most Holy One led the retreat.

King Makuk followed close behind, but he tripped, falling on his outstretched arm. The sound of fracturing bone filled the air.

The Most Holy One looked around. *Where is Makuk's bodyguard?*

"The gods have struck me," King Makuk yelled. He held his sharply angled arm protectively. "It's broken! My arm is broken!"

A bodyguard rushed to King Makuk and assisted him to his feet. Once upright, he paused to stabilize his flailing arm. Suddenly, swooshing sounds filled the air and King Makuk fell. An arrow had pierced his upper right back. He fell, struggling to breathe. Blood flowed from his gasping mouth as gurgling death sounds drew the attention of nearby warriors who looked on with pity.

Horrified, The Most Holy One moved closer to the fallen king and strained to hear the king's words.

The dying king gripped his bodyguard's wrist, coughed blood, and stared at his kneeling servant. "Go. Don't stay for me. My life is spilled. Help the Most Holy One and our warriors."

"No, My King! I can't leave you."

"Please me," the king said, a bloody froth falling from his mouth. "There . . . is another . . . sun for you. Go! I order you. Gooooo."

With tears washing away his wood-ash war paint, the bodyguard, loosened his grip on the king's arm and then crawled toward the Most Holy One who had retreated to the edge of the jungle. The guard waited respectfully as his king's *ik,* carried by the wind and gathered by the gods, departed, leaving the earth to claim the king's body. His head rolled slowly to the left. His eyes, filled with the stare of death, seemed to follow his defeated men into the jungle.

The Most Holy One wiped a tear. Turning toward the jungle, he called to the dead king's bodyguard, "Come. We must go. There's nothing more you can do."

Crying, the bodyguard fell at the Most Holy One's feet. "I must return to my king. I need to retrieve his authority necklace. I must return it to his family."

"I understand," the Most Holy One said. "Go."

Far from the enemy's village, The Most Holy One gathered the village chiefs. *I'm glad we don't have to fight again.* He looked around then took a deep breath. "Chief Sukok, count the surviving men."

Village Chief Sukok, who had sustained deep wounds to his right arm and leg, stood. "Most Holy One, I have done the count." Weary, the chief settled onto the ground. He took a deep breath and spoke in a whisper. "Of our original two-hundred-forty warriors, one hundred and three are alive. Only fifty-eight can fight."

The Most Holy One asked, "What is the count of King Makuk's warriors?"

"Twenty-three live," Chief Sukok moaned, looking dejected. "Only ten can fight. Never have I felt so defeated or lost so many men."

A grave silence fell over the leaders.

Worried, the Most Holy One sat crossed legged on the ground. He removed his feather crown, placed it in his lap, and pondered how he would tell his warriors of their situation. With downcast eyes, he murmured, "We have lost this battle." He paused then yelled, "No. *I* have lost this battle!"

Silence flooded the jungle while the king's pitiful outcry settled into the minds of the warriors.

The king slumped forward, touching his forehead to the ground. He then stared at the sky in silent prayer, *Gods of war, strike us no more*. "There is nothing more we can do with the number of warriors able to fight. The village chiefs concur—we are outnumbered and defeated."

The Most Holy One called to Chief Sukok, "Chief, take us home."

"Yes, Most Holy One."

Chief Sukok's shoulders slumped. Appearing about to cry, he raised his head. He choked back emotions and stared at his warriors. He opened his mouth to speak, but he could not.

The Most Holy One looked at the other village chiefs, who nodded. He walked to the gathered fighters and addressed them. "We must return to Dzibilchaltun. There we, and the remainder of King Makuk's warriors, will guard The Center and its food stores."

One man, with a jagged wound from his left ear to the corner of his mouth, rose and cleared his throat. "Most Holy One, I am Mak Ut, a village leader of King Makuk's Chalmuch, I thank you for all you have done to help my villagers, but some of us wish to return to Chalmuch and rebuild our homes."

"Mak Ut, I understand. You and your villagers are free to do as you wish. However, I believe we would be safer if we were united in The Holy Center.

"Home is where I belong, Most Holy One.'

"Then return, Mak Ut."

Chief Sukok gathered his division chiefs. "Men, prepare for home. See to those in need. Slings are needed. Those, whose *ik* is carried to the wind should be buried here. Take their necklaces for their wives and mothers." The chief pointed to two men who sat nearby. "Search for a waterhole. We will take its water and rest there."

Vine slings were made to carry Chief Sukok and the wounded. The warriors worked in silence. Their energy depleted and their spirits dashed, the warriors mourned the loss of comrades. Everyone knew the wounded left in the enemy's village would be tortured and the bodies of the fallen would be desecrated—kicked, hacked, clubbed and left as food for jungle scavengers, but for now, everyone focused on getting the living home.

This knowledge weighed heavily on the king's psyche. *What more could I have done to prevent this? Am I alone responsible? Oh gods, bear me up.*

Four men searched the area for spears and arrows left by the enemy. They would be needed if the enemy pursued the retreating warriors.

Chapter 6

With a signal from the Most Holy One, the weary warriors began the homeward trek. Scouts went ahead to gather information on travel conditions. With the return of each scout, a more rested one repeated the task.

"Most Holy One," Chief Sukok said, "jungle heat is building. Everyone is weary and the bearers are exhausted from carrying the wounded. The men need rest."

"I know how they feel," The Most Holy One said, raising his hand for everyone to stop. "Post lookouts. We'll rest here."

The warriors slumped to the dusty jungle floor. Some found shelter in the sparse dappled shadows cast by barren, overlapping tree limbs.

The Most Holy One used his bamboo tube to give water to the wounded. "Take comfort," he said. "Your home and your family you will see again."

The Most Holy One and his warriors used the time to gather sand for scrubbing dried blood from their limbs and bodies. Some of the blood belonged to them and some to the enemy.

One man continued to bleed from a gaping wound in his thigh. His weakened condition caught the eye of the Most Holy One.

"Chief Sukok, send men to find a *bakalche'* tree," the Most Holy One ordered. He pointed toward the injured man. "We need its sap to stop his bleeding."

"Meku. Xmu," Chief Sukok shouted, "find and bring the sap that stops bleeding."

Warriors with none or minor injuries cared for the more seriously injured while waiting for the sap. Some men cared for warrior's broken bones as others stemmed bleeding.

When the scouts returned with the sap, the doctor liberally applied it to bleeding wounds. Within minutes, bleeding slowed to a trickle or stopped.

"Doctor, put a binding around this man's thigh to close the wound's edges," the king ordered. "When that is done, care for the wounds of the others."

Out of gratitude, the wounded man reached for the king's hand to kiss it, but Chief Sukok knocked the warrior's hand away.

"You know better than touch the king," the chief said.

The Most Holy One took the injured warrior's hand. "This man has honored me. I am in his debt for the pain, suffering, and blood he has shed for me and our villagers."

The chief bowed and backed away, knowing he had angered the king.

Six days later, the weary warriors neared Dzibilchaltun. One man ran ahead to inform the high priest of the defeat and the number of wounded men returning.

Upon hearing the message, the high priest felt faint. He leaned against the wall and contemplated his people's future. *Should we fear our enemy's revenge and a raid on our center—perhaps in the dead of night? Has this happened because our king offended the gods?*

The priest recovered and called for his servant. "Send a runner to our approaching king. Tell him we wait for him and our warriors. Tell the assistant priest to prepare a sacrifice to be offered in thanksgiving that our king lives and the evil spirits of the distant land have not claimed all our warriors."

As the servant left, the priest stepped onto the upper terrace of his palace and addressed two guards. "Blow the conchs. Gather the people. I need to tell them our fighters return. Every home has a loss or wound. The people should prepare to receive and care for the injured." The priest called to another servant, "Go to the palace. Tell the house master that the Most Holy One has ordered the wounded of King Makuk be cared for by palace servants. They should prepare."

The guards stiffened with shock on hearing their warriors had been defeated.

The high priest yelled, "I said call the people! Blow your conchs!"

The guards shook their heads in disbelief then one blew his conch. At first, the sound broke because of the trembling of the conch blower's lips. The conch's mournful sounds filled the barren jungle, summoning villagers to gather on the central plaza.

The high priest turned to an assistant priest. "Inform the queen the king returns. He is safe."

The high priest sat down on a terrace cushion. With downcast eyes, he watched the plaza fill with anxious appearing villagers. The plaza droned as everyone looked toward the temple terrace.

The priest overheard some villagers ask, "Is there word of the battle? Does everyone return safely?

Has the stolen food been recovered?"

After an hour, the priest rose as if he shouldered a heavy burden. He raised his arms to quiet the crowd. "Villagers, the Most Holy One and our warriors are approaching."

A few scattered yelps of celebration came from the crowd.

The priest continued. "Our king returns with many wounded. Some of our villagers . . . do not."

A collective gasp filled the plaza.

From various parts of the plaza, wives and mothers called out. "Who doesn't return?

The high priest's voice quivered as he spoke "Prepare to receive the fallen . . . and to mourn those not with us. Those who can must assist the Most Holy One and those unable to walk."

A pall of anxiety fell over the crowd as if every breath had been stolen by the god of death. The priest watched villagers stand as if dead while many boys and older men rushed into the jungle to help those requiring assistance. The priest knew some of the villagers went to see if their family members were among the living. Most females and elderly men milled about the plaza, awaiting word of their family's fate.

The high priest remained on his terrace. As dusk approached, he heard the jungle reverberate with shrieks and lamentations of villagers who had gone to help the wounded. Unfortunately, many villagers discovered their loved ones were not among the walking or wounded.

Over many dawns, the realization of village losses settled into the consciousness of the king and his people. He spent long hours brooding over his defeat while he and the people awaited rain.

One day, Hakum quietly approached the pensive king, reading in his library. "Most Holy One, the high priest wishes your counsel."

The king leaned back against the cool library wall. *Why does he seek counsel now?* "Have him come before me."

The king moved to his throne room to await the priest.

The high priest smelled of fresh hair oil and incense. He bowed unusually low, his authority necklace rattling against the floor. His ear plugs gleamed like they had just been polished.

The king thought, *I have rarely seen this priest so groomed.*

"Most Holy One, my priests and I ask your counsel. Many dawns have passed since your holy sacrifice and Chaac's denial of rain. The jungle and even our hardy crops die of thirst. The villagers are desperate. Pray instruct us what to do, Most Holy One."

The king gripped the jaguar heads carved into the ends of his stone bench. *Does he believe crop failures are due to my loss of the god's favor?* "I know their plight," the king said, squeezing the jaguar heads. "I see leaves fall from trees. I too go without maize. My family grows hungry. I'm very aware of our problems."

"Most Holy One, I see your gaunt face and note your weight loss. We know your family shares their rations so the people may eat, but we need options lest we too shrivel and die."

The king paced, intermittently glancing at the priest, pondering a response and thinking of his kingly responsibilities. *I must control my anger. Does this priest doubt my interest?* The king stopped pacing and stared out a doorway. "High Priest, consult the shaman. Ask if the time is right for me to make another sacrifice and then bring me his counsel."

"As you wish, Most Holy One."

The king went to the queen's quarters where she sat bare breasted on a floor cushion, nursing their youngest son. "You wear the look of worry," the queen said, glancing at the king. "What bothers you, Bulek?"

The king sat down beside his wife and allowed his son to grip his forefinger. For a moment, the king smiled and forgot his troubles. Shaking his son's small fist, the king looked the queen in the eye and took a deep breath. *What would I do without you?*

"Yes . . . ?" The queen asked, expectantly. "I am your queen, but I am also your wife. What troubles you?"

The king sat upright. "I think the priests believe I have lost favor with the gods."

The queen placed her son on a cushion and took the king's hands in hers. Gripping and shaking them, she looked into his eyes. "Bulek, you are the Most Holy One. The gods do not ignore their own. Have no fear for the loss of their favor."

The king walked to the doorway and stared at the sky. After a moment, he faced the queen. "I must revisit the sacred cave. The priests are now determining the date. This is a trip I dread, but I must do what is required of me . . . to appease the gods, the priests, and our people."

The queen's face blanched as she caught her breath. She looked at the floor then at her husband. "My heart is heavy with your worry, but I know the gods, the priests, and our people hold you in high regard. We believe in you . . . your strength. Why would the high priest ask you to travel if he did not value your position and you?"

The king knelt beside the queen and whispered, "Ix Tzutz, your faith is stronger than mine. I hope mine will carry me through the trip."

"It will. Now, come lay beside me. Let the prince and me rub worries from your head."

Chapter 7

Waiting in the king's palace, the high priest, wearing the colorful regalia of supplications, rose from his floor cushion to address the arriving shaman and assistant priests. The group had been convened to consider what they might do in lieu of another sacrifice by the king. He glanced upward as if taking strength from the red image of Chaac, the god of rain, painted on the ceiling. *Chaac, send me wisdom.* "Advisors, tell me what path our king is to take."

From his smoke pot, the shaman waved smoke across his face and inhaled deeply. "We could sacrifice an animal, but they're difficult to find. If we were to hunt for one, we might as well hunt for animals to eat—meat for the whole village. In either case, we would have to travel far to the south where we might encroach on the land of others. That could be dangerous in a time of drought."

"Perhaps we should search for a smaller animal like a rabbit," an assistant priest said.

"A small animal equals a small reward," the shaman said. "Besides, we haven't seen rabbits in many moon cycles. They've been eaten or moved into the greener southern jungle. If we were to use a small animal, villagers might say we sacrificed it to get a meal only for the priests. We can't do that."

"Let us pray the night," the high priest said. "Seek the input of the gods while we are lost in sleep. Let's meet at dawn to disclose their message."

After a night and morning of prayerful deliberation, a consensus had been reached. The high priest returned to the king's throne room to present the group's decision. He bowed, acknowledged the presence of the nursing queen, and addressed the king. "Most Holy One, the priests' council offers their thoughts."

From his throne, the king pointed toward a nearby cushion. "Sit, High Priest. Share your counsel."

The high priest sat crossed legged on the cushion. He rested his hands on his knees, took a deep breath, and for a moment stared at the floor then the king. "The time is favorable to visit the sacred cave. In two days, we will be in the calendar day of Kan, the day governed by the god of maize. Most Holy One, we ask your consent to prepare for travel. We feel you must.

The king stood. *This is not what I wanted to hear.*

"High Priest," the queen said, "God Kan rules maize. He cannot guarantee rain."

"My Queen. Most Holy One. The mighty Kan works with the rain god. They will bring us rain in exchange for our king's offering. Without holy blood, I fear our jungle will die."

The king slumped onto a floor cushion. "I will do your bidding. Prepare for my journey to Xibalba. Pray the gods receive my sacrifice and honor our need."

The high priest rose, bowed to the king and queen then left the hall saying, "I know the gods will heed our prayers."

The day of sacrifice arrived. The king and his entourage, composed of the high priest, assistant priests, acolytes, shaman and servants, made their way to the sacred cave. The usual prayers and supplications rose to the sky gods.

Dead leaves, crunched under the trampling feet of the procession. The crunching reminded the king of the times when he heard similar sounds made by crickets, perched on succulent green leaves, searching for a mate.

With little shade to protect them, the men sweltered in the heat of direct sunlight that seared their bare skin.

The high priest approached the king. "Most Holy One, we must take a detour for rest at the waterhole. There we'll find shade and water, which we need to withstand this heat and for you to make your sacrifice."

The group followed Hakum who lead the group through jungle familiar to him.

At the waterhole, the king noted its river was no more than a trickle.

The high priest shook his head. "Most Holy One, the gods of the underworld wish to deny us even a sacred river. Ideally, we should have a ladder, but there isn't time to construct one. We must make vine ropes."

When the ropes were ready, the priests blessed the area and asked the gods' permission to enter the waterhole and take its waters.

After quenching their thirsts and a short rest in the damp shade of the sinkhole roof, the men filled their gourds with its murky water. The Most Holy One then asked to resume his trip.

After a short trek, the king quickened his pace. A sudden tug on the king's robe produced a tearing sound. He had snagged his feather covered robe. "Gods forgive me."

Consoling the king, the high priest said, "The gods don't see such trivial things."

"It's easily repaired," Hakum said.

Reaching the mouth of the cave, the king performed the required rituals. At the sacred pool, he made his ablations, shed his clothes, and stepped onto the sacred stones.

The high priest swung his fly wisp to drive away a fly that buzzed around the king's head.

The king frequently shifted his weight on the stones. *Great gods of Xibalba, strengthen my will, steady my hand and heed my supplications?*

The high priest said, "Bring the sacred leaf."

The king's anxiety became physical. He felt his legs shake and saw his hands tremble. *Gods give me strength for the benefit of my people.*

Taking an obsidian knife from the leaf, the high priest handed it to the king. He swallowed hard and fingered the black blade, noting its shiny, sharp edges. Several times, he turned the knife over in his hand seeking a comfortable gripping spot. He knew the priests had noted his anxiety.

In a low voice, the priest prayed, "Bless, O gods, this king and his sacrifice willingly offered. Receive it with blessings on our land. Send us rain and abundant crops."

The distant roar of the waterfall seemed to dim as everyone focused on the king.

After two deep breaths, the king stuck out his quivering tongue. He grasped it with his shaky left forefinger and thumb then pulled it forward. He gagged a few times. After another deep breath, he rested the knife point on the mid-portion of his tongue. Squeezing his eyes shut, he pushed the knife point through his tongue. As blood spilled from the wound, searing pain spread through his trembling body. "Ahhhh!"

Having pushed the blade more than halfway through his tongue, he pushed it all the way through to remove it. A stream of blood arched into the pool. With bloody hands, he compressed the wound between his thumb and forefinger. He knelt to wash the blade in the sacred pool then handed it to the high priest.

"Bring the leaf with the sacred rope," the high priest called to an assistant.

The king took the knotted rope. His apprehension grew as he stared at a thicker rope than the one he had used before.

The high priest nodded to urge the king.

Eyes closed, the king took a deep breath. After a moment, he pulled his tongue as far forward as possible. Wincing, he threaded the bee's waxed end of the coarse rope into the bloody hole. He paused several times to take a deep breath and force himself to keep his tongue extended. His jaws ached as he gagged. He felt sick to his stomach. *Gods, let me not vomit.* He wanted to swallow, but wouldn't. *Every drop of blood must flow to the gods.*

The high priest said, "Let me help keep your tongue extended."

The priest stooped to take a handful of water to rinse the tongue tip then gripped it with his thumb and forefinger. Avoiding blood, the priest pulled the king's tongue out and upward.

The king forced one end of the waxed rope though the tongue and out of the bottom hole. He shuddered on each attempt to pull the rope's first knot through his tongue. The knot stuck in the too small slit. Manipulating the rope caused blood to gush over his trembling hands as the high priest struggled to keep his finger and thumb blood free.

Empathic, the high priest released the tongue and shuddered as he and the acolytes chanted loudly.

The king pulled sharply on the lower end of the rope, ripping it through the slit. The encompassing, burning pain caused his knees to shake, yet he moved the rope back and forth. He paused only when a knot entered the hole. The rope sawed its way toward the tip of his juddering tongue. Soon, the slow-moving crystalline pool shimmered blood red. *I must give more. The gods must be appeased.*

"Most Holy One, I think you have made a sufficient offering," the high priest said. "I'm concerned you may, in your ardor, give too much of yourself.

The king repeatedly said to himself, *I must give more. I must.*

With his last ounce of energy, the king pulled the rope from the gaping, bloody hole.

The high priest's face turned ashen, when he saw the size of the hole. He muttered through his shock, "Oh gods, The Most Holy One has given of himself, his blood, and his energy in your honor." The priest shook his head. "Most Holy One, we must stop your bleeding.

Suddenly, a gush of air from the cave's depths rushed past the group, extinguishing their torches.

There was murmuring among the group as to the

meaning of the sudden darkness.

Someone said, "I hope this is not an act of the gods' displeasure."

"Nor the act of an evil spirit," someone else said.

The king prayed, *Oh gods, make us not blind in your presence. Be not displeased. I pray you show no displeasure.* He shook with pain. *Ask not for my life.*

Able only to mumble, the king said, "Bless us, oh gods of the underworld. Bless my offering."

One torch suddenly flickered into a large flame. The men questioned each other about its meaning.

The high priest raised his hand. "Quiet. The sacrifice has been accepted, but the gods desire more. The light of this one torch is to guide us to our duty. We must wait for the gods to tell us of their needs. This sacrifice is complete. Prepare for home."

While other torches were relighted, the king squeezed his tongue to stop its bleeding as he washed the sacred rope in a small blood-free area of the pool. On standing to return the rope to the high priest, he felt dizzy and steadied himself by grabbing onto the priest's arm.

The high priest allowed the king to steady himself and then handed him the special salve made from bakalché resin. The king used his forefinger and thumb to spread the gooey yellowish substance on his tongue and through the hole. He then covered his tongue above and below with flat, smooth stones provided by the high priest. Moaning, the king clinched his teeth and thrust his tongue tightly against the roof of his mouth. The pressure of the stones and the salve would stop the bleeding.

The unsteady king dressed with the help of

several priests. Then the group walked toward the cave's mouth.

The king felt dizzy as he neared the cave opening and stumbled along the narrow passage. As his dizziness worsened, he caught himself on his outstretched hand thrust against the damp wall.

The high priest whispered to the king, "I think you gave too much blood."

Chapter 8

The trek to Dzibilchaltun was slow. Heat, thirst, and walking sapped the king's strength. His feet moved like he wore stone sandals. The longer he walked, the more he swayed and staggered.

Hakum encouraged the king to lean on him, but the king refused.

Through clenched teeth, the king mumbled, "I cannot be seen as helpless."

"Most Holy One," you must let me help, Hakum pleaded. "No one will think the less of you. These men know you made a great sacrifice."

The king clutched tree limbs for support. For a moment, he paused and removed his tongue stones so he could drink water. He emptied a water tube in a few gulps, causing his tongue to bleed.

"Replace the stones," the high priest said.

The king reset the tongue stones just as his grip weakened, and the water tube fell to the dust. Almost toppling over, the king slumped. Hakum and the high priest caught the king's arms and eased him against a tree trunk.

"Sit, My King," Hakum said. "Take your rest."

The high priest yelled to a bodyguard, "Send someone to refill the king's water tube."

"I must not falter on this path," the king

mumbled while sliding down the tree trunk to sit on the ground.

"Drink this," the high priest said, offering his water tube to the sweat drenched king.

Fearing the king might die, the high priest removed the king's crown and feathered cloak then fanned him. "With your permission, Holy One, I will spread your cloak over these tree limbs to make shade. I'll carry your crown until you wish to wear it again."

The king nodded slowly. *I pray I'm not dying.*

Hakum handed the king a container of the resin so he could apply more salve to his tongue.

After drinking some freshly collected water, the king mumbled, "I . . . must . . . move on."

The high priest removed the king's feathered cloak from the tree limbs while Hakum assisted the king to his feet.

After walking two hundred paces, the high priest said, "Most Holy One. You must rest. I'll spread your cloak to make shade."

"I must continue as the others," the king mumbled, grimacing from pain after each word.

"But, Most Holy One," the priest chided the king, "they haven't made your sacrifice. You have done all but offer your life."

"High Priest, say no more about resting."

"As you wish, Most Holy One," the priest said, his face twisted with worry

The high priest turned to the assistant priests and whispered, but not so softly the king did not hear, "We must pray for the king. I fear for his life. Let your prayers be ardent."

"I heard that," the king muttered. "I promise. I will not die."

The growing heat caused the group to move progressively slower.

Every step of the king resulted in cracking sounds created by his breaking tree branches that failed to support his weight as he fought to steady himself. *Gods, bear me up*. He experienced more dizziness and turned to the high priest. "Make shade. I must rest."

Using the royal cloak, the high priest created a patch of shade where the king settled onto the ground. He and the high priest shared the shade as Hakum swatted at pesky, sweat-thirsty insects.

The king watched eight vultures circling overhead. "They think a meal is at hand."

The high priest followed the king's gaze and said, "Reminds me of an old proverb. 'Vultures are the last of the living to leave the jungle,' but not this day. Not today."

The high priest motioned to the shaman. "Take my priests to Dzibilchaltun. Two acolytes are to stay with us. Have the king's servants prepare to receive their leader. The queen should be told of his fatigue.

"I heard that," the king mumbled weakly and closed his eyes

"Return with four strong men and a hammock," the high priest said. "They are to carry the king home. Now, go."

Startled, the king awoke to the distant sounds of the recovery team. He nudged the high priest awake. "Help has arrived.

The priest stood and looked in the direction of the sounds of the approaching rescuers.

"I visited with the gods," the king said, looking at the priest.

"Perhaps," the priest said. "What did they say?"

The king thought for a moment and then mumbled, "My family ran through the jungle. Each had fear on their face. Often, they looked back, but the vision did not reveal what they saw or feared."

"And why did they run?" the high priest asked.

"I don't know; the dream thread broke when I awoke."

"Perhaps it is the gods' way of letting you know your family wants to see you. They worry for you. They ran to see you. The queen looked back to make sure the family ran together."

On reaching The Center, the high priest instructed the bearers to enter the king's palace through a rear tunnel. From there the leader could be carried, unseen by villagers, to his bed chamber.

When the group reached the passageway, the king murmured, "Gods be praised. I'm home."

He heard the queen running down the shaft before he saw her. When she reached him, she half-crawled into his hammock. Words were unnecessary. Her face revealed sentiments of worry, sorrow, love, and joy.

"Speak to me," the queen said. "You look pale. Say you are well. Word came you were dying. Say it isn't so."

"I live," the king mumbled, squeezing her hand.

Once in his bed, the queen and family moved to his side. He felt revived by the coolness of the stone walls.

Over the course of the afternoon and early evening, he drank four gourds of water. Later, he asked for more.

The king, noting some tongue bleeding, mumbled, "Hakum."

Hakum pushed the children aside and assisted the king in sitting up so salve could be spread on his tongue. The king then slumped onto his bed and slept.

Chapter 9

Four dawns later, the high priest gathered his assistants in the Temple of Chaac. They performed the required offerings, prayed for rain, and then shared a meager morning meal. Afterwards, the high priest had his servant summon villagers to The Center.

Hours later, the high priest calmed the boisterous crowd then informed them the king had made, and the gods had accepted, his sacrifice.

The weakened king, carried to the temple prior to the crowd's arrival, simply waved to the people from his portable throne.

The high priest instructed the villagers to perform their ritual of the sacrifice of a fish to the earth gods.

Afterwards, the king returned to the palace to rest and await Chaac's rain. Later that day, he heard rumors that many villagers had left the plaza thinking it strange the usual fanfare, which normally accompanied his appearance, did not occur. He wondered if they thought he had done less than he should.

Three days later, the nobles gathered for the high-sun meal in the main dining room. Its colorful images of the gods painted on the ceiling gladdened the king's heart. The meal proceeded with laughter and a relative abundance of food—one sweet fruit, a zapota, and a full cup of maize-honey mush per diner. The noblemen, high priest, and royal family rejoiced in the return of the king's strength and the anticipation of rain, which everyone believed would soon arrive.

Three flute players entertained the group with lively music, which mimicked singing birds often heard during happier, wetter days. Now, birds had no food, no water, and no shade. Some fell dead from the sky while trying to fly south.

"High Priest, what do you know about the drought?" the king mumbled, removing a sugar apple seed from his cheek pocket. "Many days have passed, but rain eludes us. You said the gods had accepted my sacrifice."

The priest placed his half-eaten fish on a clay plate, but kept chewing. "My King, I wish I knew the thoughts of the gods. Perhaps they try us."

The king nodded. *Yes. Me more than you.*

The priest continued, "We must prove we have no drought of faith. Wait the time. The gods will heed our prayers."

Days of hot destitution came and went without rain. A few clouds appeared in the northern sky then quickly dissipated, mocking villagers' expectations and prayers for rain. Hardy weeds and undergrowth withered and died. Dust devils, often rising high in the sky, darted across the empty market clearing.

Some of the king's court spoke of villagers moving south to distant, greener parts of the jungle in search of a new life. He worried his people believed the gods had withdrawn their favor or had forgotten him.

Worried for himself and his people, he sent for the high priest to seek his advice.

Hakum sat on a floor cushion in the king's receiving room, repairing the sacred feathered cloak damaged on the last trip to the holy cave.

"I had forgotten about the tear," the king said watching Hakum bind new feathers to the underlying cotton backing. "With this drought, where did you find these feathers? There are no birds."

Hakum stopped sewing. He first looked at the floor then the king. "Most Holy One, we could not provide for your pets. They provided the feathers."

Crying, the king fell onto a pile of cushions and struck them with his fists. "By the gods. What more is asked of me? The birds were a gift from Ix Tzutz to celebrate our marriage."

Just then, the high priest arrived at the king's doorway. He cleared his throat. "You sent for me, Most Holy One?"

Wiping his tears, the king forced himself upright. "Yes. Come in, Ah Kin Mai. I need your counsel. I've had a dream."

"One you wish to share?"

"Yes." Followed by the high priest, the king walked onto the terrace where a hot breeze ferried the sounds of stone masons working on a new temple. "I had a dream. A good dream. Our people were celebrating a special occasion. For what, I don't know." The king pointed toward the plaza floor. "A man sat there, on the spot where my great, great grandfather's stele stands. The king raised his hands as if playing a flute. "The man played a bamboo flute. He played cheerful music. While he played, water spewed from the flute's finger holes. The more he played, the more water flowed. It ran to our fields causing maize to grow. Trees sprouted leaves. Birds flew and sang."

"Did the dream sender share its meaning?"

"That's why I sent for you. The gods send no rain, but they have provided water in *Xlacah,* our waterhole. We are to move its sacred water to our fields and give drink to our crops, just as the waterhole gives drink to our people. We must do this miracle while waiting for Chaac to gather sky water to make rain. People in southern Yuca use surface streams to irrigate their crops. While we have no surface rivers, we have water from deep within the gods' domain."

Looking perplexed, the priest said, "Most Holy One, this use of water is a foreign thought to me. The gods gave their water for our drink . . . not to spill on the ground. That may be a sacrilege. May I counsel you in the morning?"

"Yes. Do so."

The high priest returned to the Temple of Chaac and summoned his assistants. The shaman, reportedly ill, could not attend. During the night, flickering flames cast mystery-filled shadows on the ancient temple walls as they reverberated with the murmurs of ancient prayers regarding the unusual use of water. The priests rotated prayer duty so one priest prayed throughout the night.

At the sign of the sun god's awakening, the high priest assembled his assistants. "Let us offer a joint prayer and await answers from the gods. Each of you will drop a kernel of maize into the smoke pot. The last object into the pot will be a piece of paper on which I have placed a drop of my blood."

"Gods of the worlds above and below," the high

priest prayed, "accept our offerings and answer our prayers."

Minutes later, the high priest stood and addressed the kneeling priests. "If the gods disapproved of our king using water from Xlacah for drink to our crops, we would have received a sign. I will tell the Most Holy One no sign of disapproval is a sign to proceed."

The high priest found the king pacing in his receiving room, hands behind his back and head bent low. A hot, dry breeze blew through the multiple doorways, momentarily increasing the room's warmth.

"Most Holy One, why are you in this hot room?"

"I like having the images of god Chaac above me. What word do you have for me?"

"Most Holy One, my priests and I prayed the night. We believe no sign is a sign to proceed."

"Then so be it." The king motioned to Hakum who sat nearby. "Send for my builders. Sound the conch and summon the people to the plaza. There is work to be done."

The engineers and builders listened quietly as the king presented his idea of using bamboo tubes to move water to nearby fields. By dusk, the builders were to report on the feasibility of his plan.

Late in the afternoon, the builders returned to present their plan. Before entering the king's hall, the sound of conchs echoed across the plaza, summoning villagers.

The head engineer led the way, bowed, cleared his throat, and then stood erect. "Most Holy One, we will first direct water to those areas where maize clings to life. From there, we have selected two additional areas to receive a portion of the water."

"This is an addition to my plan," the king said. "I had not thought of proportioning water to other fields."

Most Holy One, "Village men will harvest the largest bamboo logs. They will be split lengthwise and segment walls removed to make a half-tube to carry flowing water. The receiving end of the water tube will be the height of four men and then slope downward. This will allow water to flow to where the earth will drink. Smaller bamboo trunks will be lashed to the larger tubes to create a supporting lattice."

Hearing the report, the king smiled then donned his royal robe and feather crown. He appeared happy as he smiled and headed for the palace terrace to greet villagers waiting in the central plaza.

Seeing their leader on the palace terrace, the crowd shouted his praises and slapped their thighs.

The king raised his arms, bidding his people to be quiet. "People of Dzibilchaltun. Listen. We have much work to do. You are accustomed to building with stone and stucco. Today, Chumbulum, my engineer, will tell you about building something new. This we do while Chaac gathers sky water to make rain. We must work swiftly!"

The crowd cheered Chumbulum's appearance on the terrace. He waited for the crowd to quiet down then said, "Villagers." He moved to the front of the terrace. "My friends. All the men who cut trees, for baking limestone, will stop their work. We will work in teams as we do when building a temple. One team will harvest bamboo, another will split bamboo, and another will remove bamboo segment walls. Others will collect vines to bind the bamboo, and others will build lattice supports for the water carrying tubes."

Chumbulum paused to accept questions from villagers. Having satisfied their questioners, he said, "Each household will donate one water jug to the project. They will be used to carry water from Xlacah to the highest point of the tube." Chumbulum glanced toward the king who nodded his affirmation of the presentation. Chumbulum continued. "Since women are the water bearers for their households, they need no training. They will carry water-filled jugs to men who will hoist and pour the water into the half-tube. The jugs will then be refilled and emptied again and again until the selected fields have drunk their fill. Several days later, we will repeat the process until the crops grow and bear their bounty. Then we will feast again."

The villagers shouted their approval.

The king knew the people were happy to have a plan that would provide the equivalent of rain even if manmade. He had long watched his people sit helplessly, watching their crops die while awaiting rain. Such waiting led to depression and worry. He knew the drought had weakened their faith in him but believed this dream meant the gods still favored him.

The king visited the worksite to monitor the progress of his project.

Workers cut, stacked, and prepared bamboo faster than builders could shape supplies to the task. In a matter of days, the first section of the irrigation tube stood ready. Within ten dawns, the half tube reached the first field.

During the king's daily visit, Chumbulum explained his men's work process. "Temporary dams will sit in the largest half tubes to retain water until its desired release. We need enough force to cause the water to reach the farthest field not trickle to the nearest one and stop."

Days later, while the high priest and king read in his library, word of the completion of the tube arrived.

"High Priest, search the writings of the scribes. Find the most propitious day when we should start the flow of our sacred water."

"Most Holy One, I have anticipated this day. The scribes tell me the best time is two suns from today."

"Then we must move quickly." The king walked to the doorway and looked to the sky. He smiled and looked over his shoulder at the priest. "I praise your forethought. We must inform the villagers. They will want to prepare a celebration for the day we give drink to the earth."

"With your permission, I will share the plan with the villagers. I know they will be happy to hear it."

Chapter 10

To mark the occasion, the queen asked the women, designated to carry water jugs, to dress in festival clothing. A few found short lengths of leaf-bearing vines, which they twisted together to make celebratory crowns.

Every member of the villages had gathered for the momentous occasion.

While waiting for the jug bearers to begin their task, the queen sat on a temporary throne near the waterhole. The hem and shoulder straps of her long dress bore elaborate decorations of shells and pieces of glimmering jade and gold. Her black hair, gathered in a ponytail, glistened with sage scented oil. Her long gold earrings and authority necklace flashed in the sunlight and clanked against each other as she moved her head.

She held an ornate water-filled bowl containing the ashes of a piece of paper stained with blood from her fingertip. Her prayers, associated with the burning of the paper, imbued the water with a blessing. She would use this sacred water, flicked from her fingers, to bless the jug-carrying women as they transported the water-filled jugs.

The women appeared happy to play a role in

promoting the return of life to the gardens. They saw their job as a gift to fellow villagers.

Mothers and stronger female children shifted empty water jugs over and over from head to ground while waiting for the ceremony to begin.

The matriarch of the community, Xma, yelled to the jug bearers. "Form a single line behind me."

She led the smiling and giggling women, past the queen, to the waterhole where two of the strongest dipper-women awaited the women's arrival.

On hearing the king's conch blown to announce his arrival, the queen stood.

Slapping their thighs, the crowd shouted his praises and bowed as he passed.

He wore gold arm and wrist bracelets, his finest loincloth, sandals with gold eyelets, his authority necklace, and his gold encrusted jade ear plugs. His crown had new, longer quetzal feathers and new blue, red, and yellow feathers woven into his ceremonial cloak. Hakum had polished the center gold-encrusted shell clasp on his cape to a gleaming luster.

The king appeared stoic as he and the noblemen passed the queen then walked toward the receiving end of the tube. The smiling king took slow, measured steps toward his temporary throne. He waved to his people who bowed and cheered. He paused in front of his throne so Hakum could hold the royal cloak aside as the king sat down. Hakum then stood to the right of the king and smiled.

The king nodded to the nearby high priest. He and the assistant priests made offerings, blessed the water tube and crowd with incense, and then he bowed toward the king and blessed him.

The king watched several smoke pots being

swung in a celebratory blessing as he whispered to Hakum. "Tell the priests not one ember should fall from their smoke pots. We don't want our jungle to become an inferno." The king rose, raised his arms, and looked toward the sky. "Gods, we use your water for our people and your praise." Looking at the waiting water bearers, he said, "Draw and carry the holy water."

As the women passed the queen, she blessed them with holy water and prayed, "Gods of Xlacah, carry yourself in these drops of sacred water and bless those who assist. Bless their labor and grant life to our crops."

The king turned to the high priest. "Where is our shaman? I don't see him."

"I will speak of him later, Most Holy One," the high priest said. "He's still ill."

The king smiled at seeing the water bearers contribute to the needs of the village. They carried the heavy water-filled jugs to the tower where each woman handed her burden to one of eight waiting men.

The men, wearing their best loincloths and valuables, stood barefooted at various levels on a bamboo ladder placed on each side of the receiving end of the tube.

"Let the water jugs be emptied," the king said.

The man receiving the water jug at ground level passed it to a man stationed higher on the ladder. When the jug reached the top-most man, he poured its water into the receiving end of the half-tube then dropped the jug into the hands of a man at the foot of the ladder. He handed the jug to a woman who took it to the waterhole for refilling. She then returned it to a ladder man.

The king walked to the tube to watch water flow down the half-tube to the first temporary dam, creating a long shallow pool. Farther up the tube, another temporary dam found a home. After several lakes were created, the man assigned to each lake waited for the command to remove its temporary dam.

On the king's order, the dams were sequentially removed, allowing water to gush toward the fields. The king and crowd cheered on seeing the water flow without a break.

These cyclical activities were repeated throughout the day. However, after only a few cycles, the junction of two of the widest half-tubes weakened. The joint buckled, spilling valuable water. Uxtub, the tallest villager, rushed to the tube and supported it with his extended hands. He held it until workers could reinforce the joint.

Uxtub smiled as he received the accolades of the king and villagers. They slapped their thighs and shouted his praises for saving the tube.

The high priest and engineer Chumbulum followed the king as he walked a thousand paces to the discharge end of the water tube. Chumbulum called the king's attention to the tubes, which branched like tree limbs. "These three tubes will carry the water's flow over a field three hundred paces long and two hundred paces wide. Much will grow in this watered ground."

The king smiled then said, "I have lived to see my dream. Its presence is the sign of favor I sought from the gods."

"High Priest, you sweat too much and seem worried," the king said. "Why no smile or expression of happiness?"

"I'm concerned for the shaman."

"What? I thought you were worried about me, not our shaman."

"Word comes he has been ill for days. He sweats even though he hasn't worked, nor has he lain in the sun. He speaks of strange things and strikes at the air. He is like a roped animal. His words are strange and mysterious. I fear he is possessed."

Puzzled, the king stared at the ground for a moment. *The shaman is much respected. I trust his age is not against him.* "What can we do for him?"

"Most Holy One, his family does all they can but to no avail. An evil spirit holds him."

The king clasped the priest's arm. "Report to me regularly about his wellbeing. If there is more to be done, I want to hear of it."

The king glanced over the wet fields and smiled. He picked up a lump of soil and rolled it between his fingers. "Let us leave this field with expectations of bountiful provisions."

The drought continued. The already low water level in the Xlacah waterhole continued to fall. The water-bearing women were taking its strength to give drink to the gardens of maize and fruit trees.

The king smiled on seeing the garden show signs not only of life but a young crop. He sent men to the sea hoping to catch a few fish during the poor fishing phase of the moon. The fish were to be used as fertilizer and an offering to the field gods.

Two moon cycles later, the king wanted to visit the fields to see their bounty. Hakum arranged for the local chieftain to receive the Most Holy One and the high priest to see and bless the crops.

The royal visitor and local chieftain were joined by the nobleman who owned the fields. Dressed in his finery, he beamed with pride on seeing the Most Holy

One walking in his field, fingering tassels of young maize

Pleased, the king smiled on seeing his god-sent dream realized. He held an ear of maize for the high priest's examination. "The field god has smiled on this land and us. See his gift. He welcomes our drink." The king looked at the damp ground. "The earth is no longer dry. It yields imprints of our steps. We are on sacred ground. Let us remove our sandals and trod with bare feet."

Hakum removed the king's and then the priest's sandals. Next, he assisted the local chieftain and the nobleman in removing their sandals before removing his own.

After walking barefooted along several rows of maize, the height of a man, the high priest said, "Most Holy One, we should seek refuge from the heat of the sun god. We sweat too much. Your palace awaits your return. There you'll be cool."

The king nodded.

The priest waited for the king to finish examining an ear of maize and then said, "Since we are near, and with your permission, Most Holy One, I will visit our shaman."

"Priest, we will all be more comfortable under the coolness of our stones but do visit the shaman."

"I will have my assistant run ahead to inform the local chieftain of my visit."

The high priest waved goodbye to the king then headed into the barren jungle to visit the shaman.

Chapter 11

Shamans had no access to the temple nor did they compete with temple priests. They served as low level intercessors for villagers.

On entering Dzilmak, the shaman's village, the high priest noted an eerie silence permeating everything. He slowed his pace on seeing village chieftain Dzilmak walking toward him along with the high priest's assistant.

The elderly chieftain smiled then nodded. Out of respect for the high priest, the chieftain removed his simple three feather crown. "Welcome Ah Kin Mai." The chieftain bowed to the high priest. "I hear you wish to see the shaman. May I escort you to his home?"

"Please. How is he today?"

The chief held his palms to the sky and looked into the priest's eyes as if to answer but dropped his arms. "I'm not sure." The chieftain shook his head. "The shaman speaks strange words. We understand none of them. It is like he's held captive and speaks with evil spirits. At times, he must be restrained for fear he will leave, hurt himself, strike someone, or release his demons on the village. Come, see for yourself."

The high priest followed the chieftain past makeshift altars whose smoke almost blocked their path.

"The villagers use these simple altars to burn meager offerings to the sky gods in hope of rain," the chieftain said.

"Who do they honor?" the priest asked, between coughs caused by the foul smelling smoke.

"Chaac."

"So everyone prays for rain, not just priests and the Most Holy One. Perhaps the rat on that altar should have been eaten instead of burned," the high priest said. "I notice the people have a disheartened look. They suffer the effects of starvation even more than the Most Holy One and the royal family."

At the shaman's hut, his friends and family bowed to the high priest.

The shaman rested in a hammock strung between bare limbs of two trees. Using dry palm fronds and an old cotton dress, the family had made shade for him by supporting the items over vines tied to tree limbs.

The haggard old shaman sweated profusely. He had a sparse, scraggly grey beard, and wore an old, tattered loincloth. His long, matted hair hung over the edge of his hammock.

The shaman's elderly wife stood at his side. Her leather-like skin blended into the brown of the dry jungle. Trying to cool and comfort him, she poured seawater on his head and chest and fanned him with a tree bark fan.

The shaman's body had a covering of dust mixed with sweat and sea water. Together, they created a thin coat of mud on parts of his torso. Flies flocked to his chest and face, but he seemed unbothered by them. Instead, he tried to eat them. He frequently licked his lips, which were crusted with thickened saliva and dust. He mumbled meaningless sounds while his eyes appeared to follow an unseen object.

The high priest ducked under the shaman's shading boughs and approached the old man. "Great shaman, speak of your health," the priest said. "The Most Holy One has sent me to inquire about you."

The shaman widened his reddened eyes and stared at the priest. The small group of visiting friends grew quiet. The old man seemed to focus his vision, while attempting to sit up in his swaying hammock.

The high priest assumed the shaman wanted assistance and pulled on his arm to help him sit up. *His skin is so hot,* the priest thought.

Suddenly, the shaman pulled free of the priest's grip and screeched, "Eeeh wa nahab gil mack uk seni amachu ke nohdo mas huk no ma!"

The shaman's outburst so frightened the high priest he jerked his arm backwards, almost falling. He visibly shook from shock and fear. "You are free, Shaman," the priest said, collecting his composure as the shaman continued to mumble.

"What did he say?" the priest asked the village chieftain then the shaman's wife.

The chieftain replied, "We don't know."

As the shaman quieted, the chieftain repositioned the shaman's loincloth for his modesty.

"Holy High Priest, his words are unknown to me," the wife said, bowing and wiping a tear. "Never in our thirty-three great sun cycles have I heard such sounds from him or any visitor to our village."

The shaman pulled himself upright, held onto his hammock, and then stood. He tottered for a moment then steadied himself and stared at the high priest, striking fear in his heart. Suddenly, the shaman lurched toward the priest. The shaman gripped the priest's throat, causing him to scream in horror as he tried to pry the shaman's hands from his neck.

Two villagers grabbed the old man and pried his hands from the priest's neck. Another man held the shaman while his hands struck the air. Exhaustion from starvation and his illness caused the shaman's thin legs to buckle. Terrified, the restraining villagers permitted the old man to slump to his knees. From the dust, he railed at the high priest and shook his fist at the sky while shrieking, "Eeeh wa . . . nahab gil . . . mack uk . . . seni amachu ke nohdo . . . mas huk no ma!"

As his last word flew to the heavens on spittle, the shaman slumped to the ground unconscious. Shocked, the high priest stared at the crumpled man. The priest waited to see if the shaman would wake and shake himself free of the demon believed to dwell in his heart, but the old man didn't move. With his sandal, the priest tapped the shaman's shoulder then withdrew his foot for fear the shaman might grab it, but the old man remained motionless. The priest knelt and placed his hand on the man's chest. The hand barely moved.

"He breathes," the high priest said, "but his skin is hot. Place him in his hammock and give him water when he awakens. Send for more sea water so he may be bathed and cooled."

The local chieftain stared at the high priest. "What can we to do for our shaman?"

The visiting friends became silent, awaiting words of healing for their shaman.

I wish I knew, the priest thought then said, "See to his needs. Care for him. He should be seen by the medicine man. In one day, send me word of his health."

The priest turned to his assistant. "We must report to the king. Bring a tube of fresh water from village reserves. We're leaving."

On their way home, the high priest and his companion discussed the shaman's strange behavior. The priest said, "Perhaps the shaman was not vigilant enough in his acts to keep evil spirits at bay."

"He knew they're everywhere," the assistant said. "We all do, but for some reason, one has taken hold of him."

"I'm afraid you're right, and it is deep within him. I hope it is not in his heart."

The high priest made his way to the king's reception hall. The king sat on a floor cushion fumbling with his authority necklace and staring into space.

"Most Holy One," the priest said, "I have news."

The king patted a floor cushion. "Come sit with me. Tell me what I need to know."

"I have seen our shaman. I believe he is possessed by a demon—one whose evil I have never seen. It is strong and causes our seer to speak a strange tongue, raging against the gods, me, and the sky."

"What?" The king gasped. "I had no idea he was so overtaken. Is there more?"

The priest shook his head. "The shaman is filled with fear and hate. He strikes at everything—even me. I think he wanted to kill me." The priest thought for a moment. "I ask permission to send a priest to Chichen Itza to consult with the great high priest. He has much experience. He will know of a cure for this possession."

"Do as you wish," the king said. "Send a young priest who can withstand the rigors of many days travel and heat. He should travel with a guard in case he encounters devils, foes, or the black panther. The king looked at the images of the gods on the ceiling. For a moment, he seemed to focus on the red image of Chaac. "Our shaman is dear to me. He helped care for me as a boy. Learn what we can do to rid him of this demon."

At the hour of the god's sleep, the young priest and his guard paid their respect to the king then left on their journey to Chichen Itza.

Tossing and turning on his bed, the king could not clear his mind of the shaman's demon. After an hour, he stilled his mind and found rest in the blessings of the god of sleep.

Halfway through the night, Hakum awakened the king. "Most Holy One. There is something horrible in the jungle. You must see this."

The naked king roused himself from his bed cushion, yawned, and then walked toward the doorway leading to the top-most terrace of the palace. On the way, his nostrils filled with the smell of smoke. He coughed on inhaling the hot air laden with foul vapors.

Hakum tried, without success, to place clothing on the uncooperative leader who rushed to the edge of the terrace. To the north, he saw the shaman's village and to the east the irrigated field. In horror, he watched the jungle around the maize field being consumed by a great fire that roared through the dry jungle. In shock, the king held his breath and watched broad columns of fire soar into the night sky, framing the barren jungle in stark silhouette against the searing backlight of the fire. The normally cool sea breeze felt hot against the king's skin.

Looking at his king with horror-filled eyes and

fear shaking his voice, Hakum said, "The dry leaves have caused the fire to spread to the fields. Most Holy One, our holy center is threatened."

"Have the conch blown. Gather the villagers to fight this fire. They can scrape away the dead underbrush near The Center to starve the flames.

Hakum ordered a guard, who stood in apparent shock and disbelief, to blow his conch. The king donned his loincloth then he and Hakum ran down the ninety palace steps, crossed the plaza, and then headed for the gardens. On the way, several noblemen and the high priest joined them. The men of lower status slowed their pace to allow the king to be first to arrive at the fields.

On seeing the burning crops, the king screamed and shook his fist at the sky. "Gods, do not let this be! Do not punish me or my people." Barefooted, the Most Holy One walked toward the young maize now engulfed in flames. He beat his chest and yelled at the sky. "Why oh gods have you damned my effort to feed the people? Why destroy our fields with fire?"

The king fell to his knees, buried his head in his hands, and wept. The high priest, moments behind the king, rushed to his side. With a hand under each armpit, the high priest and a nobleman pulled the sobbing king to his feet. The high priest whispered in the king's ear, "Most Holy One . . . stand before your people. Weep not for this loss. Show no weakness to the gods. They test you."

The king stood tall, trying to compose himself, but his emotions overtook him. He hung his head and cried. *What evil have we done? Why strike us like this?*

After a moment of silence, the king raised his arms toward the sky and yelled, "Burn me, oh angry gods. Burn me—not our maize." With this utterance, he raced toward a column of fire roaring like the thunder of a herd of charging boar.

The high priest yelled to the nobleman nearest the running king. "Stop him! He doesn't know what he's doing. Stop him!"

A nobleman threw himself in front of the Most Holy One causing him to fall. As though transported by a levitating force, the high priest suddenly stood beside the fallen king, helping him to his feet.

"Most Holy One," the high priest said, "I ordered the nobleman to act out of respect for your sacred being. He did as I ordered. Cast aside any desire to strike him or his family for causing your fall."

Brushing ashes and soil from his face and body, the king turned to the priest who visibly shook. "I know what the nobleman did and have no desire for revenge." The king faced the nobleman. "Thank you for your love of your king. I had no thought for myself when I ran toward the fire. I felt a great loss for the work of the people and the strength of hope mixed with the toil of growing this burning maize. You, nobleman, are blessed for your act of love.

Having regained his composure, the king asked the group, "From where did this fire descend? Did someone become careless with a cooking fire? Did the gods drop lightening?"

"No, Most Holy One," the priest said, his voice trailing off.

"Spare me nothing, Priest. Tell me everything."

"Most Holy One, I have heard something horrible. Our beloved shaman caused this fire."

Shocked, the king yelled, "No." Disbelief tinged his words as he shook his head. "That cannot be."

"Most Holy One, a villager saw the shaman burn the maize and the underbrush encircling the field."

"This cannot be," the king said, staring at the ground and shaking his head. "The shaman is a good man, a holy man. He has never angered the gods or countered his king or our people."

"Most Holy One, two villagers captured him when they saw he had set the fire. He called upon devils and screamed curses at those who made what he called artificial rain. The shaman screeched another curse then yelled, 'Only Chaac can make rain for the earth. To mimic Chaac is a sacrilege and cannot be permitted for fear of angering all the gods.'"

"Your words are stinging," the king said. "They hurt my heart.

The priest continued. "The captors said, 'The shaman screamed like a possessed man and said, Only fire can purge the evil of man-made rain. Crops so grown must be destroyed lest The Center and its people be cursed.' Those who restrained him said, 'He raged and cursed those who designed and built the watering tube.'"

"Where is my old friend now?" the king asked the high priest. "What has become of him?"

"The shaman has been returned to his hut. Two villagers guard him. I have sent for the medicine man to give him the sleep plant."

"Good. Bring him to me tomorrow at the time of the high-sun meal. I wish to question him. I ask that you seek council with the gods about his needs and what justice we should order for his misdeeds."

The king watched villagers frantically fight the flames. Some beat burning bushes, others tossed sand and stomped burning debris blanketing the jungle floor.

Occasionally, a rope sandal caught fire and required its own stomping. Several men used tree limbs to rake debris from the edge of the fire to starve it of fuel. Others braved the flames in order to pour what little water they had on fruit trees yet untouched by the fire.

Over several hours, the flames were extinguished. Villagers who wore sandals stomped embers to prevent reigniting of debris.

A thick cloud of smoke masked what had once been a verdant field. The air hung heavy with the smell of burnt maize, making it difficult to breath near the area.

Despondent, the king returned to the palace.

The queen sat on her heels in the doorway of her bed chamber, weeping over the disaster she had witnessed. The king sat beside her and attempted to console her with an embrace. "Fear not. This is not the anger of the gods."

The next morning, a hot, dry breeze blew from the south as a new day dawned. The king, high priest, nobles and curious villagers were on site to evaluate the damage. Clouds of ash rose high into the air as the leaders moved through the burned fields. Morning light revealed near total destruction of the maize. The fruit trees which stood in the midst of the maize had lost most of their leaves and smaller limbs.

The king painfully acknowledged the field would produce no food in the near future. Although depressed, he mustered the courage to address those who had helped extinguish the fire and joined him in surveying the damage. "Our beloved, demon-possessed shaman has struck a great blow. I am saddened by this loss, but

I thank you for your efforts. Nobleman, post two men to watch for hot embers. We can't afford another fire. Villagers, return to your home and rest. We consult the gods for a path to our future."

The king and high priest returned to The Center.

The distraught king paused at the door of his palace and knocked dirt and ash from his feet. Inside, he slumped into his hammock and wiped a tear as Hakum washed his feet.

The queen approached her dejected husband. "What caused this loss?" she asked, hugging her husband.

"The shaman cursed our work. He set the fire."

The queen released her husband, stood upright, and stared at him. "Not the shaman." She turned away and asked, "Why would he do such a thing?" She wiped a tear. "What are we and our people to do until Chaac sends rain?"

The king paced. "The shaman thought I caused a sacrilege by using Xibalba's waters as false rain. Now, I question what path I am to take. We must rely on our priests for directions. There is nothing more we can do now. Go. Take a nap, comfort our children, and pray the gods send a dream to guide us."

The queen kissed her husband and left for her quarters where their children played.

Lost in thought, the king paced his bedroom. *What must I do? Gods guide me.* He paused and stared out the doorway. *Gods guide me!*

The king had a fitful sleep until the next day's high-sun meal when he awoke with a start. Half asleep, he looked out the doorway and noted the sun high in the sky. *Why did no one awaken me?*

He dressed then walked toward the dining room from which he heard animated conversations.

"You're up?" the queen said, burping her son over her bare shoulder.

The noblemen stood and bowed as he entered.

"Why did no one awaken me at sunrise?"

"I instructed Hakum to let you sleep," the queen said. "Your worries are best solved with sleep. Come. Join us."

The king sat down on a cushion painted with images of Chaac and Huracan.

While the diners shared the fare of a small fish and three red *xac pac* berries per person, conversation centered on the fire and the shaman's role in the disaster.

Hakum entered the dining hall and addressed the king. "Most Holy One, you asked the shaman be brought to you at this time."

"Bring him," the king said, placing a berry in his mouth.

A hush fell over the diners on seeing the scruffy shaman stumble into the room. He smelled of urine. Two guards half-dragged the distraught, mumbling man to the center of the room as he struggled to escape his captors.

"I don't want to be here! Not in the presence of heretics!" the shaman shouted, eyes glaring so much they appeared about to fall from their sockets.

The guards pushed the shaman to the floor. One held the old man's arms behind his back while the other put his foot against the shaman's neck, keeping him prostrate and preventing any attempt to attack the king. Sunlight, streaming through a doorway, illuminated the downed man's weathered face and caused dust particles, stirred by the shaman's squirming, to glisten.

"Guards," the king said, "let the shaman stand. An old friend should not be treated this way."

"Yes, Most Holy One, but we should hold him," a guard said.

The king walked around the standing shaman and examined his body. He looked for a physical answer to explain the shaman's behavior. He still bore dirt from his village, and his brow bore a thick crust of darker dirt. His tattered loincloth had multiple urine stains. His knees and elbows had multiple scrapes.

The shaman, glaring at the king, scowled, raged, and murmured incomprehensibly.

The king faced the shaman and stared into his reddened eyes. "My old friend, why have you done this horrible thing of fire?"

Suddenly, the shaman shrieked the unfathomable words he had screamed earlier.

Shocked and perplexed, the king glanced around the room. "Can anyone decipher these words?"

Silence and stares filled the space as each guest looked questioningly at his neighbor.

The shaman shrieked and then muttered in a low, guttural voice, "Cursed be those who mimic the gods and make rain. To mimic the gods is sacrilege. Cursed be those who take for themselves the role of Chaac. They and their works must be destroyed!"

The king fingered his necklace while pondering the shaman's words. He then looked past the doorway, past the tops of gleaming temples and palaces toward the sea, and then back at the shaman. "Shaman, your king consulted the priests, and they approved building the water tube, which I saw in a dream sent by the gods."

"My thoughts were not sought on this profanity," the shaman said. "If you had, I would have told you of the sacrilege."

"You doubt our high priest?" the king asked.

"Your priests and acolytes did not hear the gods say to make artificial rain! Your so-called holy men heard nothing. The absence of rain is a way of testing you and our people. You have failed the gods, but I have saved you."

"Shaman, your illness—or demons—have caused you to act in ways never seen before. You have done great harm. What am I to do with you?"

The shaman stopped mumbling and raised his head. "Do your pleasures, but nothing undoes the evil wrought by you in making rain. Chaac will not forgive your blasphemy."

"Enough!" the king yelled, shocking his guests. "You speak counter to our priests and counter to a dream sent to me by the gods. You are one against many and heed only demons." The king walked to his cushion. "Guards, take the shaman to his home and keep him there while we consider his fate. See that he is bathed and dressed anew. Hakum, get my hair oil for the shaman's use."

The struggling shaman had to be dragged from the room.

The king picked up a berry, stared at it, and then threw it at a wall. He shook his head and murmured something under his breath as he rose. He called to the standing noblemen, "Come with me to the council room. We need to decide the shaman's fate."

The queen grabbed the young prince who ran after his father. "Hakum," she called, "Take the children to their play area."

The queen joined the men in the council room and listened while they deliberated the shaman's fate.

The high priest looked right then left at the council members. "Most Holy One, I urge caution of you and the noblemen. Take no haste in deciding the shaman's fate. We should await word from Chichen Itza. The priest who traveled there for consultation should soon return."

After much discussion, the group recommended the king wait for the input from the great high priest. They also agreed the shaman should be given the sleep plant to prevent him from harming himself, or others, and to prevent him from starting another fire.

The king overheard one of the noblemen say, "Postponement is easy for me. I don't look forward to deciding the fate of an old friend."

The king could not concentrate on anything while awaiting word from Chichen Itza. Days seemed to drag. The sleepless king pondered possible solutions to the problem regarding the shaman, but none seemed appropriate.

Late in the fourth day following the council's meeting, Hakum informed the king, "The priest has returned from Chichen Itza. He has word from the great high priest."

"Send for my council and the queen."

Within a short time, the group met in the council room to hear the young priest's message.

"Tell us, Priest, what does the great high priest suggest?" the king asked.

"Most Holy One, the great priest sends blessings and holy advice for the removal of the curse from our shaman. The great priest's words are hard, Most Holy

One."

"Spare me. What is his advice?"

"The demon dwells in the shaman's heart. We must cut it from the shaman's body."

The council uttered a collective gasp.

The king dropped his head. "This is not what I expected or wanted to hear."

Glancing at each nobleman, the young priest said, "The great high priest consulted the stones and concluded the shaman's demon-containing heart is to be offered to Chaac in two sun rises when the calendar is right for removing evil."

The king, queen, and council gasped at hearing the mention of two sun rises.

The Most Holy One stood up from his throne, palms to the sky, and stared at the priest. "Your words pain my heart. Are you sure the great priest had no alternate solution?"

The young priest looked at the king then lowered his eyes. "No, Most Holy One . . . only the words I have spoken. A failure to do so will allow the demon to beguile others."

The king looked skyward. *Why this message. I had hoped for a way to spare the shaman. Gods, why do you let evil so attack us?*

"High Priest, make ready the ceremony in two dawns." The king stepped down from his throne, shaking his head. "How can I do this thing I care not to do?"

The noblemen stood until the king and queen had left the hall.

In his quarters, the king fell on the shoulder of the queen and wept. "The gods hurt me with this news, for I am the one who must order and see the deed done."

"Bulek . . . I share your sorrow and the weight of your obligation." The queen stroked the king's head. "I too love the shaman."

The king ordered the impending ritual be announced throughout The Center and surrounding villages. He then summoned village chiefs and noblemen to the palace, so the high priest could inform them about the impending ceremony. The king invited the officials to spend the night in the palace and required they attend the ritual. Common villagers would not be permitted to enter the central plaza during the ceremony.

Minutes before the dawn of the ritual day, an eerie stillness hovered over the jungle. Torches sputtered in the predawn breeze as priests, noblemen, and village chiefs gathered on the terrace of the rarely used Temple of Heart Sacrifice located at the far edge of the plaza. They dressed in their finest clothing, jewelry, earplugs, and crowns. Standing quietly, they stared straight ahead.

The king and queen climbed the temple steps. Each wore gold jewelry, elaborately decorated loincloths, crowns, and a jaguar skin over their shoulder. Her servant held her long feathered robe aside, to prevent it from being stepped on. Hakum carried the train of the king's longer robe.

The king stared toward the top of the temple. The short queen often leaned against the steep steps, which she climbed with difficulty. When the royal couple stepped onto the terrace, the nobles bowed. The royals quietly took their seats, six paces from the north end of the stone altar stained brown with blood from previous sacrifices.

The king's crown of tall bluish-green feathers fluttered in the warm morning breeze as Hakum tucked the king's and queen's feathered capes aside to protect them from the expected splatter of blood. He then stood behind the king's throne.

The rattle of various authority necklaces and an occasional cough broke the silence of the early dawn. The sad looking noblemen shifted their weight, waiting for the dreaded ritual to begin.

Once the king had settled on his throne, the high priest ordered the conch blown. Its mournful sound echoed across the jungle while two guards escorted the shaman up the temple steps. The sleep plant had obviously left him drowsy. He complied with the guards physical commands but had difficulty negotiating the steps. On reaching the last few steps, the shaman slumped to his knees. A collective gasp echoed around the empty plaza.

The king thought, *Gods, don't let him fall.* He whispered to the queen, "The shaman shows the effect of the sleep plant. For that I'm thankful."

Once on the terrace, the shaman looked around. He had been bathed and dressed in a new loincloth. His hair had been washed and rubbed with the king's own fragrant oil. The shaman nodded his recognition of the king.

The king stood out of respect. His heart ached as he thought, *Even now, the shaman shows me respect.*

Suddenly, the shaman shrieked, "Eeeh wa . . . nahab gil . . . mack uk . . . seni amachu ke nohdo . . . mas huk no ma!"

The shrillness of the sounds startled the noblemen who jumped back as if a curse had been hurled at each of them. Everyone, except the king and queen, seemed frightened by the shaman's words.

The king and queen had steeled themselves for anything unusual. Each drew in a deep breath and attempted to exhale their angst. Unperturbed, they stood straight and still. The king knew the high priest and his acolytes believed the outburst to be demonic—presumably directed at their king—possibly everyone.

The Most Holy One took a few steps toward the shaman. "Shaman, do you know who stands before you?"

The shaman shrieked, "Eeeh wa . . . nahab gil . . . mack uk . . . seni amachu ke nohdo . . . mas huk no ma!" He then spat at the king.

The king kept his composure. Without a word, he turned and walked to his throne, moved his cape aside, and then sat down. He hung his head, thinking, *This is more than I can bear.*

The queen squeezed her husband's hand several times. He returned the gesture but held his grip. The queen used her other hand to wipe a tear and still her quivering lip while staring at the floor.

The drowsy shaman gathered his strength over several seconds. Staring at the king, he yelled, "You mocked the gods! You dared to make rain. You are cursed!"

The king whispered to the queen, "I don't want to be here."

The queen squeezed the king's hand. "I know. I know."

Eyes closed, the king raised his head. His lip trembled as he said, "High Priest, remove the shaman's heart as the great high priest instructed. Free the shaman and our village of his evil spirit."

The high priest bowed then waited as assistant priests removed his ceremonial clothing. The celebrant of the ritual should wear only a white, cotton loincloth that would be burned after the ceremony.

An assistant approached the high priest, bowed, and offered a folded sacred banana leaf containing an obsidian knife.

The king swallowed hard on seeing the blade. He squeezed the queen's hand so hard she moaned.

Four chac priests, with the assistance of the shaman's guards, walked the old man to the altar. Over the years, he had been on this platform many times, assisting in other sacrifices. His eyes widened, as he stared at the blood stained altar stone.

Suddenly, the assistants lifted the startled shaman, face to the sky, while the high priest said a prayer. The assistants lowered the trembling shaman, face up, onto the altar. He offered no resistance. His stiffened neck muscles held his unsupported head upright. With wide eyes, he appeared to search the sky and his surroundings while muttering unknown words.

The king knew the shaman remembered the chain of events about to happen. The shaman and king winced when the shaman's arms and legs were stretched downward. They were held by six men, not the usual four because no one wanted the shaman to create a problem.

Taking the knife from the banana leaf, the high priest walked to the altar. He stood motionless beside the shaman whose arms and legs were stretched to the point of being dislocated. The high priest murmured incantations, which were repeated by assistant priests.

Suddenly, a cool wind blew in from the north, instead of the usual hot wind from the south. It bore a sense of dread and relief from the morning heat. The priests' ritual words were ferried beyond the plaza to the ears of villagers who waited beyond the plaza.

The shaman let his head dangle over the end of the altar. He stared to the north, the direction of the sea and his home. For a moment, he stared at the king and queen who sat five paces away. The gaze of the king and shaman met for a moment. The king struggled to maintain a blank stare, but he knew his face revealed his despair. He mouthed, 'Forgive me, old friend.'

The shaman lifted his head. His and the gaze of his friend, the reluctant high priest, met. The high priest abruptly broke eye contact and looked skyward. With both hands, he raised the knife overhead. He showed it to the king, queen, and then the noblemen who stood in a semicircle behind the altar. Everyone faced east and waited for the first rays of the sun to appear over the tree tops.

The blue-grey morning sky suddenly sparkled with the first golden rays of sunlight. The sun god had awakened and waited.

The shaman's eyes appeared fixed on the obsidian blade held over his torso. Without warning, the knife was plunged into the shaman's upper abdomen.

The king, queen, and noblemen uttered a co-mingling sound of empathetic pain. They could no longer restrain their emotions on seeing their beloved shaman's mouth gasp on his demon-freeing journey.

The shaman stiffened his extremities against the grip of those who held him. His last utterance—a sky-filling scream. Blood gushed from his wound. The old man raised his head and, with horror filled eyes, stared at the blood flowing from his abdomen. He dropped his head and went limp as the priest cut through the shaman's diaphragm. Unable to breathe, the shaman lost conscious.

The king burst into tears and looked away.

The assistant priests released their hold on the shaman's extremities and stepped back as the high priest cut free and then held high the shaman's beating heart.

Seeking a blessing, those who had held the shaman on the altar walked under a stream of blood squirting from the heart. Another stream of blood found its way across the high priest's face.

The king forced himself to watch the high priest place the shaman's quivering heart in the sacred vessel on the lap of the stone statue of Chaac, which stood behind the altar. The heart would remain in there until it had disintegrated or had been ferried by birds to the sky gods.

Keeping with custom, the high priest ordered the corpse be rolled down the temple steps.

The assistant priests prepared to execute the order, but the king raised his hand. "Stop!" he yelled. The priests paused and looked at the king. He said, "The shaman's body is not to be treated this way. Take him to the jungle and bury him in the place of his family's honored dead."

Four priests lifted the bloody corpse, hoisted it onto their shoulders, and then began the trip down the temple steps.

The king stared at the shaman's dangling head, gaping mouth, and staring eyes. Suddenly, the Most Holy One wailed. He called to the priests. "Wait." He tore a jade bead from his authority necklace. "I want to place this in the mouth of the shaman so he takes it to his grave. Let his family know I have done this in keeping with rituals for a loved one who travels the river of death. Tell his wife of this act."

"A moment," the queen said, tugging at her authority necklace. "I too wish to add a bead to that of the king's."

The two jade beads rolled in the king's hand. He wrapped his fingers around the gifts, uttered a prayer, and then placed them in the shaman's mouth, which the king closed.

"High Priest, inform the shaman's wife his wooden idols are to be kept in her home. Those idols are temple property and are usually returned on the death of a shaman, but their return to the temple is not required. For her care, I ask you take to her a measure of royal gold. Now, bear the shaman's body reverently to his resting place."

The king, queen, and noblemen removed their sandals and, according to rank, walked barefooted through the blood on the terrace.

"Conch man, blow your shell," the king said. "Notify The Center's people that the ritual is over."

With the dispersal of the despondent and reluctant attendees, the king and queen left the terrace, adding to the multiple bloody footprints left by the assistant priests who had carried the shaman's body down the temple steps.

As the assistant priests carried the shaman's body into the jungle, their mournful chants lingered in the ears of those who loved him.

The high priest and his assistants retired to a sacred chamber where they would pray for one day without bathing or eating.

Speechless and saddened, the king returned to the palace, his heart filled with a great sense of loss. *I still remember games we played when I was a boy . . . his hugs and smiles.*

In the royal quarters, Hakum wanted to remove the king's ceremonial clothing, but he refused. He sent Hakum away, collapsed onto a pillow, and wept. Hakum reentered the room carrying two small pieces of fruit and a cup of water, but he left on order of the queen who moved to the king's side. She loosened and then removed his cape. She tried to console him with an embrace as she rubbed his back. "Don't cry for the shaman," she whispered. "He is freed, his demon is destroyed, and our center is saved."

"Yes, free of his demon," the king sobbed, "but I am without a shaman—without my friend. My heart aches. Perhaps it is gripped by the shaman's demon."

Offering the cup of water, she said, "Rest awhile. Sleep. Still your mind, and then I'll send your prince."

Moments later, Princess Sac-Nicté entered the room. "Why are you crying, daddy?" she asked as she approached her father. "Are you hungry?"

The king forced himself to look at her and shook his head.

The princess cocked her head and said, "I have four berries in my room. You can have them."

The king sat up, wiped a tear, and embraced his daughter. "Thank you, but you eat them."

Chapter 12

Four full-moon cycles later, a worried Hakum visited the high priest to seek his counsel. "High Priest, The Most Holy One has lost his will. His spirit, dry as the drought, has become life-sapping. He eats little and drinks almost nothing. Even the queen has become concerned for his wellbeing."

"I know of his condition. We priests pray for the gods to send him peace."

"Despite his sacrifices, the drought persists with only the hint of rain from a few scattered clouds that blow over The Center then dissipate. Day-after-day, the king receives villagers who ask his permission to move away." Hakum paused to shake his head. "In his heart, he knows they will never return. Each time he grants the requested permission, he loses a piece of his soul. He asked me, 'Will anyone remain in Dzibilchaltun, besides my family, to comfort me?'"

"Thank you for your concern, Hakum. I will think on your concerns and speak to the king."

On a particularly hot day, the high priest sent word to Hakum that he sought audience with the king. No longer did the king, noblemen, and priest meet for a high-sun meal. They had nothing new to discuss and little food—certainly not enough for a group meal.

The high priest entered the king's quarters, bowed, and then stood motionless for several seconds.

The king leaned back against the wall, stared at the priest, and then said, "I am curious. After all this time, why do you want an audience? We have not seen each other for many dawns. Has there been a disaster?

"No. No disaster, Most Holy One."

"Come," the king said, patting a cushion. "Sit beside me. Tell me of your need?"

"Most Holy One." The priest's voice broke as he spoke. "I come with a heavy heart. In our temples toil seven priests. We have gold, silver, turquoise, shells, and worldly goods, but we have little food and none to purchase. I cannot care for my priests. Permit me to send four of the older priests to Chichen Itza to work in its temples."

"I sense the concern in your voice. We all feel hunger. Yes, send them to Chichen Itza. May the gods bless their travel.

"Thank you Most Holy One."

The priest stood, bowed, and then walked in a small circle, a hand on each side of his face as he stared at the ceiling.

The king watched for a moment then asked, "Is there more?"

"Most Holy One, we priests have prayed for three days. All agree the gods require a special sacrifice. I am here to ask your aid for our people and The Center.

"You cannot ask me to make a blood offering greater than my last.

The priest stopped circling, cleared his throat, and stared at the king.

"No, Most Holy One, but I ask that you listen with your intellect and not your emotions. With the departure of the priests for Chichen Itza, I ask they be joined by . . . Princess Sac-Nicté." *This is also my opportunity to get back at you for denying me Ix Tzutz. She should have been my wife.* "There, the princess should visit the gods in the sacred well."

The king gasped, went pale, and then stood motionless.

The priest said, "She can carry an offering to the gods who deny us rain, deny us crops, and drive our people from our beloved center." The priest paused, waiting for his request to settle into the king's mind. "Only a great sacrifice will assuage the gods. Only then will they send rain to make the jungle green and our crops grow. The princess must make this journey."

The king reeled when he heard the priest say, "You must sacrifice your daughter."

Sweating profusely from the day's heat, the king sweated even more. He began to sway. Extending his hand to make a point, he fainted.

A loud, hollow thud filled the room as the king's head struck the floor.

"Gods, don't kill our king," the priest yelled as he shuddered. Fearful, he knelt beside the king and examined his head. "Thank the gods, no blood." The priest watched for chest movements then exclaimed, "He breathes."

The priest cradled the king's head in his lap, yelled in his ear, and rubbed his face. "Awake, Most Holy One! Awake."

The high priest's yelling reached the ears of the queen and Hakum who ran into the room.

"What happened?" the queen asked, her face filled with fear. She dropped to her knees beside her husband and placed a shaking hand on the king's chest and then stared into the priest's eyes. "Say he is not dead."

"No, my queen," the priest said. "He sleeps. See. He breathes. Fear not. He will awaken."

"I pray this is not the deed of the Shaman's demon," she said, looking questioningly at the priest. Her eyes begged for an answer. "Say it isn't. Say the shaman's evil is destroyed."

"This is not the work of a demon, my Queen. The shaman's demon is dead."

"Allow me, High Priest," Hakum said, indicating he would care for the king. He then cradled the king's head in his lap and rubbed his cheek.

The queen spoke into the king's ear, "Wake up, Bulek.

The high priest sat on the floor praying and waiting for the king to awaken

Moments later, the king regained consciousness and looked around. "What happened?"

Almost in a whisper, the high priest spoke in halting words. "I had just asked that Princess Sac-Nicté accompany the priests departing for Chichen Itza."

The queen asked, "Why would you want her to go to—? Oh no! No! No! Not that." The queen's face blanched. Her jaw dropped as if ready to speak, but her tongue remained motionless for a moment. "My daughter cannot be sent to visit the gods. Not there. Not anywhere. No. Never!"

"My Queen, the gods require a major sacrifice if they are to be assuaged and send rain," the priest said. "The princess must visit the gods in the sacred well. She is the only hope for our people and The Center."

The queen rose from her crouched position and, for a moment, stared at the priest and then her husband.

Her entire body shook as she collapsed on the floor, sobbing. The floor darkened as her tears were absorbed by its stucco. Between sobs, she said, "High Priest, how can you ask this of the king or me?"

"My Queen," the high priest whispered, "the gods have not answered our king's prayers. It troubles me to say so, but the king's blood was not enough."

The queen made a fist, tightened her jaw, and glared at the priest. "How can you say his blood is not enough? He is *the* Most Holy One—the one who speaks with the gods. The one to whom the gods send dreams. Great dreams! *He* is my king, your king . . . a god-man."

The priest stood erect, his chin set. He tightened his jaw muscles and sucked air through clenched teeth. "My Queen, we need an offering of *great* worth. It *must* be of great worth if the gods are to grant our needs. There is no gift more valuable than the princess."

"Yes," the queen murmured, "nothing is more valuable to the king and me than our daughter, but is *she* valued by the gods?" The queen took several deep breaths then asked, "Why do you think she can persuade the gods to send rain?"

"My Queen," the high priest said, "the gods cannot deny a request from your daughter. She is our only hope for rain. Surely she, if anyone, can convince the gods to send rain. They cannot—they will not—deny her."

Crying, the queen begged, "Bulek, I have to leave this discussion. Its pain is more than I can bear."

The queen shuffled to the doorway where she slumped against the wall, weeping uncontrollably.

The king stared at the high priest. "You know the princess is our first born. She is the love of my life. Her visit to the gods would leave a great void in our lives and leave me with a life of heartache. There are female orphans in the village who could visit the gods. If they did not return with a god-message, there would be no mourning family to suffer her loss. There must be someone other than my beloved princess for this visit."

"Most Holy One, great needs require great gifts. I'll wait in the temple for your reply."

The king sobbed as he watched the priest back from the room. The king said, "Hakum leave me."

The king paced from one doorway to another, sobbing. *Have the gods sensed a waning of my faith? True, I've questioned why they haven't sent rain, but I meant no disrespect. Have I been selfish? Concerned only for myself? Have I ignored the gods too much?* The king sobbed and leaned against the wall. *Has the priest sensed a flaw in me? Is my blood worthless?* The king stared at the image of Chaac on the ceiling. *For many sun cycles, you have sent us rain and spread your love over this land. Do you desire my daughter? Will you look upon her with as much love as I have for her? Perhaps you are testing my faith through your desire for her.*

The king stood still for a moment, seemingly lost. *Without you, I have no place to turn, so I will do this deed. I pray you will find her so beautiful and full of love that you will return her to me and her mother. As the leader of our faith, I can do nothing more. I will send her, but I pray you return her.*

Crying, the queen had fled to the comfort of her room. In anguish, she paced in a wide circle while waiting for the king to arrive. She prayed he would tell her their five-year-old daughter would not go to

Chichen Itza.

Princess Sac-Nicté entered the room carrying a game board. "Do you want to play. . . Why are you crying, mommy?"

"I have a grain of sand in my eye," the queen replied. "I see you want to play your favorite game."

The queen tried to play the game but repeatedly broke the rules.

"Mommy, you can't do that," Princess Sac-Nicté said then pushed a game piece back to where it had been sitting. "Don't worry. I won't tell daddy you did it."

"I'm sorry, dear. Mommy doesn't feel like playing now. Go play with your brother."

The king entered the queen's quarters. She sat near a doorway sobbing and staring toward Chichen Itza. He sat down on a cushion beside her then took her hand. He caressed her fingers, kissed them, and then moved closer to her side and hugged her. For what seemed like an eternity to the queen, they stared in silence toward Chichen Itza.

Finally, the king squeezed his wife's shoulder and spoke in a shaky voice. "Ix Tzutz, we are leaders. We are called upon to make a great sacrifice." A tear traced its way down his cheek. "My heart is sad, but I'm glad to know our daughter can visit the gods. She will look down on us and our people knowing she has convinced them to send rain when all else failed. She must make this trip . . . tomorrow."

"Tomorrow!" the queen cried out then burst into tears. She sobbed against the king's chest. "No! Not tomorrow. Not tomorrow." She stopped sobbing then said, "I still remember how she cared for the younger children, her hugs, her smile and her laughter." The queen rolled on and banged her fists against the floor, tears flowing onto its ancient plaster. She wanted to yell but couldn't release the grief welling inside. She writhed and scratched at the stucco like digging a grave. "No. Not her . . . Not her."

The king stood, wiped his tears, and tugged at the queen's arm. "Please get up. You are above this display. We are royals and leaders." After a long silence, he said, "The high priest asks we travel with the princess to Chichen Itza so the people know we willingly offer our daughter. We want to please the gods on whom we call for rain. If we want them to return our crops, the jungle, to hear birds sing again, then this gift, this trip, is one we must make.

"I cannot witness this thing required for the gods and the priest. Don't ask me to make this trip."

"You're her mother; you must go." The king knelt and pulled the sobbing queen against his chest. "It is your duty, our duty to our daughter, to The Center, the people . . . the gods." The king took the queen's hand and pulled her to her feet. "Come. We must prepare to leave at sunrise."

The queen slid down the king's body and lay face down on the floor, hammering it with her fists. "No, no."

The king knelt and hugged her for a moment and then pulled her into a standing position, but her legs buckled, and she slumped to the floor, sobbing. He lifted her in his arms and carried her to bed. He whispered, "My heart is also broken but don't make this harder than it has to be. Please, Ix Tzutz, you must try to understand.

Because the queen's servants worked at the far end of the palace, the king called for Hakum.

"Yes, Most Holy One?" Hakum asked, running into the room as if a disaster had occurred.

"Get the queen's servants. They are to help the queen prepare for travel to Chichen Itza at sunrise. She will accompany our daughter who will visit the gods of the sacred well."

Hakum appeared shocked on hearing the princess would travel for a sacrifice. "As you order, Most Holy One."

Despondent, the king placed the queen on her bed then forced himself to his bedroom where he collapsed on bed pillows and wept, contemplating his impending loss, the sorrow of Ix Tzutz, and the sacrifice of Princess Sac-Nicté. "Gods, if you must—take her, but I will miss her."

Hearing scuffling sounds outside his bedroom, he looked up to see the queen being semi-dragged to her dressing room by hand-maidens. She wept with such grief she could not stand. He sobbed as her wailing faded in the distance. Just then, Princess Sac-Nicté ran past the king's bedroom. A second later, he heard her tip toe to his side.

Stroking his head, she asked, "Why are you and mommy crying?"

Lost for words, he sat up, faked a smile, and looked into his daughter's questioning eyes. He searched his soul for a way to tell her about Chichen Itza.

She obviously had not yet gone to play for she smelled freshly bathed. Her soft hand caressed his cheek as he looked deeply into her eyes. He took her hand in his, kissed it, and then held it against his cheek. She appeared perplexed as she looked into his eyes.

Clearing his throat and wiping tears, he placed her

on his lap, hugged her, and spoke softly. "We are going on a trip—at sunrise. I wish we didn't have to, but we must. You, my princess, will go with us."

"That sounds like fun," the princess said, eyes widening with anticipation. "Where are we going?"

Choking tears, he said, "Chichen Itza. Where the gods live and where you will meet them.

"Oh, I want to go," the princess said. "It sounds like fun."

The speechless king tried to swallow the lump in his throat. In broken words, he said, "The trip is necessary for the good of The Center and our people. We seek rain from the gods so our crops will grow and we will have food."

"Can I help, Daddy?" the princess asked, stroking the king's arm that embraced her.

Standing his daughter on the floor, the king stood then stared at the ceiling. He placed his hand on her shoulder and choked back tears. *I can't let her see me cry.* He swallowed hard, looked at his daughter, and said, "Yes, you can. Your mother and I want you to take our request for rain to the gods. They will listen to you. They must listen to you."

"Don't cry, daddy. I'll do it."

The princess scratched her bare belly.

Against his will, the king cried. He slumped to his pillows and dragged his loosening grip down his daughter's arm.

Appearing perplexed, the princess muttered, "I said I'd help."

"Thank you." *How can I make you understand what is before you?* "I know you'll help. Thank you."

Night fall came too swiftly for the king, for at its end came morning and the beginning of the fateful journey.

The king and queen slept on the same bed pillows. For the first time in many weeks, the princess slept between them. The queen often touched the king's arm to comfort him.

He found his bed uncomfortable and the air hot. Unable to find a spot where he could rest, he retired to his hammock. There he contemplated life without his daughter and tried to imagine how her visit with the gods would help her people.

At daybreak, Hakum backed into the bedroom, out of respect for the queen's modesty, and then shook the king.

"Most Holy One, you must prepare."

"I'm awake, but don't wake the princess or the queen. Sleep has been too short for them."

"As you wish, Most Holy One."

"Go to the priests and see that all is ready."

The king placed his ceremonial robe over his arm. He failed to notice it dragged a path through the ubiquitous dust and ash that covered everything since the fire. Suddenly, he stopped in the doorway, dropped his robe, and stared at the sky. *Great gods, why haven't you heard my pleas? Haven't my sacrifices been enough to satisfy you? Have I or anyone so sinned against you that my people must suffer this plight? What wrong has been done and by whom?*

Wrists crossed behind his back, he paced in silence.

The queen awoke, stretched her arms, and smiled. "The gods sent me a dream."

"Spare me. I'm too troubled."

"But listen," she said and tugged at her husband's hand. "Our daughter returned from the gods with a message. Pulled from the well, she ran into my arms, smiled, and said, 'The gods promise rain.'"

The king shook his head. "I wished I had had your dream, but it troubles my heart. Why would the gods send *you* a message? I'm their messenger."

"Don't fret." The queen smiled and stood. "The way of the gods is not as important as their message. Maybe you were too troubled to hear them. Besides, you didn't sleep."

The king stopped pacing and stared at his wife. "You know only one in forty persons return from the fall to the well-gods, and not all taken from the lake live to share the message the gods gave them."

"The gods do what they will," the queen said and shrugged. "Their reasons are not for us to know. You must believe."

"I'm afraid your dream is a wish—not a message from the gods." *Could her dream really be from the gods?* "Don't the gods know I gave blood until I had no more to give short of death? My sacrifices produced not a single rain drop. My blood simply flowed to the world of the gods while they looked away. They don't know me or my sacrifice."

"Don't say they looked away," the frowning queen said. "They simply saw not the right sacrifice. You gave blood, much blood, but they don't want blood. They want—no, demand more. It is in Chichen Itza where the gods will acknowledge *our* gift. They will return our daughter and send rain."

The king sat beside the queen who had fallen back on her bed. He took her hand and kissed it. "Strange how your faith grows while mine weakens. You shook with terror when you heard the priest ask that Sac-Nicté visit the gods. Now, you ask me to share your certainty that her trip will be a blessing."

"But you are our king," the queen said in a soft, firm voice. She shook his hands. "You must believe, Bulek. You are our intermediary. I know no other way. Don't abandon your faith, me, or our people and certainly not our gods."

"My heart hears your plea so still your mind. Let's prepare for our trip. It's a long one."

The queen smiled, left the room, and called for her servant to complete packing for the trip. To another, she called for assistance in dressing.

The king summoned Hakum. "We need many water tubes. There will be many thirsts to be quenched. Most of the jungle is barren and the distance between waterholes is far."

The king's preparations for the trip required the embarkation time be changed to a night departure.

The royal family ate the high-sun meal then sent Princess Sac-Nite to take a nap. She would need the rest to endure the trip starting at dusk. The group planned to sleep during the day to escape the day's heat.

At dusk, a wreath of dried vines, along with the last fresh flower from her mother's private garden graced the princess' head. The king smiled as the princess looked into his eyes and grabbed his hand. "I've never slept outside the palace," she said.

"Then we'll make it fun. We're lucky the moon god shares his light. There is much to see and learn. You'll have fun. Let's get started."

Skipping ahead, the princess smiled and said, "I like fun."

Short legs caused the princess to struggle to keep

up with the adults. Occasionally, she skipped or stopped to examine a jungle mystery, causing her father to say, "Keep up."

Early in the night, the king said, "Hakum, the princess needs a nap. Look ahead for a place where we can rest. Find a spot open to the sky so the princess can see the stars. The high priest will tell her about the place where the sun god sleeps."

The king and queen watched as the princess walked the ancient dusty path. She kept her gaze fixed on the moon-lit ground, searching for unknown things.

Half buried in the dust, she discovered a dead bird. She started to pick it up, but her mother shook her hand and said, "No."

Until this time, the princess had never seen an intact dead animals. Death had never been discussed in the children's presence.

"What is it, daddy?"

"That's what is left of a beautiful bird—like those that used to fly over the palace."

"Why doesn't it fly?" the princess asked, staring at her mother. "Why is it on the ground?"

"It couldn't find food, water, or shade, so it died," the queen said. "That's why it doesn't fly. It has lost its life."

"Life? What's life, mommy?"

The queen took the princess' hand. "Life is something given to us by the gods when we are born. It lets us see, breath, walk, talk, hear, smell, taste, love, and enjoy life. It makes us who and what we are."

"Then I have it?"

The queen choked up then cleared her throat. "Yes. You do." She knelt and embraced her daughter. "You have life. A long one."

Overhearing the conversation, the king slowed his pace.

The princess smiled and then walked ahead playfully dragging a stick.

The king whispered to the queen. "Why do you speak of such things? Speak of this no more. She is too young."

"But I shared the dream the gods sent me. Our daughter will have a long life."

"Speak no more of life or death to my daughter. Don't create uncertain thoughts."

"Your daughter?" the queen asked, short of outright rage while slapping her breast. "She's my daughter too. I will speak as I wish—with words from my heart."

The king shook the queen's arm. "You will speak *NO* more of life or death to our daughter."

The queen wrenched her arm free and stared at him. "Our daughter *will* visit the gods and *will* return with their message. It will be a message to strengthen your faith and bring favor to our people."

Suddenly, the king heard his advance guard running toward him. "Most Holy One, " the guard said, "the great high priest of Chichen Itza and his entourage approach. His guard told me the priest has been visiting priests of a nearby village and now returns to Chichen Itza."

"How far ahead is he?" the king asked.

"Not far."

The king called to his high priest, "Prepare to receive the great high priest."

A buzz of excitement filled the group on hearing the great high priest might join their group.

The king and his high priest traveled ahead to

intercept the approaching dignitary. On seeing the great high priest, the king and high priest bowed and kissed the palm of the elderly man's shaky hand. A short man, he had a hunched back. While he wore no crown, he wore several gold bracelets, an authority necklace containing numerous thumb-size gold images of gods. He also wore a gold ring on each of his knobby fingers.

"Great High Priest, this is the high priest of Dzibilchaltun," the king said. "We humbly ask to join your group for our mutual travel to the holy city."

"You and yours are invited to join us," the great high priest said. "There is safety in numbers. Evil roams the jungle in search of food and gold."

"We are blessed by your presence," the high priest said.

"I know of you through the priests you sent to Chichen Itza. We have all prayed for your needed rain."

"We travel with Princess Sac-Nicté," the high priest said proudly. "She will visit the gods in Chichen Itza's well to ask them for rain."

The elderly priest looked at the small girl and smiled. "I am sure the gods will send a message from her lips. Bring her to me."

Reluctantly, the queen nudged the princess toward the elderly priest. "Great High Priest, this is Princess Sac-Nicté, and I am her mother, Ix Tzutz, Queen of Dzibilchaltun."

Patting the princess on the head, the priest said, "Beautiful Princess, I am happy to meet you. I am sure your mother and father are proud to be able to present you to the gods. I know you will serve them well."

The presence of the great high priest increased the tension between the king and queen. They tried to whisper while they continued their heated discussion about the princess.

The high priest approached the royal couple, bowed, and addressed the king. "Most Holy One? I thought I heard doubt regarding the princess. The great high priest must not hear such things. You must clear your mind of these matters. Set an example of worthiness for this group and our peop—."

"I see Hakum ahead," the king said. "Let's hurry to our resting place."

"Yes, my King," the priest said, "We all need drink and rest, but think about what I said."

As the sun set, the king awoke, sat up, and mumbled, "I needed that sleep." He nudged the sleeping high priest. "How was it with the princess?"

"I instructed her about the heavens and the stars. She knows of the place of the god's travel and the special place for the sleep of the sun god."

Shocked the king asked, "What did you tell the princess about Chichen Itza?"

"She knows she is going to visit the gods. I spoke of nothing more."

"Say nothing more to her about the reason for this trip," the king said through clenched teeth. "I order it."

"Most Holy One, I know this is a trip you do not want to take, but I pray your doubt-stricken heart will be filled with the same faith as our queen."

"Careful with your words, High Priest. Make sure this trip is for the gods and not revenge. For years, I have felt you resented my marriage and children. Say nothing more to feed this feeling."

"But Most Holy One—"

"Quiet."

The queen walked between the two men. "High

Priest, two moons ago, I had a dream about my daughter's visit with the gods. In it, she returned from the well with a positive message about rain. The dream filled me with joy—"

"My Queen," the high priest said, "you were favored with that message, and my ears were blessed to hear it. You were truly blessed."

On hearing the priest, the king dropped his head and stood motionless for a moment. "Careful, High priest." The king saw the servant of the great high priest moving about and said, "The great high priest is breaking camp. Let us join them. Leave nothing behind.

Hakum gathered supplies while the queen and king went to awaken their daughter.

The princess rubbed her eyes and whimpered, "Do I have to get up? It's dark."

"Yes," the king said. "You must get ready to travel."

Chapter 13

Crunching sounds awoke the king. He alerted a guard then watched him investigate the distant disturbance. One after the other, various members of the group awoke. They appeared anxious for their safety on seeing the king scanning the area.

The guard returned and said, "It was a toucan scavenging our discarded seeds. The crunching sounds came from the bird hopping on dry leaves."

The group laughed at the size of the "enemy."

"How strange to have a toucan here," the king said. "I hope its presence is a good omen.

"Let's go back to sleep," the queen said.

The sun-god moved to the noon sky, and sunlight found its way under the group's awnings. A guard quietly rearranged the largest one to prevent sunlight from awakening the royal family.

As the day drew to a close, the guard awoke Hakum who would prepare food.

The king watched Hakum's activities and shook the queen's shoulder. "Wake up. We eat and travel soon."

The queen anxiously looked around.

"What is it?" the king asked, noting a look of uncertainty on her face.

"I was dreaming, and you broke the thread."

"Do you remember the dream?"

"Some." The queen looked at the sky. "Strange."

"What do you mean—strange?"

"I stood in a dark cave, carrying a torch. I saw a hole in the ceiling through which I could see a raincloud. From the cave's depth, I heard birds singing. Their song grew louder as they flew closer. Each had the face of people we knew but are with us no more. One had the face of our princess."

The king felt faint. "What was she doing?"

The queen waved her right hand in a circle overhead. "The birds circled the cave then flew out the hole and toward the cloud. They linked up their wings, wrapping them around the cloud. They squeezed it, but no rain fell. The bird with the face of Sac-Nicté appeared to have a broken wing and flew with difficulty. She flew around my head several times then fell dead at my feet. When I bent toward her, you woke me."

"What does this mean?" the king asked.

"I'm not sure. Should I mention it to the high priest?"

"No," the king said. "Not until we are sure what it means."

Hakum called, "Most Holy One. My Queen. Your meal is ready. May it be pleasing."

The group gathered to eat a few berries. The king noticed the queen seemed pensive, looking at nothing except her food.

"What's bothering you?" the king asked.

"My dream comes to me even though I am awake. I ask myself if I'm really awake."

"You aren't dreaming. You are awake. Put the

dream from your mind and eat your fruit."

"I can't. The dream bothers me. If the gods speak to us through dreams, I am bothered when the dreams differ so—first a good one and now this."

"Then pray about it while we walk tonight, but now, we eat."

The meal finished, the king suggested the sugar apple seeds be left in an open space for animals. After handing his pillow to Hakum, the group set out on the night march.

Several times, the group stopped to rest. The king sat beside the queen who napped beside the princess. Soon after, the trip resumed.

The queen whispered in the king's ear. "Let's walk at the rear. I don't want the others to hear me."

The king stepped aside and let the high priest pass. He stared at the couple and seemed to question why they had stopped.

The king motioned for Hakum to walk several paces ahead with the princess.

"What is it?" the king asked the queen.

The queen whispered, "My dream returned. The same birds flew in my new dream, but our daughter did not. Remember, she had a broken wing. I think her injuries grew worse, and she flies no more. I am afraid of the gods' dream. This one portends something bad."

"I don't know what to think of this."

"I believe the gods battle among themselves. One sent a good dream. Others send a bad one. They tell me our daughter may visit the gods, but she will not return with a message. Our sacrifice, her sacrifice, will be no more than a sacrifice—a blessed but simple offering."

"I think it's time to speak with the high priest," the king said, shaking his head. "Share your thoughts with him when we stop for the next rest."

"Maybe," the queen said, shaking her head.

The king took the queen's hand and returned to their place in line, but the new dream troubled him.

The princess lagged farther and farther behind as the group trudged through the hot, barren jungle. The queen asked for a break so her daughter could rest. Once she had rested, the king summoned the high priest to counsel with him and the queen.

As the high priest sat down, the king said, "The queen has had troubling dreams. We want to share them for guidance."

"Please. Unburden yourself," the priest said, cupping his hands to his ears. "My ears are to serve you."

The queen took a deep breath. "Two dreams came to me. My daughter will go to the gods, but she will not bring us their message. Her sacrifice will not bring the favor of rain."

For a moment, the priest stared silently at the queen then said, "You recently brought me word of a wonderful dream of joy. You said, 'The princess *would* bring a message from the gods and in turn much needed rain.' Now, you tell me of dreams with no messages from the gods and no rain. Perhaps the king's waning faith has contaminated your dreams. Speak no more of this pollution. I will pray for the gods to strengthen the royal family's faith and block evil thoughts in your dreams. Most Holy One, do you wish to share more?"

The king glanced at the priest then the queen. "No. No more."

"Then rest, Most Holy One." The priest bowed and turned to leave. "The night walk is long. Rest well, My King."

The high priest returned to his resting spot where he spoke with the assistant priests. "I am troubled by the royal family."

"Why?" a priest asked.

"I fear the Most Holy One's faith is waning. In the past, I have overheard him say troubling things to the queen, and now I've heard of dreams which bother the queen *and* the king. The queen's dreams bring doubt to the king. I fear his doubt may bring peril to our mission."

"What are we to do?" an assistant priest asked.

"We must pray and watch. There is little more we can do. Just pray and watch."

After a mentally and physically exhausting trek, the king suggested a rest. He lay quietly staring at the star-filled morning sky. He rolled toward the queen and whispered, "My faith is weak, and now you bring me troubling news. Worse yet, the high priest is uninterested in our dreams. I don't know what to do. Do the gods battle over our thoughts—our future? Worse yet, our thoughts battle each other and in doing so suggest there are no gods. If they exist, why don't they acknowledge my sacrifices? I have no fear of death in protecting our people, but I won't die for gods who ignore our prayers and oblations."

The queen stroked his face. "Clear your mind of such thoughts."

"I can't." He rolled onto his back. "Do we offer our daughter for naught? To which god do we ask her to speak? From which god do priests desire messages? Perhaps, we pray to the wrong god." The king raised a trembling hand toward the sky and sadly whispered, "I don't know where to turn for comfort."

Taking his hand in hers, the queen held it against her cheek and whispered, "I know the ache in your heart. We doubt our gods and have a high priest whom we doubt because he will not hear my second dream. I, like you, wonder what we are to do."

"We need sleep. Perhaps the greater god will inform our dreams or enlighten our thinking, but for now, we should clear our minds with sleep."

The day's heat grew in intensity. On day eight of an expected twelve-day journey, the king noted the sparse vegetation had taken on a green hue. A few trees had budding leaves and occasionally a bird could be heard, singing in the distance. He took heart in the jungle's recovery.

While the king prepared to sleep, the high priest approached him. The priest appeared happy and waved his hands. "Most Holy One, have you noticed the gods of Chichen Itza have extended their benevolence to this part of the jungle. Everything is greener."

"I've noticed. May they grant such favors to The Center."

"I too pray for such favors. Soon, we'll be in Chichen Itza and prepare the princess for her visit with the gods. We will soon have their message and rain for The Center."

The king forced a smile. "The queen and I are happy for that day, not only for The Center but our people."

The priest bowed. "I wish you and our queen a good sleep."

After the priest left, the queen asked, "What are you doing? Has your heart changed?"

"No, but I won't share my concerns with him. Not yet. Let's sleep and pray the greater god will direct us in another dream."

For the first time in twenty-seven full moon cycles, the king had tree-shade in which to sleep. The wind blew from the east, filling the air with the faint smell of dampness and verdant growth. Nature's signs portended a day good for sleeping and one filled with expectations.

The day passed quickly. The king arose and prepared for the night's march. He stopped gathering his possessions to hear the queen whisper, "My dream returned. The bird with the face of our daughter spoke to me. She spoke with a weak and distant voice. Her words were delivered as the song of a bird—"

"What did she sing?"

"She sang,

'Force me not from my nest;
I cannot fly at my best.
Care for me on your tree
and someday I'll care for thee.'"

"Strong words," the king said, frowning. "I too had a dream. In it, I carried a small tree limb on which were many smaller branches. On the branches sat evil-looking black birds, but one branch had no bird. From the direction of Chichen Itza flew a multicolored bird. I had never seen such beauty. It perched on the empty branch and sang,

'You have given me perch,
for this, I am happy.
If you let me stay,
I will bless you every day.'

At that moment, the other birds fell dead from their roosts."

Fighting excitement, the queen whispered, "Only the great god can send a similar message to different hearts. The nest and branch are our home, the palace!"

The king grasped the queen's hand and looked her in the eye. "I heard what you heard. This trip cannot continue. We must return our daughter to the palace."

"What are you saying?" We can't just leave--not without the blessing of the high priest, and I know he won't give it." The queen shook her head. "He is the one refuting the gods?"

The king shrugged. "Since he refused to hear your last dream, he will not hear these dreams. His duty is to be a priest, not hear words counter to his way of thinking—even if misdirected. I fear he has, or will, poison the minds of others causing them to turn against us after we heeded his request to offer our daughter and now withdraw the offer. She is part of his jealousy over our marriage. No. He is too skillful with words to trust."

"We can't go forward, and we can't go backward, neither up nor down."

"Then we must move sideways," the king whispered. "After the normal night's journey, I will insist we travel farther. I'll say I'm anxious to get to Chichen Itza. After the longer march, everyone will be tired and should sleep soundly. When all are asleep, we will take Sac-Nicté and escape to another part of the jungle."

"Steal away?"

"Yes. We'll follow the arc of green jungle south and then north to Chalmuch, the old village of King Makuk." The king looked deeply into the queen's eyes. "We'll face hardships, but we're more likely to find food and water along that route than if we backtracked. Some of Makuk's people returned to their village after that disastrous war. I'm sure the older village leader, Mak Ut, still lives there. He will help us. We'll be safe with him."

"Do you think the people of Chalmuch will be offended by our deserting this mission? They worship gods similar to ours."

"They do, but we worship only two similar gods. Chalmuchans will have no concern for gods they don't acknowledge."

"Should we tell Hakum, and can we trust him?"

"Hakum has been a trusted servant all my life. While I won't order him to follow us, I hope he will continue to serve this family."

"What will we tell Sac-Nicté?"

"Tell her we're going to play a game of hide and find. We are going to hide from the others and don't want them to find us. If they do, we lose the game and she won't get a prize. She'll understand."

"Have you thought about the prince?"

The king sighed and shook his head. "I'll miss his happy face, his laughter, his smile, and his hugs, but I have no fear for him. The high priest will declare him the new Most Holy One. Someday, we'll be reunited, but now, my fears are the dangers for you and Sac-Nicte."

"What dangers?"

"The priest will declare our actions a sacrilege worthy of our being sacrificed on The Center's altar. All he has to do is convince enough people he is right, and it could happen."

"We must pray he doesn't find us."

The king settled in for a day of sleep but could

not. He tossed and rolled as the sun and heat reached its zenith. He sat up and looked around, wondering if the others were asleep.

The queen rolled onto her left side and faced her husband. "Can't sleep?"

"No," he whispered. "My mind is filled with thoughts of our problem. My heart is racing."

The queen held out her hand. "I too am shaking."

"Don't worry," he said, squeezing her trembling hand. "Everything will be alright."

"Why wait another sunrise and night?" the queen asked. "That would take us farther from our new destination. Why not leave today?"

"I haven't asked Hakum if he will join us."

"Then ask—no, tell him."

The king rolled onto his back and stared at the sky. He felt pained and pensive. "I conceived my plan without fear, but its execution could be dangerous. Once we leave, we can't return." Gathering his thoughts, the king sat upright. "Maybe we *should* act today. I'll speak with him."

The king removed his authority necklace and placed it in a pouch. He didn't want it to rattle and awaken someone.

The queen gathered her clothing, food pouch, and water tubes.

While the king crawled toward Hakum, he paused and looked back at his family. The queen tiptoed toward the princess. He watched as the queen took a deep breath, no doubt to quiet her anxiety, and then placed her hand over the princess' mouth. The princess awoke and tried to pull the hand away but couldn't.

The king smiled on seeing the princess awake without sounding an alarm.

The queen put her index finger against her lips and whispered, "Shhhhh. We're playing a game of hide and find with the high priest. You must be quiet, or we'll lose. If we win, you get a prize, but you have to be as quiet as a falling leaf."

"Where will we hide?" the princess whispered.

"Shhh," the queen whispered, "we must travel far away to find the right place, and we must be very quiet. This will be fun."

The princess smiled then whispered, "I know a special place where we can hide." She pointed in the direction of The Center. "He won't find us there. I'll show you."

Shaking her head, the queen said, "We can't go to the palace. That's the first place he'll look. No, we'll hide in the jungle for a while. Then we can visit your special hiding place."

On reaching Hakum, the king placed his hand over his servant's mouth and a finger to his own lips.

Hakum awoke with a start and mumbled, "Hmmmm."

"Shhh," the king whispered.

Hakum grabbed the king's wrist and sat up. He started to speak, but the king tightened his hand over Hakum's mouth.

"Shhh," the king said. "Listen carefully. I have need of your service, but I can only *ask* for your help." The king removed his hand and said, "The queen and I had dreams that told us we must not go to Chichen Itza. Sac-Nicté must not visit the gods. The high priest won't hear us and speaks only of *his* interests. I must take a separate path despite the priest. I ask you to go with us but at your own peril. I do not command you to go but ask you as a trusted friend and servant."

"Most Holy One, I, like my fathers before me, swore to serve and defend the royal family, but I cannot go as your friend. I cannot be the friend of one who speaks with the gods. I am your servant. I must travel with you."

"Thank you, Hakum. The queen has gathered our supplies, and we are ready to leave."

"Then I will gather my things, some weapons, and extra water tubes."

The king saw the queen nod, indicating she and the princess were ready to leave. The king helped Hakum gather his supplies and hoist them onto his shoulder. He and the king tiptoed toward his family who had left camp. For defensive purposes, Hakum followed several paces behind the king.

Someone in the camp coughed.

Everyone in the king's group stopped mid-stride, fearing any noise would cause their discovery.

After a few moments, Hakum nodded and whispered, "All is good."

The king led the trek that would take his family from everything they had known. He repeatedly said to himself, *Gods keep us safe. We follow your dreams.*

The king whispered to the queen, carrying the princess. "We must quicken our pace, but move like a deer, so we make no disturbance." He looked into the inquiring eyes of his half-asleep daughter and said, "If anyone hears us, we lose the game. Be as quiet as your pet mouse."

The sleepy girl nodded, while exploring the

inside of her mouth with a dirty finger.

The king's soft-leather sandals carried him quietly over the remnants of an old path. He was careful not to step on debris whose sounds might awaken the sleeping group.

Arms fatigued, the queen placed Sac-Nicté on the ground. Several times, the group slowed their pace, so the princess could catch her breath and rest her legs. The queen and king alternated carrying her so they could avoid rest stops that interrupted their flight.

Driven by generations of duty and responsibility, Hakum continued his pace without a whimper. At one point, he carried not only supplies but the sleeping princess as well.

"My Princess, I am proud of you," Hakum said while shifting her in his arms. "You have been quiet, brave, and strong. Some day you will be an esteemed queen."

"Thanks for your confidence, Hakum," the king said and tousled the hair of his sleepy daughter.

The midday heat and humidity caused everyone to sweat and tire. Nevertheless, they pushed on. Their route took them through a greener part of the jungle. This meant fewer dry leaves to be noisily crushed under foot or leave a visible trail, making it more difficult for the high priest to follow—if he had chosen to do so.

The queen stopped often to wipe sweat from her brow and take a moment's rest. "Go on. I'll catch up."

"We should all rest and eat," the king said.

Hakum placed his bundles on the ground then cleared a resting spot. He spread a cloth on which the princess could nap after eating. The royal family stretched out on another ground cover and stared at a strip of blue sky made visible by a breeze parting the jungle canopy.

"Hakum," the king said, pointing overhead. "I think I see fruit."

"You do, Most Holy One. From the few fruits lying on the ground I can see this is a young mamey tree. I'll climb it and collect the fruit that can be eaten."

The queen smiled. "This is a sign from the gods."

Hakum collected fifteen fist-sized mameys, dropping them into the hands of the king and queen. He then returned to the ground.

"Now we can kill our hunger," the king said then smiled. "Thank you, Hakum."

"Most Holy One, I simply did my duty. We must scatter our seeds far away to disguise our trail in case the priest follows us."

After the meal, Hakum stood watch while the family slept.

Chapter 14

The king awoke with a start. He cupped his hand to his ear, but he heard nothing. Moments later, he heard strange, distant sounds. He whispered to Hakum, "I think I heard something."

"What do you think it is?"

"I'm not sure. Listen! There it is again," the king said, his voice shaking. "It's coming toward us. We have to leave."

The king awoke the queen and princess. "We have to leave. I've heard strange sounds."

With fear on her face, the queen glanced at her daughter then the king. "You carry Sac-Nicte," she said. "I'll gather our things."

Hakum threw supplies on a cloth door then picked it up by its corners. He threw the parcel over his shoulder and followed the family who ran deeper into the jungle. The king moved as quietly as possible with an occasional backward glance to see if anyone pursued them.

The king frequently stopped to listen for danger but heard only his heart, pounding like a war drum—partly due to running, partly due to fear. After traveling a distance, he stopped. The king's arms cramped from carrying Sac-Nicte. He put her down and listened for any hint of pursuit, but he heard nothing. He got a water tube and offered the family a drink. As he drank, he cocked his head toward the part of the jungle he had just left. With fear cracking his voice, he said, "Hakum, I hear something. It's what we heard before. It follows us. We should go."

"I agree."

The king picked up Sac-Nicté who looked anxious, perhaps by contagion.

The exhausted queen took a deep breath, and using a tree trunk, pulled herself to her feet. Panting, she ran beside the king.

The king switched the princess to his left arm and looked back to see Hakum throw the bundle of supplies over his shoulder then run toward the king.

The queen dropped her water tube and stopped to pick it up. Suddenly, a crashing sound came from a few hundred paces behind her and moved toward the group.

"Leave it," the king yelled. "Run! We don't want to be captured."

No longer was the king trying to avoid stepping on twigs or breaking branches. Unconcerned about noise, he broke everything impeding the family's path. The broken limbs created a trail easily followed, but it had to be done.

The king's breath came in loud pants, mixed with moans and groans whose intensity equaled the fear and pain causing them. Just as he reached his limit of speed and stamina, the jungle filled with the sounds of blown conch shells. Fear gripped the king's heart. The drive to live spurred his fatiguing legs.

Sac-Nicté jostled about so much the king held her head to prevent breaking her neck. She cried perhaps from being jostled, her father's tight grip, or the fear she undoubtedly sensed in her father.

The king's fatigue surged. His arms could no longer carry Sac-Nicte nor could his legs support him. He stumbled, dropped his daughter, and then tripped over her as he fell. *Gods don't let me be caught like this.*

The queen, close behind the king, tripped over him. She screamed as she fell. Too tired to get up, she bit her lip, trying to be calm so she would not upset her daughter.

Hakum yanked the king and queen to their feet. Their gaze met. For the first time, the king saw fear on Hakum's face. Neither man said anything. The queen rose and placed her hand over her daughter's crying mouth. The king took Sac-Nicte in his arms. *Gods, give me energy to run. I must protect her.* He took a deep breath and began the run of his life.

The sounds of conchs again rumbled through the jungle like an ensnaring noose.

The princess squeezed her father's neck. He knew she sensed something bad could happen. She scrunched her mouth and cried, "I'm scared."

"Shhh," the king said, his words broken by the stress of panting. "Don't cry. You're safe. They're not going to find us."

Hakum mumbled something about capture then said, "The royal family will not die in the jungle. Not here. Not now."

Despite his fear, the king could run no farther. He stopped, looked to the sky and prayed, "Gods protect us." He placed Sac-Nicte on the ground and slumped to her side. On his knees, he kissed her cheek, hugged her waist, and then wept. *Spare us pain, oh gods. Spare us pain.*

The princess appeared perplexed as she stroked his head. "Why are you crying, daddy?"

The king couldn't speak. He couldn't tell her she might be killed. The queen knelt on the other side of Sac-Nicte. The king and queen wept while hugging their bewildered daughter.

Facing the sounds of pursuit, Hakum stood erect in front of the royals. His spear in one hand, axe in the other, he shifted his weight from foot to foot. For a moment, he put down his axe and took a knife from his bundle. He stuffed the knife inside his loincloth then picked up his ax and readied himself for an imminent attack. "I may face death," he said looking at the king, "but death protecting the royal family is my duty. My honor."

"We don't want to die on our knees," the king said, assisting the queen to her feet, thinking, *May we die swiftly.*

The royals stood defiantly, quivering chins held high. The king placed Sac-Nicte between their erect bodies as they embraced each other with trembling arms and awaited the inevitable.

"Gods, may we die without pain," the queen prayed.

Hakum looked at her. "You will not die. Not if I can help it."

The princess gripped her father's hand. "Daddy, I'm scared. What's happening? Is something bad coming?"

He picked up Sac-Nicte and hugged her tightly. "Don't worry. Your mother and I are here to protect you." *I will forever remember your giggles and your smile.* He tightened his embrace. *I loved to hear you laugh and pray I hear it again.*

He and the queen stared silently into each other's eyes and tightened their embrace.

Hakum shifted his weight faster and faster as the sounds of conchs grew louder and closer.

"Those are thrashing sounds," the king said, fear rattling his voice. "They fill the jungle. Their loudness means many pursuers. If this is our fate, I want our deaths to be quick."

Dense underbrush prevented the group from seeing the threat, but the undergrowth leaked the sounds of approaching danger.

The king tightened his hold on the queen, drew his daughter closer, and then stiffened himself with resolve.

The princess whimpered, squeezed her father's neck, fingered her hair, and glanced between her parents and the noise.

Hakum raised his spear to a defensive position and lowered his body, bracing himself for attack.

The thunder of pounding feet and fracturing branches grew closer. Tree branches just beyond them shook and then gave way.

The princess screamed and looked away as she tightened her hug on her father.

The queen squeezed her eyes shut.

Eyes closed, the king prayed, *Great gods, give me courage. Do not let me show fear in front of my family.*

Running toward the startled family sped a herd of deer. They suddenly veered east, avoiding the royals, and then headed south. Behind the deer came the sounds of conchs and running feet. Within seconds, several hunters darted past. Glancing at the group, the hunters continued to run probably wondering why the fancily dressed group traveled in this part of the jungle.

The royal family sighed and went limp—almost falling to the ground. Death had passed them by. The king let his daughter slide down his torso to stand on the ground. *Thank the gods we are safe.*

Hakum looked at the king, dropped his ax, and exhaled a long breath. "That was *not* the high priest," he said then smiled.

"Yes, and for that I thank the gods," the king said, staring at the sky.

The queen buried her face in the king's chest and wept.

With her hands still covering her face, the princess asked, "Mommy, are we still playing?"

The queen nodded, trying to stifle her sobs. "Not now."

A lone hunter brought up the rear of the hunters. He stopped and stared at the group. "I am Citu," he said and bowed. "We hunters are from Chalmuch. What brings a group dressed as noblemen to the jungle?"

The king noted Citu had no shortness of breath even though he had been running. *This is a very fit hunter. Somehow he looks vaguely familiar.*

"I am the Most Holy One from Dzibilchaltun," the king said.

Citu looked at the king in astonishment and then bowed. "Most Holy One, I and my people know your office. You have been our ally for many moons. You once spared me and later helped King Makuk in defense of our village's stolen food stores. I and our villagers are forever indebted to you."

"Now I know why I remember you. You had stolen some fruits, no?"

"Yes, Most Holy One but no more."

"I regret your king fell in that battle. Who leads your people now?"

"Most Holy One, I provide some leadership to our people in the absence of a king or chieftain. I am one of ten leaders chosen by our people to provide guidance."

"Then they have a strong leader." The king nodded in the direction of the other hunters. "Why have the men of Chalmuch come to this area?"

"We come to hunt. Only in the green jungle can we find sufficient game and fruits."

The distance sound of a conch, followed by a chorus of shouts, interrupted Citu. "Most Holy One, my men have killed a deer." He raised his arm and shook his fist in celebration. "We have meat. Most Holy One, allow us to feed your family."

The king nodded. "We thank you. My servant is offered for your assistance."

Stepping forward, Hakum bowed. "I am Hakum, Citu. I too remember you."

Citu bowed to each family member. "King, Queen, Princess, Citu is pleased to offer his service."

Hakum asked, "My King, should I prepare a fire in this clearing?"

The king looked at Citu. "Would you have the deer cooked here?"

"As you wish, Most Holy One. We will prepare the deer as soon as the men return."

Citu blew his conch, apparently signaling his men to return.

In a short time, two hunters returned lugging a deer carcass tied to a tree limb carried on the men's shoulders. Soon after, two more hunters returned, carrying another deer.

Smiling, the king said, "Your hunters have been greatly rewarded for their efforts."

"Yes, Most Holy One. Our villagers will be well fed. It is becoming more difficult to find meat near Chalmuch, so we hunt deeper in the jungle." Citu motioned to the deer bearers and then pointed to a small clearing. "Gut the deer there. Most Holy One, once the deer is cleaned and eaten, we will return to the village to share our bounty."

"You'll be greeted with great jubilation," the king said, swatting a fly, which had followed a trail of dripping deer blood.

"Most Holy One, why do you travel here? You aren't dressed to hunt."

"Citu, I'll share our plight over our meal. For now, my family and I need rest."

"Take your rest, Most Holy One. It will be some time before the meat is cooked."

Away from the cooking area, Hakum spread cloths on which the family could sleep. "Most Holy One, your resting place awaits. I will awaken you when the meal is ready."

The king and then the royal family awoke to the aroma of roasted deer.

"That smells so good," the king said to Citu who attended the rotisserie. "We have had fruits but no meat for many days."

Citu rose then bowed. "Which cut would you prefer, Most Holy One?"

"The queen and I can share a front leg with the princess. Its meat is enough for us."

"Don't worry," Citu said, while cutting the requested portion and handing it to Hakum. "There is enough for another portion if you wish."

"Thank you, but the leg is enough," the queen said.

The king joined the hunting party who ate their meal some distance away. While they ate, Hakum served the queen and princess. After serving them, he moved ten paces away and ate alone.

The aroma of cooked meat and fallen scraps attracted flying and creeping insects. "Look," the king said, pointing to a swarm of ants. "The entire jungle attends our feast."

"I see them," Citu said. He licked deer meat from his fingers and turned to his eight hunters. "Throw your bones far into the jungle. We don't need any more hungry mouths here."

As the meal ended, the king shared his story about the royal family's travel through the jungle. He ended his tale and said, "So when the high priest refused to hear our dreams, we had no choice but to leave."

The hunters sat quietly, appearing dumbfounded. One-by-one, they spoke among themselves about the unbelievable treatment of the Most Holy One.

"Most Holy One, I am shocked," Citu said. "I don't understand how a priest can deny the advice of one who speaks with the gods."

The king whispered to Citu as if talking to a trusted friend. "It is possible the priest had bad motives, but I'm no longer sure I speak to any god—not yours or mine."

"But if you don't speak to the gods, who does?" Citu asked, worry crossing his face.

"I'm not sure. Your question is a good one, but it has no certain answer."

"Most Holy One, I know the gods speak. It is we who don't hear. Often we don't like the message. Other times, we choose not to hear. Sometimes, we hear only our silence and believe it is the gods'."

"Citu, you are a wise man. You have more wisdom than my scribes or priests." *I wish you served in my palace.*

Citu stood for a moment then paced around the fire. "I believe some gods listen to some kings and not others just like a child may listen to one parent and not another. That doesn't mean both parents don't love the child, or the child doesn't love both parents. Only one ear, or heart, can listen at a time. With time, ears get tired and voices grow weak, but the gods are always there."

After his fifth circle, Citu faced the king. "Most Holy One, we of Chalmuch have no king. Come live with us. Speak to our gods. We have only one infirmed priest who performs only the most simple rituals and prayers."

The king rose, and for a moment, stared at Citu. "Perhaps the gods have spoken to both of us this day. They sent the queen and me certain dreams that caused us to divert our path. We were making our way to your village, seeking safety from a spurned high priest, and then *you* suddenly appear."

"I understand your meaning, Most Holy One."

Citu, I believe the gods sent us here for a reason." The king looked at the queen for confirmation. "The gods have ordained we meet, at this time, this place. There is need in each of us for the other."

Citu faced his men. "Would not the Most Holy One be welcomed in our village?"

Each hunter stood, nodded, and then bowed to

the king.

The king swatted a pesky fly from his lip and nodded to the hunters. "Your acceptance is most heartening, but I must hear from the elders of Chalmuch. There are many differences between our people. My people fish, harvest salt, grow cotton, write, and read. Yours do not. Nevertheless, they do have talents to share. My family and I wish to visit Chalmuch. I would like to hear from its people about becoming their king."

"As you wish, Most Holy One," Citu said, bowing. "We are honored."

"If your village honors me with this agreement, we can meld in an alliance, for I have need of your hunters' skill and their strength. My doll and my son remain in Dzibilchaltun, and I want them returned to me."

With a look of delight, Citu said, "I expect no refusal of your request to seek counsel with our people, Most Holy One."

"Citu, there may be repercussions for your people if they take us as their royal family. In fact, there may be problems this day if the high priest returns to Dzibilchaltun and gathers an army to pursue us."

"Fear not, Most Holy One. We're great in strength and stealth, if not in numbers, but enough of this discussion. Let's rest. At dusk, we leave for Chalmuch."

"Agreed. My family and I have walked for days and ran for what seemed a thousand awakenings of the sun god. We need rest before undertaking such a trek."

"As you wish, Most Holy One. I will post guards. We sleep until the gods sleep."

For the first time in days, the king rested,

feeling safe.

Perhaps, the king thought, *the gods know my way better than I. I should not have doubted them.*

Chapter 15

Hakum shook the king awake. "Most Holy One, the sun god prepares for sleep."

The king arose and assisted the queen and princess prepare for the night trek.

"Do I have to go?" the princess whined, rubbing her eyes.

The king stared into her eyes. "Yes. It isn't safe to stay here. We might be found by the high priest, and then we'd lose the prize. We don't want to lose do we?"

"No, but I want to sleep," the princess said, yawning.

"Well, you're a big, strong princess. You can do this. I'll carry you."

Hakum gathered the family's goods as the king informed Citu they were ready to travel.

"Most Holy One, permit me to lead. I'll position hunters at the rear for a defense."

"Thank you for your concern, Citu, " the king said. "We're ready.

The trek began at a slow, but steady, pace. Sac-Nicté seemed uninterested in walking and had to be pulled along by her mother. After a long walk, the king took Sac-Nicté in his arms where she rested her head on his shoulder and slept. Caressing her head, the king kissed her cheek and glanced at the queen. "She's very tired. I'll let her sleep."

An advance guard broke obstructions from the path, causing a howler monkey to screech its ire at the intrusion. Startled by the group's activities, the king heard a flock of unseen birds fluttering overhead.

After walking for what seemed liked two sun cycles, the queen said, "I need a rest."

The king instructed Hakum to tell Citu the queen needed rest.

Citu sent a hunter ahead to search for a clearing.

Once there, the king placed the sleepy princess on a ground cover. Despite the hard ground, the soft murmurings of the jungle lulled the queen and princess to sleep. The king leaned against a small tree. His head bobbed to and fro, as he battled the god of sleep.

Citu had just finished his turn at guard duty when he heard distant male voices. He woke the group.

"What is it?" the king asked.

"I'm not sure, Most Holy One, but I hear men's voices."

Citu motioned for his hunters to take a defensive position. They stood in front of the royals and waited—weapons at the ready.

The muffled voices grew closer. It soon became clear a group of many men approached the hunters. The king saw two torches through the underbrush. The torches and voices grew nearer.

Citu moved in front of the royal family. He shifted his stone ax from one hand to the other, ready for any eventuality.

Hugging his daughter, the king embraced the queen and whispered, "I can't believe we're having another encounter." *I pray it's not the priest.*

The unidentifiable travelers drew closer and their voices louder. Suddenly, the king recognized one of the voices.

"Citu," the king whispered. "That's the voice of the high priest from whom we fled."

"Fear not, Most Holy One. I and my men will protect you and your family."

The oncoming group sounded as if they were a few hundred paces away.

Citu backed to within two paces of the royal family and held his ax across his chest. Readying his club, Hakum stood at Citu's side.

In seconds, the king and the high priest were almost face-to-face. Even by torchlight, the king could see the high priest's face blanch in apparent surprise. The priest raised his hand to signal his assistant priests and four bodyguards to stop.

Weapons raised, the hunters created a semi-circle around the royal family then moved a few steps forward.

"Dare not approach me," the high priest shouted at the hunters. "I am the High Priest of Dzibilchaltun." Staring at the king, the priest bowed. "Most Holy One, we are here to rescue you from these evil men who have kidnapped you and your family.

"We are not captives," the king said, placing Sac-Nicte on the ground behind him. "We are here of our freewill. We have been fed and protected by these Chalmuchan hunters."

The priest gasped and clutched his authority necklace. "How can that be, Most Holy One? Why come to this place, with these people?"

"We asked you to hear our dreams, but you did not. You refused to hear our wish to abandon the trip to

Chichen Itza. The queen and I chose to obey the will of the gods, so we left because the gods demanded it." The king took a few steps toward the priest. "You said we doubted our faith. We didn't. We acknowledged our faith and followed the god's instructions."

In the torchlight, the priest's face reddened with anger. He grimaced and so tightened his grip on his ceremonial wand his fingers blanched. The king had never seen the priest so angry and wondered if the priest would strike him.

Voice breaking, the priest said, "Sacrilege! You have disgraced the gods, Dzibilchaltun, me, and our people." The priest paused for a moment then raised his wand to a striking position. "You have committed blasphemy!"

The priest swung his wand at the king, but Citu grabbed the priest's wrist and twisted it with such force he cried out and dropped his wand.

Those traveling with the high priest gasped and stepped back, not knowing what to do.

Citu's hunters stepped forward and raised their clubs in defense of the king. The king asked, "Ah Kin Mai, why do you do this?" The king moved closer to the priest. "Have I not given you rank, comfort, and my amity?"

The priest glared but said nothing.

"I confirmed your holy position and treated you well even though I have long thought jealousy filled your heart. I fear you have poisoned the hearts of your assistants against me because you believe the gods have abandoned me. I did not challenge you earlier because I feared your men's poisoned minds would cause them to rebel against me. I thought it better to leave than risk harm to my family alone in the jungle."

The high priest glared at the king and leaned forward. "You are not my king. You have willfully ignored my holy orders and those of the gods. It is you who have brought a curse on Dzibilchaltun."

The priest gestured with his free hand then shook it as a fist in the king's face.

Citu twisted the priest's arm even more as the priest continued his rant. "*You* are the reason there is no rain, no crops, no food, no animals in our jungle." The priest's voice grew louder and angrier. "You have brought nothing but desolation and despair to our land. Through your stubbornness, there is no future for The Center—not until your heart is on The Center's altar will our glory be returned."

The queen bolted upright, clutched the king's arm, and gasped on hearing the priest's threats.

The king stood stoically, presenting a stone face to the priest.

Citu further twisted the priest's arm and stared the angry priest in the eye. "How dare you disparage the Most Holy One? Your only desire is for authority over Dzibilchaltun."

The king and queen backed away from the priest as Citu continued to stand toe-to-toe with the angry, red-faced man.

Citu said, "You obviously seek only that which elevates your power. You don't care for your village or villagers. The Most Holy One is the only person who speaks with the gods of Dzibilchaltun. You merely ask of the gods. It is the king's will that is to be obeyed, not yours." Citu raised his club. "With this club, I should crack your unholy head like a nut whose meat is to be eaten."

The priest protectively covered his head with his

free arm.

Grabbing Citu's raised club arm, the king said, "Do not strike him, for he is no longer a priest. The gods once instructed me to elevate him to be Ah Kin Mai, our high priest, but the gods have now spoken differently to me through you, Citu. This man is no longer high priest to any chief, to any king, or any people. He is stripped of all rights, lands, and privileges. To his family he is dead. His wife is free to marry another. He is a man condemned to exile."

The assistant priests and the high priest's bodyguards gasped on hearing the condemnation.

The king looked at them and said, "Stand back." He extended his hand toward the priest's authority necklace.

Snarling, the priest reached for the king's wrist, but two hunters pinned the priest's arms to his side. The king grabbed the center gold image on the priest's necklace and gave it a sharp tug, pulling it free of the priest's neck. The priest lunged at the king, but unable to wrest himself free, spat on him.

Conquering his anger, the king wiped his face and glared at the ex-priest. "Citu, remove this man's gold bracelets. They belong to Dzibilchaltun's people. Take his jaguar skin. A villager killed this cat. Its skin I gave to this priest. It now belongs to the people of Dzibilchaltun." The king pointed to the priest's ear plugs. "Remove those. They were a gift, but they belong to The Center. His deerskin sandals and loincloth are to be given to one of your hunters chosen by lot. The priest's feather crown is to be burned on this spot and the ashes scattered on the ground."

On hearing his sentence, the priest struggled against his captors' grip.

"Hakum," the king said, "take the priest's authority necklace and symbols of office. Prepare them for transport to Dzibilchaltun. Someday, they will be given to a worthy high priest."

The king faced those who accompanied the high priest. "This man is priest no more. From this day forward, he will be known as Heregesob, the heretic. He is exiled from Dzibilchaltun, never to return. If you choose to follow him, you too are exiled. Make your decisions now, for my group travels tonight. We will first go to Chalmuch then Dzibilchaltun."

"Citu," the king said, "have Heregesob tied to the tree against which I rested. In time, he will free himself, but he will struggle to do so. While he struggles, he should ponder his actions. I will burn his crown at his feet to teach him all things are transient.

The king addressed the four assistant priests. "You and your bodyguards. What say you? Do you side with your king?"

Lamul, the elder and first assistant priest, limped forward on his walking stick. "Most Holy One, we knew nothing of your dreams or the high priest's failure to heed them. We are priests. We follow a high priest, but our high priest is no more, so we cannot follow him. We are at your side, Most Holy One."

Lamul and the other assistant priests stepped beside the king.

"Guards of Dzibilchaltun, what do you say?" the king asked.

"Most Holy One, we are sworn to protect The Center and the royal family. We believed we traveled tonight to rescue you—not harm you. We knew nothing of your conflict with the high priest—Heregesob. We remain steadfast in our oath and serve only the Most

Holy One and his family."

While The Center's guards spoke to the king, he watched Citu's men tie the struggling, naked Heregesob to the tree where the king had rested. The bonds were made of green vines. In time, they would slip or break, giving him his freedom.

The men who tied Heregesob returned and bowed to the king. "Most Holy One, the bonds are made as ordered."

"Hakum," the king called, "bring a flame from our campfire."

Hakum removed a smoking stick from the fire pit then blew on it. Within seconds, it flared into a flame.

The king dropped the ex-priest's feather crown at Heregesob's feet.

Heregesob stared in horror as the king set fire to the crown's tallest feather. The burning crown produced a short lived flame, an acrid smell, and then crumbled into an ash heap. Heregesob shook his head while the king, using his sandal, dragged the crown's ashes over the ground—the most despicable thing one could do to a priest's honor.

The king looked into the eyes of each man from Dzibilchaltun. "Those of you who are with me are to walk through these ashes."

Every man in the ex-priest's group walked, single file, through the ashes then bowed to the king.

"Citu. We are ready to go to Chalmuch," the king said. He turned to the assistant priests. "Return to Dzibilchaltun and tell the people of The Center and the former priest's family the once high priest is no longer a priest. He is Heregesob and forbidden, ever again, to enter Dzibilchaltun, for he has displeased the gods and angered the Most Holy One. Anyone seeing him in our land is commanded to kill him on sight. Citu, give the returning priests and guards water and a portion of meat for their trip."

Lamul, the elder assistant priest, said, "As you command, Most Holy One. I and our people await your return to our holy center."

The priests bowed to the king and then left for The Center as the king and Citu's men headed for Chalmuch.

The king snuggled the princess in his arms where she slept, her head resting on his shoulder. *I can now relax. My precious one is safe.*

Citu scanned the sky through openings in the canopy, searching for stars to guide the way. He led the group until the awakening of the gods and dawn's sunlight painted the sky beautiful hues of red. He raised his hand to stop the group. "Most Holy One, we should rest. This area is flat, and I see no ground walkers to pester us."

"Then make it ready," the king said.

"Clear a space," Citu instructed a hunter, "and start a fire, so deer can be cooked for the morning meal.

After eating, the royals and others fell asleep, while a hunter guarded the camp's periphery.

Citu had given little thought to the group's refuse of deer bones left at each campsite, but he should have known animals would devour the organs of the deer.

A jaguar had found and eaten the discarded deer organs and wanted more than rotting guts. For two days, nose to the ground or sniffing the air, the jaguar followed the trail of deer bones and the scent of deer carcasses left on tree limbs, shrubs, and an occasional fleck of dried blood.

The jaguar stealthily planted its broad paws, disturbing neither leaf nor twig, silently tracking the deer's scents. Now, the distant, lingering aroma of roasted deer meat attracted the jaguar like children to a honey apple.

Full bellies helped everyone sleep except for the king. Concerns about meeting Citu's villagers, and their decision regarding the adoption of the royal family, filled the king's thoughts. He stared at the full moon, scanned the stars, listened to the sounds of the jungle, and contemplated the future. Hearing strange, distant sounds, he turned to see a guard checking the deer carcasses stored in a tree. The guard shook the supporting branches and tugged at the carcasses. All seemed secure from scavengers.

Appearing tired, the guard moved slowly as he patrolled the far side of the camp. The king thought, *That guard must force himself to keep moving to stay awake.*

A short time later, the guard's watch came to an end. He walked to the sleeping relief guard and shook him awake.

"Okay, okay," the awakened guard said. "I'm getting up. Be patient."

"Shhh," the retiring guard said, "You'll wake everyone."

The relief guard got to his feet and grabbed his spear. He and the current guard walked away from the campfire whispering. Moments later, the retiring guard found a sleeping spot.

The king watched as the new guard shook the deer carcasses to make sure they were secured. He placed wood on the fire then moved to the far side of the camp to keep watch.

As if he had heard something strange, the patrolling guard suddenly turned toward the east. He cupped his ear. "Who's there? Who is it?"

Apparently hearing nothing, the guard returned to patrolling but carried his spear at the ready.

The king closed his eyes. *Hope that guard heard nothing significant.*

Suddenly, the roar of a jaguar and shrieks of the patrolling guard filled the jungle with bloodcurdling screams.

Hunters, guards, and the king ran toward the agonizing sounds. They arrived just in time to see a jaguar bite the guard's neck. The cat shook the guard while holding him in its jaws. The full-moon's light revealed blood flowing from the guard's wound.

The seized guard pulled at the animal's jaw with one hand and grappled for his spear with the other. Spear in hand, the guard tried but could not thrust it. After a struggle to position it, he managed to push its point into the jaguar's lower jaw. The cat loosened its bite and slapped its claw-extended paw against the spear. The paw knocked the spear free, but the paw's trajectory left four bleeding slashes on the guard's chest.

The king winced as he watched the struggle.

The lure of the guard's blood was too much for the jaguar to ignore. It re-attacked the guard, biting his bleeding neck.

A hunter rammed a spear into the cat's right flank. The startled cat released the guard then directed its attention to its new wound. It roared and pawed several times at the spear stuck in its flank. Finally, the cat dislodged it, leaving a gaping hole, spurting blood.

Hunters, with clubs and spears at the ready, surrounded the hissing jaguar. Limping in a small circle, the cat bared its bloody teeth, roared, and then lunged at the nearest hunter. He jumped back, escaping the brandished claws, but the cat lunged at a taunting hunter opposite the downed guard.

One hunter grabbed the injured guard's heel and pulled him to safety. Suddenly, the yelps of hunters filled the jungle as a barrage of spears impaled the cat. Looking like a giant porcupine, the cat roared and clawed the air, nearing collapse. Wanting to be the one who "killed" the cat, Xtan rushed forward and clubbed the head of the whimpering cat. The jaguar fell to the ground—dead. A communal shout of thanksgiving filled the jungle while the group congratulated and hugged each other.

Citu rushed to the wounded guard bathed in his and the jaguar's blood. Citu cradled the guard's head in his lap and pressed his hand over the neck wound. The pressure momentarily stopped the bleeding. "Luckily, only a superficial tube has been opened," Citu said.

The slashes on the guard's chest had begun to develop a thin, sagging clot and their bleeding slowed.

Citu appeared uncertain about what to do to permanently stop the bleeding from the guard's neck.

Hakum and the Most Holy One moved beside the fallen guard and assessed the situation.

"Hakum," the king ordered. "Bring my salve and ten green leaves from that Ficus tree. Citu, continue to press on the wound."

Hakum returned with the king's special salve and leaves.

The king knelt in the guard's blood then spread

the yellowish salve over the chest wounds while Citu continued to apply pressure to the neck wounds.

Leaves in hand, the king said, "Hakum, spread salve on the glossy side of this one." He then placed the leaf's salved surface against the guard's neck wound while Hakum stacked the other nine leaves on top of the first. The stacked leaves were then held in place with hand pressure.

While Citu held the guard's head off the ground, Hakum wrapped vines around the guard's neck and the stacked leaves to keep them against the wound. The king then pressed on the bundle until the bleeding stopped.

The guard's wounds prevented him from speaking, but he mouthed his thanks and squeezed the king's arm.

"Thank you, Most Holy One," Citu said then called his men together. "Go far from camp and use sand to remove the dried blood from your body. We want no contamination to attract another cat."

The king sized up the dead jaguar. "Citu, let this jaguar's skin be taken to the temple in Chalmuch. It will make a great cloak for a Chalmuchan noble. As for now, little of the night has passed. We should sleep. We need to be rested for travel."

The king headed for the campsite. *Sac-Nicté and Ix Tzutz must be worried after hearing the guard's screams and yelling.* He found the queen hugging their daughter and wearing a fearful face. Her face lit up on seeing the king approach her with outstretched arms. He knew she wanted assurance they were safe. "All is well," he said. "We killed a jaguar that attacked a guard."

Citu approached the king and bowed. "My men

send their thanks to the Most Holy One for his salve. They will flay the jaguar then salt its skin and carcass. Its meat will be added to our trove and shared with our villagers."

"The salve is a small gift. It is a king's duty to help his people. I thank the gods no one died."

The king looked at his daughter. *You have been spared a trip to the gods of the well, and we have been spared an attack by the jungle cat. I hope you and I have many sun cycles together, and I pray my prince is also safe. I want to see him become a man, marry and have a son of his own. Gods, let me see him soon.*

The king woke first. A brilliant morning sun stole the night while a land breeze rustled tree tops and awakened animals. He watched as Citu and Hakum searched for twigs to kindle a fire. Once started, a guard cut a strip of meat from a deer and roasted it. The rest of the group was soon stirred by the aroma of cooked meat.

"Citu," the king said. "I would like to stay a few days in Chalmuch before returning to Dzibilchaltun. The queen and princess need the rest, and I would like to meet your people and speak with your leaders."

"As you wish, Most Holy One. I will send a runner to Chalmuch, to alert the villagers we arrive in half a day. He will arrange for a meeting of the elders, after you have had a night's rest."

"Will you have the villagers gather water? The queen and princess wish to bathe."

"I will order it, Most Holy One."

"Thank you, Citu," the queen said, having overheard the request.

Following breakfast, the supplies and carcasses

were collected. The group started the last leg of their journey at a pace faster than normal in anticipation of reaching Chalmuch.

Chapter 16

Citu held up his hand to stop and quiet the group. "Most Holy One, hear that? Those are the sounds of conchs blown in Chalmuch. They alert the villagers of our arrival."

A young, panting runner from Chalmuch approached the group. He bowed and panted. "Most Holy One. Citu. I bring a message of thanksgiving for the arrival of our guest and the hunting party's safe return with meat. The leaders will gather at dawn for an audience with the Most Holy One."

"Give this runner meat and water," Citu said to a hunter.

In need of rest, the group stopped long enough for the runner to eat and regain his strength. Afterwards, the group resumed their trek. The hunters, carrying the carcasses, sang a song of thanksgiving to Ek-Zip, the god of hunting. The song's rhythm lifted everyone's spirit. Soon, everyone sang. Their steps seemed to grow lighter, for they would soon be in Chalmuch.

A short time later, the weary group marched into the village square long deserted by the warring raiders who had years earlier stolen its food stores. The king looked around the village. Its appearance had changed significantly since his visit two years before the war. Now, there were fewer huts but they looked new. The thatched roofs of the rooms at the top of the important pyramids such as the royal palace, the main temple of worship and the remaining noblemen's homes were new.

The villagers cheered, slapped their thighs, and yelled shouts of welcome. They voiced their gratitude to Citu for bringing the Most Holy One and meat.

Citu climbed six steps of the royal palace once used by King Makuk. He faced his people, and raised his hand to quiet the crowd. "Greetings. I thank the gods we have returned safely and with meat." Citu gestured toward the king. "And in the company of the Most Holy One of Dzibilchaltun." The crowd roared their welcome and slapped their thighs. Citu continued, "Tonight we feast, drink, and celebrate. An important happening will be announced after the awakenings of the gods, but now know that the Most Holy One resides in our village."

Climbing three steps, the king raised his right hand in a welcoming salute and benediction. "Thank you, people of Chalmuch. The queen, princess, and I thank you for your hospitality. We will meet after the morning sun, but tonight, we feast."

The king and queen coaxed the princess in front of her mother. With one finger in her mouth and one twisting her hair, she bowed, and then waved to the villagers who repeated their shouts of welcome.

"Most Holy One," Citu said, pointing to the upper palace terrace, "I welcome you and the royal family to enter and rest. The queen and princess will find water for their baths."

From the palace terrace, the king watched the

preparatory activities for a feast on the plaza. As the sun settled on the horizon, villagers started two bonfires—one for cooking meat and one for social activities. Beside the social fire sat four men, wearing celebratory face paint of green with two black bands painted below their eyes. Other men beat long drums made from hollowed tree trunks. Minutes later, other villagers arrived carrying food baskets, which they placed near the social fire.

Citu arrived and asked his guests to join the villagers at the social fire. Meanwhile, the princess slept in the palace under the watchful eye of a local female guardian.

This celebration would not have occurred on the plaza of Dzibilchaltun. Such festivals would only happen in The Center's outlying villages where common people lived.

The king and queen sat on temporary stone thrones. A jaguar skin, belonging to Chalmuch's former royals, covered the king's and queen's seat.

Entering the social area, two teams of two men carried bamboo poles on their shoulders from which two jugs, the size of a man in the fetal position, swung back and forth. The jugs held a fermented mixture of maize and water, containing low levels of alcohol. Taking care not to spill the contents, the men placed the jugs into shallow holes near the social fire then bowed to the royals.

The Most Holy One nodded.

Using a hollow gourd, a woman ladled the drink into gourd cups, which were distributed and quickly emptied by thirsty merrymakers needing no excuse to drink.

The Most Holy One found the liquid foul

smelling and unsavory. "What do you think of this drink?" he whispered to the queen. "Its appreciation must be an acquired taste."

"It's horrible," the queen whispered. "It is sour and bitter but I know I have to pretend to like it."

"Thanks for your diplomacy, but I think the locals love it. They lick their lips and smile after each gulp."

The king preferred his celebratory drink made from maize and honey, but he politely sipped the local brew.

The villagers rapidly consumed the liquid, causing Citu to send for more.

With the social fire roaring, several drunken men prepared to dance.

Citu leaned toward the king. "I think you will like this. It's the Dance-of-Favorable-Hunts and is performed to thank the gods for our bounty."

One intoxicated man assumed the role of a hunted deer. He tried to move about on all fours but kept falling over, necessitating he assume a half-upright posture instead. Five intoxicated men played the role of hunters in the mock hunt. The hunters staggered around the fire and among the seated villagers who were symbolic trees through which the hunt occurred. More than one hunter, and the "deer," had to be pushed off a "tree" or prevented from falling into the fire.

Laughing and slapping his thigh, the king said, "Citu, I think the deer has had too much drink."

"It makes for a funnier hunt, Most Holy One."

The villagers symbolically beat the deer with their fists. This act represented stone throwing—the villager's contribution to the kill. An intoxicated hunter thrust his blunt spear between the deer's arm and chest, symbolizing its kill. The deer yelped and thrashed about on the ground in a poor representation of dying.

"Good kill," the king shouted and slapped his thighs while laughing.

"Most Holy One," Citu said, "I am glad you enjoyed the hunt."

Suddenly, a co-hunter snatched the "killing" spear and threw it to the ground. The interloper then used his own spear to make another symbolic slaying of the same deer. Villagers booed and beat their fists against their palms. The first spearman sprang to his feet, grabbed the second spear, and threw it far away. The second slayer ran at the first, tackled him, and knocked him to the ground.

The king jerked backwards and emitted an empathetic "Ouch" as the first spearman hit the ground with a thud.

Wrestling on the ground, the spearmen raised a cloud of dust as they attempted to throw meaningful punches. One man got to his feet and tried to pummel the other who had risen to his knees. Fists flew, but most missed their mark or caused the puncher to lose balance and fall.

Citu watched for a while then stepped forward. He simply glared at each man who returned his stare then stopped fighting.

"Ak Se, go to your hut," Citu said to the second spearman. "You dishonor us before the Most Holy One."

Ak Se's less-intoxicated wife forced herself upright and assisted her reeling husband to his feet. The two then staggered away—presumably to their hut.

Cheering with abandonment, the crowd lifted aloft the first spearman in praise of his hunting skills and readied him for a congratulatory parade. He received a cup of drink and the crowd's affirmation as two men carried him, precariously perched on their shoulders, around the social fire.

"Citu," the king said, "it has been many moon cycles since I have laughed so heartily."

"I am happy you laugh, Most Holy One, but wait for the next dance."

Not to be outdone, several village women would perform the Evil-Reed-God-Dance.

An older woman rose to join the dancers, but her intoxicated husband pulled her down. "You're too old," he said. "Sit down."

Citu said, "Most Holy One, only the prettiest women are permitted to perform this dance."

"Then I will watch closely," the king said, smiling at his wife.

"Four women will dance the role of basket weavers sent to gather reeds from the marshes," Citu said. "The reeds are needed to make baskets for use in the village or bartered with inland people. The story starts in a reed patch. In it lives an animal with two heads, large mouths, sharp teeth, and bulging eyes. Its skin is covered with large green bumps whose colors blend with the reeds. In the past, the reed god killed and ate women who went too deeply into its domain. Over time, one of the gatherers started to carry a spear. She stood guard against the evil god while others gathered his reeds."

"I look forward to seeing a successful hunt," the king said.

The royals watched gatherer-women stagger among the crowd who represented the reed marsh. Stumbling about, the dancers giggled while making mock gathering motions then tossing their imaginary reeds onto an imaginary pile.

The woman playing the role of the evil marsh god crawled on all fours, dragging her bare breasts on the ground while growling.

Occasionally, one of the gatherers would mimic the god's presumed warning sounds then giggle. The women's bad acting caused the king to laugh.

If gatherers got to close to the evil god, the demon raised its head, snarled, growled, and attempted to attack the gatherers. The spear carrier feigned striking at the reed-god, forcing it to back away. Finally, the speared god crawled away leaving the gatherers to collect reeds in peace.

"The wounded god always recovers and returns to guard his reeds," Citu said, leaning toward the king. "No one has ever captured the god for all to see."

At the end of the dance, the gatherers received a heroine's celebration for surviving the attacks. As a thank you, the gatherers received an extra drink for their exemplary enactment. Two drinks were given to the spear carrier.

The women liked the drink so much they pleaded to be allowed to reenact their dance to earn an extra portion of mush.

Citu stepped forward and thanked the gatherer-women. "We have all the reeds we need. Sit with your family and enjoy the festivities."

Villagers, age fourteen and above, were allowed to drink, but the elixir and their inability to handle drink caused many of the young celebrants to lose their inhibitions. The king watched several boys and girls steal away, hand-in-hand, into the jungle.

The evening grew late and most villagers were

intoxicated. Soon, there were few people standing or interested in eating the roasted deer. However, the scent of charred deer fat filled the air, attracting small animals to the periphery of the village. Their silvery or green eyes glowed in the dark.

"Citu, you had better secure the uneaten meat," the king said, "or those animals just beyond the fire's glow will eat it."

"It will be done, Most Holy One."

One-by-one, the villagers fell asleep near the social fire, which slowly burned itself into a heap of smoldering ash. Several villagers managed to retreat to their huts where they awaited morning light and regrets for over indulging.

The king had intentionally limited his drink and left the affair having had an enjoyable time with his senses intact.

The king, wearing his royal feathered crown, stood on the central plaza, waiting for the sun god to awaken. As it did, Citu and Hakum followed him up the steps of the partially ruined Temple of Cacoh, the creator god where the king would meet with village leaders.

Every village center of moderate size had a similar temple but none as large as in Dzibilchaltun. Part of Chalmuch's temple roof had collapsed, but a portion remained intact and displayed two intact red and green images of Dubdo, the god of maize, and Chaac, the god of rain.

As the king entered the building, Citu said, "Most Holy One, our nine leaders were elected based on their wisdom, prowess, strength, wealth, hunting skills, and family size."

The leaders, wearing simple loincloths and featherless head-bands woven of red and white cotton, stood and bowed as the king entered what had been the local priests' outer room of the main sanctuary.

"Please return to your cushions," the king said.

Citu bowed to the elders. "Please sit. Leaders, the king has a story to tell— one of sadness and one of joy. Later, the Most Holy One will share the entire story."

At that point, Hakum handed the folded jaguar skin, taken just days earlier, to the king. Salted for preservation, it still reeked of dead animal. The king raised it overhead. "May the gods, whose images smile on us from this ceiling, recognize this jaguar skin and imbue it with sacred powers. Leaders of Chalmuch, I want your village to possess this skin, but I want it be owned through Citu."

Looking surprised, Citu, the now honored leader, stood and stared at the king. The Most Holy One draped the skin over Citu's shoulders. He bowed to the king and then to the village leaders who cheered and slapped their thighs in approval.

One leader fingered the skin. "This was a large jaguar. From the holes I count in its pelt, it must have given a great fight. Most Holy One, I and the village is honored through this gift."

Hiding the hint of a tear, Citu cleared his throat and said, "I am unworthy, Most Holy One, but on behalf of my people, I thank you."

The village leaders shouted and slapped their thighs in adulation.

Finally, the adulation subsided. Citu paced the stone floor. His jaguar cape swayed behind him, spreading its scent and attracting a few flies. He stopped and faced the village leaders. "Leaders of Chalmuch, the Most Holy One came to our aid during the war. Though we did not return with our king, we returned with the aid of this king and leader of the holy center. Without his assistance, our warriors would not have survived."

The villagers slapped their thighs in appreciation.

Citu swatted at a fly and continued. "You chose me to be this group's leader. I have attempted to lead and care for your needs, but I am not a chief, nor do I speak with the gods. I'm a simple hunter and leader of hunters. I cannot do otherwise."

"And a good one," Muchal shouted.

"Thank you, Muchal," Citu said. "With authority given me as your leader, I have asked the Most Holy One to be our king. He can restore our temple and bring us a high priest. He has agreed to serve us but only with your approval. I ask that you council among yourselves and bring me word of your decision by the time of the high-sun meal."

One leader bowed then said, "We will consider your counsel, Citu."

Citu bowed to the leaders then the king. The leaders rose, bowed to the king, and then left, talking among themselves.

"Most Holy One, let us retire to the palace of Chalmuch's king," Citu said.

The Most Holy One thought, *Never had I imagined such a day would come. I thank the gods for this blessing.*

The king scanned the receiving room of the former king's palace.

"The villagers have kept the palace in repair," Citu said, pointing to new stucco on the ceiling of the receiving hall. "The images of our gods remain here. Its floors are whitewashed and all its cloth doors are repainted. I have prayed for a benevolent king with kingly leadership to fill this palace and bring us a high priest. We have no priest to do similar repairs to the temple.

"Citu, your work, deeds, and love honors your dead king, but I could not live here permanently. I have responsibilities in The Center, but we should consider our peoples to be one. I could visit regularly, and when my prince is older, he would live here. In time, your people would come to know and love him. He could help meld our peoples."

"Most Holy One, your plan is sound. We could provide harvests of the jungle and you could provide fruits of the sea and salt, but we also need a high priest."

"I recently sent priests to Chichen Itza, because we had little food. I couldn't feed them. I can recall one to serve as your high priest."

"Most Holy One, your plan is acceptable to this humble servant, but I must discuss this with the other leaders for I fear objections by one man. Come, let us rest until the high-sun meal."

Village leaders conferred about Citu's proposal.

Mak Ut, the oldest leader, spoke first. A long facial scar slightly retracted the left corner of his lips. The deformity affected the clarity of his speech. "I don't approve the surrendering of our sovereignty to any king or Dzibilchaltun. We don't need a king. We're a small group, and we have enough of what we need. We don't worry about losing gold or silver—we have none. Look around you. We are blessed. Our families are happy, and we rule ourselves. We pray to gods who hear our pleas."

Alew Ik, the youngest village leader rose and rubbed his shaved head. "Mak Ut, we can't hide forever. We have a proud heritage, but few people know of us. In time, we may grow and prosper, but how we do that will depend on outside forces. If we knew writing, we could improve our lot, but we don't. There are many things to learn. Our people have ideas but don't know how to share them. That knowledge is in Dzibilchaltun and would be shared. I beg you, think of our future."

Mak Ut frowned and said, "Alew Ik, you *say* you think of our people. How will this alliance—no, this surrender to Dzibilchaltun—help me, my family, or our people?"

"Sir, we are far from the sea. Our women would not have to risk their lives gathering reeds. Women of The Center do this. We have fruits we could exchange for reeds and salt. We could exchange meat for fish. We could learn the ways of the stars, the moon, and the sun god. We need a better channel for the gods to bless our efforts—"

Padraig said, "I favor having ties to Dzibilchaltun. We need to learn better building methods; to learn writing to honor the gods and our people; to learn to grow better cotton and make finer cloth. We wouldn't have to wear these leather loincloths anymore. There is much to learn from the holy center."

Discussions raged for most of the morning. At times, they were heated and tempers flared.

Miso presented the concept of intermittent visits

by the Most Holy One.

Mak Ut countered, "If we need a king, he should live here."

"For me, "Elun said, "the prince would be suitable for a short time."

Mak Ut argued, "No one of such young age is acceptable to me. I could better serve our people."

Those who chose the conservative path argued the loudest, but in the end, eight of the nine leaders agreed to meld with Dzibilchaltun and prepared their presentation for Citu. Mak Ut dissented.

The leaders moved to the king's palace and called to Citu. He motioned from the doorway of the reception room that the leaders should join him and the king.

The Most Holy One rose and said, "Citu, honored elders, I take my leave so you may consult freely."

Citu bowed as the king left. "As you wish, Most Holy One."

The leaders sat on pillows moved into a circle. Standing, Citu cleared his throat. "Leaders, what is your counsel?"

"Citu," Alew Ik said, bowing, "we have consulted and ask you to extend your request, now our request, to the Most Holy One. This day he is our king."

Smiling, Citu said, "Elun, will you welcome back the Most Holy One."

Elun left the room while the leaders spoke among themselves. Within minutes, the king entered the room.

Citu bowed and said, "Receive the Most Holy One, King of the holy center of Dzibilchaltun and

Chalmuch."

All stood, bowed, and said in unison, "Welcome, Most Holy One, King of Dzibilchaltun and King of Chalmuch."

Hakum then escorted the queen and princess into the room. The leaders bowed and said, "Welcome Queen and Princess of Dzibilchaltun and Chalmuch."

The king said, "Citu, I will spend two days with your people before leaving for Dzibilchaltun. In time, the prime prince will live here. Until then, my lieutenant will be Citu. He has proven himself to be wise, a good hunter, and a leader worthy of trust. Salute him, your chieftain. He has the power of life and death when he speaks in my name."

Eight village leaders cheered heartily and slapped their thighs in gratitude and submission to Citu. Citu noted Mak Ut withheld his praise and barely tapped his thighs. He knew Mak Ut had been angered by his peers' willingness to surrender independence to the Most Holy One.

Mak Ut had often spoken of his interest in becoming the chieftain, but he had not gained the support of fellow elders. He had argued that Citu knew nothing of leadership, or ruling, and lacked the wisdom to do so. His only skill was hunting. Mak Ut felt his years of service and wisdom should have garnered him the post.

"Citu, will you tell the village of their leaders' decision?" the king asked. "I will give audience to anyone wanting such.

Chapter 17

For two days, the Most Holy One listened to the praises of his new people and considered a multitude of requests. At the end of the second day, villagers had another feast to mark his rule.

The king spent his last afternoon in religious rituals and fasted to be purified before praying throughout night in the Temple of Chaac. With his prayers and rituals, the old temple had again become a proper place to worship. The next morning, the infirmed local priest and the king prayed in the temple for his safe travels and a blessing on the Chalmuchans.

At high sun, the king's travel preparations were interrupted by Citu. "Most Holy One, we wish to give you four baskets of maize for the people of Dzibilchaltun. I will send men to carry them and one basket of meat to be eaten during your trip."

"Citu, I will return this favor with salt harvested from our salt flats.

The king's entourage prepared to leave the village plaza but his chanting subjects wished to pay their respects. They bowed to the ground as he passed. Some extended a hand to touch the king's sandal, a sign of respect.

Mak Ut, the oldest Chalmuchan leader, had set

out for Dzibilchaltun two days earlier than the king. Mak Ut wanted to find the priest known as Heregesob and from him learn what had happened between him and the king. Somewhere in this knowledge, Mak Ut hoped to find reasons he could use to dissuade his people from serving Dzibilchaltun's king.

At the end of the second day of travel, Mak Ut approached the zone known as The Center. He encountered a local villager and asked if he knew the whereabouts of the former high priest. The man informed Mak Ut he had heard Heregesob had been seen in northern villages, asking for food and water and telling lies about the king."

The villager shared rumors he had heard from the assistant priests and guards who had been with the king in the jungle when the confrontation occurred. "Few believe Heregesob," the villager said

"Thank you, villager, but I want to find this Heregesob."

"Careful. If you do, don't let anyone see you speak to him. The king has ordered the death of anyone who helps him."

"Thanks for the warning," Mak Ut said. "I bid you good travels."

Hoping Heregesob might be in the area, Mak Ut searched for him. After roaming the northern jungle for four days, he caught a glimpse of a half-naked man walking ahead. He wore a leather loincloth too small for a man of his size. Mak Ut quickened his pace, and with the stealth of a mouse, approached the man from the rear.

Feeling uneasy, Heregesob stopped and turned. Ninety paces away he saw a tired looking older man carrying a walking stick. His facial scar conveyed fearsomeness. Heregesob yelled, "Who comes at me. Show your intent." Heregesob raised his fists. "Are you friend or enemy?"

"Stranger, I am Mak Ut, Village Leader from Chalmuch. I come in peace. Who are you?"

"I am the high priest of Dzibilchaltun," the man said, eyeing Mak Ut. "I know your ornaments. You are Chalmuchan. I prayed for you, your people, and your king during the war. Why are you here, and why do you speak to me?"

"I've been searching for you."

"Me?" Heregesob asked in disbelief. "Why?"

"The Most Holy One is in Chalmuch and has convinced my people to surrender their independence to Dzibilchaltun. I warned them, but none heeded my words. The king, using magic, made a young hunter, Citu, our village chieftain over my objections, so I have searched for you to learn the reason for your being exiled and, hopefully, use that information for my purposes."

"So, you've heard the lies about me?"

"I claim no truth or to have listened to lies. I seek truth—my own truth."

"Then you are wise. I know the truth, for I suffered the king's lies. To begin, the gods spoke to me and to my priests telling us the princess should go to the sacred well in Chichen Itza." Heregesob clench his fist, sensing his anger grow. "As we traveled to Chichen Itza, the royals stole the princess in the night!" *I have to add something to the story so this Chalmuchan will believe the king's actions are sacrilegious. I'll say Bulek wanted selfish control of Chalmuch.* "The king wanted to expand his kingdom so he would have a greener jungle—Chalmuch's jungle."

"I've heard of your story but without these details," Mak Ut said.

Heregesob motioned they should sit down on nearby rocks then said, "The king's sacrilege should have caused him to be rejected, but the king scorned *me*, the high priest. He stripped me of my position, took my clothing, and tied me naked to a tree. I am forever exiled from the holy center. I may never see my family again." For a moment, Heregesob stared at the ground, then stood and shook his head. "Now, I wander where I know the location of water holes, but I have no friends. A few strangers have shared their meager foods and water, thinking me to be a lost traveler. One charitable man gave me this loincloth for my nakedness."

Heregesob stopped ranting and sat down on his rock. He picked up and fingered a small stone then shook his finger in Mak Ut's face. "This jungle is cursed by the king's ill will. He's responsible for this forsaken, barren jungle. His evil heart must beat on the altar in Dzibilchaltun for this wretched drought to be lifted." Heregesob stopped fingering the stone and threw it aside. "Well, you've heard my story. Why do you seek my truth? There is nothing I can do for you."

Mak Ut stared at Heregesob then touched his and Heregesob's chest. "We can help each other."

"And how would we do that?" Heregesob asked.

Mak Ut stood. "I can tell your story of the king's sacrilege to the people of Dzibilchaltun along with my story of his takeover. Hopefully, I can convince The Center's people of the king's blasphemy." Mak Ut struck his palm with his fist. "If the King is cast out, the prime prince becomes the new king."

"I know the rule," Heregesob said.

"According to tradition, a child prince will have a guardian—a high priest. In Dzibilchaltun, you might regain your post and your status. You could again be high priest, the one who teaches the prince about the evil deeds of his father. Your office would be secure."

Heregesob thought, *I doubt this man is capable of anything so important, but what do I have to lose?* Heregesob kicked at dry leaves. "Why do you think the people of Dzibilchaltun will heed your words?"

"I can speak as a village leader. I could share the truth of your king's selfish ambition to rule Chalmuch through false diplomacy."

"And what do you want from me?" Heregesob wondered how to he could strike back at the Most Holy One. *I must convince this man that Bulek has bewitched the young Citu through magic.*

"Travel with me to Chalmuch," Mak Ut said. "There you can relate your story about the unworthy king and his thoughtless exile of a sacred priest. Help me convince my people that their surrender to Dzibilchaltun is not in their interest. I should be their chieftain, and Citu, the hunter now in charge, should be one of nine leaders loyal to Chalmuch's chieftain—me—not some intruder from Dzibilchaltun."

"I like your plan, Mak Ut. I have everything to gain, but first let The Center hear your words. Seek the ear of Assistant Priest Canche. He was my most trusted and valued assistant. I pray he heeds your truth. I'll wait here for your return."

Mak Ut walked along Dzibilchaltun's *sacbe*, the long, sacred avenue, to the central plaza. It had been many moon cycles since he had visited The Center.

Little had changed. Reflected sunlight from the whitewashed sacbe almost blinded him. He saw the king's palace, far across the plaza. He shifted his gaze to the priests' palace. He walked past the Temple of the Six Dolls and noted the current king's doll stood on a pedestal in the temple's central portal.

Mak Ut walked into the shade at the foot of the Palace of the Priests where a strolling man read a book. The fact he could read and had gold icons sewn to his white loincloth identified him as a priest.

"Acolyte, I am Mak Ut, a village leader from Chalmuch. I would like to speak to Priest Canche. Will you relay my request for an audience?"

"I see from your squared leather loincloth and headband you are from Chalmuch. What business do you have with our priest?"

"I bring grave concerns from Chalmuch about Dzibilchaltun."

"Wait here. I'll ask if Priest Canche will see you."

"Thank you."

After moments of pacing, Mak Ut looked toward the upper terrace. A young priest with a partially shaved head and long pony tail stood at its edge. The man motioned for Mak Ut to come up.

The man's face bore white paint, and his eyes were outlined with green dye, an indication he was a priest and had been recently involved in a religious ritual. His simple clothing reeked of sweet incense, and his authority necklace contained the largest sea shell Mak Ut had ever seen.

Mak Ut bowed. "Priest Canche, I am Mak Ut, village leader of Chalmuch."

"Come in from the sun, Mak Ut, and share your

concerns."

The men entered the priests' reception room. A ray of sunlight, reflected off the white stucco floor, illuminating niches containing religious relics of gold, silver, turquoise, and sea shells.

Awe struck, Mak Ut glanced from treasure to treasure. *I have never seen such treasures.*

"Our people have been generous," the priest said, gesturing toward a multicolored cushion bearing images of the serpent god, Kukulkan. "Please. Sit."

"Thank you. In the king's absence, I would deliver my message to the prince, but since he is not of age, I believe you should hear my words of warning."

"Warning?" the priest asked, looking concerned. "Why a warning?"

"It's about your king. He, not your high priest, has committed sacrilege."

"Mak Ut, I have heard the king's story from a priest who traveled with the king in the jungle. Why should I hear your story? You weren't present at his confrontation."

The priest rose, walked to the corner of the room, took his staff and struck its end on the floor. A servant rushed in and bowed.

"Xuult," the priest said, "summon the other priests and our village leaders to hear this man's story. I wish to consult with them by the time of the gods' sleep. See that this leader has accommodations, food, and drink."

Xuult bowed and then escorted Mak Ut to a sleeping space.

Mak Ut sat in the doorway of his room watching the setting sun paint the sky a kaleidoscope of purples and oranges. He knew the chieftains were just returning to their homes after a day of searching for food. He would have a long wait before they gathered in The Center.

The leaders gathered at the foot of the Palace of the Priests awaiting Priest Canche's appearance.

A servant, holding a flaming torch, stepped onto the palace terrace and motioned for the leaders to enter the priests' council room.

Mak Ut stood out of respect for the chieftains. Each took a seat on a floor cushion and listened while priest Canche introduced his guest. "Mak Ut, may it please the ears of these leaders to hear your words."

Mak Ut cleared his throat and told his tale. His short story had apparently astonished the leaders. He bowed and then sat down on his cushion. Although he sat still, he appeared to shake as flickering torches caused his shadow to dance on the whitewashed walls.

The elders and priests were stone quiet.

After several seconds, Canche stood. "Mak Ut, our king is a man of honor and courage. If he wanted to subdue your people, why did he not do it when the war ended? Your people were in chaos, weakened, and without a king. Why would he wait until your people were stronger and have a leader?"

"Most honorable leaders and Priest Canche, that time was not right."

"Why then is this time right?" a chieftain asked.

Mak Ut gathered his thoughts. "Your king has found a young and physically strong Chalmuchan—one who can be manipulated—controlled. His name is Citu. Citu surrendered our people's destiny so he would become chieftain and head village leader. With Citu's help, my village will be ruled by your king, and my people will be no more. He will speak for the Most Holy One in Chalmuch. This gives much power to Citu, an inexperienced leader.

A young priest said, "Leader of Chalmuch, this act could be good for Dzibilchaltun."

"Yes, Chalmuchan," the oldest chieftain said. "Your village has much we could use and need."

"But honorable leaders of Dzibilchaltun, we could exchange goods without Chalmuch losing its identity."

"Chalmuchan, why should we care about your identity?" another chieftain asked. "You are a small village."

"But why do I care for your identity, honorable Chieftain of Dzibilchaltun? I do so out of respect, and that is all I ask of you."

"Why should we care if the Most Holy One appoints a high priest for Chalmuch?" Priest Canche asked. "He is the Most Holy One. We, or our people, are none the worse for such an act. The gods might be pleased with such piety. Besides, your village has no high priest. Isn't something better than nothing?"

Mak Ut thought for a moment, rubbing his chin. "Your king has the right to appoint a high priest in *his* territory. Chalmuch was beyond your king's territory, so he took my territory by bewitching Citu. This is evil making, for it lacks the blessings of the gods or a high priest." Mak Ut felt his face warm red with anger. He shook his finger in the direction of Chalmuch while addressing the chieftains. "Your king must rule Chalmuch in order to appoint its priests, but he did not and therefore had no authority to name its high priest. Only the great high priest of Chichen Itza could do that. It is for this, and other reasons, your high priest is exiled. His objections were an obstacle to your king's controlling my community and naming a high priest there."

The chieftains sat quietly shaking their heads and looking questioningly at each other.

Priest Canche rose. "You have told your story, Mak Ut. Please return to your quarters and wait the council's decision."

Visibly shaking as a reaction to his emotionally charged presentation, Mak Ut bowed toward each leader, the priests, and then took his leave.

Mak Ut sat in his small terrace-level room. He watched the priests return to their quarters. The Center's village leaders huddled on the far end of the Mak Ut's terrace to talk among themselves. After much debate, they sent a servant away. Moments later, Priest Canche arrived. He and the oldest leader walked a few steps away from the group of village leaders. They spoke for a while and then reentered the palace.

After minutes of unsettling thoughts of what might happen to him, Mak Ut paced the terrace hoping for a favorable outcome.

A servant approached Mak Ut. "Leader, please return to the council room."

Mak Ut followed the servant into an empty room then sat down on a floor cushion to await the council and priests. When they entered, he stood.

Priest Canche said, "Be seated, Mak Ut. The king arrives tomorrow. We await his arrival to hear his words. If he speaks truth, you do not." The priest glanced at two guards, nodded toward Mak Ut, and said, "Take him."

The guards grasped Mak Ut's arms and held

them behind his back. Startled, he struggled to free himself as the guards forced him to his knees then pushed his head against the floor.

Fearful and angered, he yelled, "Priest Canche, village leaders, I have done nothing to deserve this outrage. I am a *leader* of my people. I know of what I speak. Don't doubt my words. Your king bewitches my people and spreads venom."

Canche said, "Chalmuchan, say no more until our king arrives and can defend his honor. Guards, take Mak Ut away."

As Mak Ut left the room, Priest Canche said, "Chieftains, you are my guests until the king arrives."

Chapter 18

The Most Holy One sent a runner to inform the prince and Priest Canche of his arrival time. The runner was to inform the priest that he should call villagers to The Center to receive the king and gifts of maize from Chalmuch.

On reaching the first crossroad leading to Dzibilchaltun, the king, anxious to get home, quickened his pace and sent several men ahead to help with preparations required for his return.

When the king reached The Center's outer limit, conch sounds filled the jungle as conchmen, posted on each of the main temples, announced the king's return. He donned his feather crown, adjusted his ceremonial cloak, and then led the group toward the Temple of the Six Dolls. Cheering villagers slapped their thighs as the king strode along a path opened by the receding and bowing crowd. He smiled and waved like a conquering leader. *I once thought I would never return here, but the gods interceded. I wished they would now send rain.*

The queen, princess, and a bodyguard left the entourage and went ahead to the palace.

The food bearers stopped at the base of the Temple of the Six Dolls as the king climbed to its terrace.

A strong wind blew over The Center as the king

raised his arms to silence the cheering crowd. His upraised arms, billowing cloak, and fluttering crown feathers gave the appearance he had taken flight. "People of Dzibilchaltun, I return with good news. We have gifts from Chalmuch. Tonight, we celebrate our good fortune."

The crowd cheered on hearing *celebrate*.

The king waited for the crowd to quiet down. "After the next awakening of the gods, I will speak to our leaders of a new plan for our people. For now, feast, sleep the night, and await word from your leaders."

The queen put her daughter to bed and repeatedly glanced out the doorway, looking to see if the king approached.

Suddenly, Prince Hiayalael ran in and hugged her. She picked him up, gave him a hug then kissed him on the forehead. "And how is my Prince? Looks like you need sleep. Want to go to bed?"

"Yes." He put his head on her shoulder and fingered her hair. "*Oma*, your hair stinks."

"Don't worry. When I bathe, I'll add incense and it will smell better, but let's get you to bed."

At that moment, the king entered. Hakum followed, bowed to the queen, and then removed the king's crown and cloak.

"How's my prince?" the king asked, rubbing his son's head.

"Good . . ."

"I think he needs sleep," the queen said, placing him in his father's arms.

"Okay," the king said. "Let's get you a nap. We'll play later. It is so good to have you in my arms. For a while, I thought I would never see you again."

"Most Holy One," Hakum said, "village leaders wish to speak to you. It's urgent."

Rubbing his son's head, the king asked, "What is their issue?"

"I don't know, Most Holy One, but they say it's urgent."

"Tell them I will hear them in two hours—in the council room after I have rested. Take the prince to his bed."

As the king approached the council room, he heard the buzz of conversation. On his entry, the leaders rose and bowed. He nodded his recognition, walked to his throne, and sat down. "What is this urgent matter?"

"Most Holy One," the eldest chieftain said, "We have a visitor. He is Mak Ut, a leader from Chalmuch. He arrived yesterday. He said you had corrupted the minds of the Chalmuchans."

Shocked and astonished, the king stood. "What? I know this man. What nonsense did he speak?"

"Mak Ut said, 'In exchange for naming a head village leader, or chieftain, and providing Chalmuch with a high priest, you gained control of the village and its people. You exiled your high priest because he would not bless your naming a high priest to Chalmuch whose people worship different gods.'"

Has my heretic priest caused Mak Ut to do this evil? "Enough! What does this liar want of us?"

"Most Holy One," the eldest chieftain continued, "Mak Ut claims the title of Chief Leader of Chalmuch should be his and not the hunter Citu. Mak Ut believes his village needs no high priest except one appointed by Chichen Itza—if the great high priest wishes to do so."

"Where is this liar?"

"Priest Canche holds him prisoner, Most Holy One."

"Hakum," the king yelled, "have Mak Ut brought to me. Now!"

"Yes, Most Holy One."

While waiting, the king paced, pounding his clenched fist onto his palm. *Why has Mak Ut disparaged me? What have I done to him to cause this sacrilege?*

Moments later, two guards pushed Mak Ut into the room.

On seeing him, the king clenched his jaw, made fists, and stared intently at his new enemy.

The guards forced Mak Ut to his knees. One guard used his foot to press Mak Ut's face against the floor, flattening his left cheek.

"I remember you from the leaders' meeting in Chalmuch." The king said. He walked to Mak Ut, placed his toe under the man's jaw, and lifted his head.

Mak Ut's gaze remained fixed on the floor. "Most Holy One. I am innocent."

"Mak Ut, face me. Tell *me* I have duped Citu and the people of Chalmuch."

"You know what you have done," Mak Ut said through crunched lips. "You exiled Dzibilchaltun's high priest because he would not bless your appointment of a high priest to serve Chalmuch. With your high priest exiled, you could control my people with the help of Citu and a high priest—loyal to you—assigned to Chalmuch. I should be chieftain of Chalmuch, but I refused to bend to your will as did Citu. You bewitched him."

The king withdrew his foot and looked at his

chieftains. "This man lies. The ex-high priest struck at me because the dream I received about the princess' visit to the gods in Chichen Itza differed from what he wanted to believe." The king paced. "Citu stopped the priest's hand from striking me. Our former priest committed a sacrilege against *me*." The king stopped pacing and stared at Mak Ut.

"Despite the priest's sacrilege, I did not take his life although I own it. Instead, I took his necklace and exiled him." The king took a deep breath and looked at Mak Ut who jerked his head under the guard's foot.

"Citu asked me and this royal family to rule Chalmuch—to be *their* royal family. I exerted no force. Citu's proposal gained approval of all the leaders of Chalmuch—except this miserable liar." Mak Ut muttered as the king continued. "Of their free will, the leaders of Chalmuch invited this royal family to be their royal family. To dispel any doubt, I will send for Citu and his leaders. They will bear witness to my words." The king motioned toward the guards. "Take this liar away to await the arrival of my witnesses."

The temple guards grasped Mak Ut's wrists and dragged the struggling man from the hall.

Mak Ut staggered ahead of his guards. One guard carried a torch to light the way as the other kept Mak Ut on his feet, easing the burden of half-dragging him the last hundred steps along a dark, narrow passageway. Each guard held one of the prisoner's wrists against the other behind his back and pushed him ahead as the three men negotiated the restricted corridor. "Not so tight," Mak Ut shouted. You're hurting my arm." As the corridor grew narrower, one guard moved close behind the prisoner, and the second guard followed the first, each gripping one of Mak Ut's wrists. The awkward column of three men moved slowly along the narrowing passageway.

Taking advantage of his position, Mak Ut used a backward facing palm to squeeze the testicles of the guard immediately behind him. As the guard yelled and retched with pain, Mak Ut jerked free his other hand so quickly the second guard had no time to realize what had happened.

The writhing guard tried to pull Mak Ut's squeezing hand from his crotch but couldn't. Mustering all his strength, Mak Ut elbowed him in the head, knocking him backwards onto the second guard who fell, striking his head on the floor where he lay motionless.

Mak Ut bolted down the passage whose ceiling got lower and lower. At the end of the corridor, he came to a forked intersection. Looking right, he saw daylight and raced toward it. He soon found himself outside the palace. He scurried down its steps as fast as his old legs allowed then ran into the jungle, losing a sandal along the way.

The injured guards staggered into the council room, prostrated themselves on the floor and informed the king of their injuries and Mak Ut's escape.

"Idiots!" the king yelled. "Go to your quarters." He pointed to several other guards and shouted, "Go after Mak Ut! I want him here before the god's sleep."

The king followed the newly dispatched guards as far as his terrace where he watched them scamper down palace steps to the plaza where they spoke to several locals, asking if they had seen the fleeing man. A woman pointed toward the rear of the palace. The guards ran in the direction indicated by the woman. A hundred paces from the palace, the guards bent over and picked up an object. They waved what looked like a sandal to the king then ran in the direction of Chalmuch.

At the juncture of two jungle trails, Mak Ut ran two hundred paces to the east where he left his remaining sandal in the middle of the path. He then backtracked along the edge of the path to the intersection where he took the west path.

Barefooted, Mak Ut ran a zig zag pattern for half a day toward the area where he had left Heregesob. On the way, he noted a sea of three-foot-high piles of leaves and jungle debris. *Villagers must have created these while searching for something to eat.* Walking between the piles and scanning the jungle hundreds of paces ahead, Mak Ut hoped to find Heregesob.

As Mak Ut searched, something grabbed his ankle and pulled him to the ground. Falling on his right knee, he sent leaves and dust skyward. A man, clad in a loincloth, rose from beneath a pile of debris.

"Why are you here, Chalmuchan?" the man asked.

"Don't you remember me? I'm Mak Ut."

"Oh. Sorry. I heard someone running toward me and feared they meant me harm. I had no place to hide but this pile."

"Help me up? I've injured my knee."

"Sorry I didn't immediately recognize you," Heregesob said, scanning Mak Ut's body, "not in this disheveled state. What happened? Did you speak to Canche?"

"I spoke to him and the council. I shared your

story concerning the Most Holy One, but the king called me a liar and sent for Citu to verify his story. The king ordered me held prisoner until Citu arrived, but I escaped."

Heregesob's shoulders sagged. "I hadn't expected the king to be there. This is bad. I dare not visit Chalmuch *or* Dzibilchaltun again."

"No," Mak Ut said. "Now is an excellent time to visit Chalmuch. Citu and the elders will be away. We can address my people without Citu's objection. They know and respect me, and they will respect you, a high priest. Let my people decide the truth after you disclose how the king duped them and Citu."

"Mak Ut, you *are* a politician. Why not? I have nothing to lose in Chalmuch. Let's go, but we must run if we are to capitalize on the time your leaders are away."

Mak Ut avoided the direct route to Chalmuch for fear of encountering either the king's guards or Citu and his elders. At nightfall, he persuaded the priest to rest a while then resume their trek. He hoped to reach Chalmuch before the time of the gods' sleep the next day.

Exhausted, Mak Ut arrived in Chalmuchan territory where he encountered three locals searching for fruits.

"Men, forgive my appearance, but I am Village Elder Mak Ut," he said, panting. "May we have a drink of your water?" Mak Ut then Heregesob drank. Addressing the youngest man, Mak Ut said, "Run to the village and call the people to the palace to hear important news. My fellow traveler, a high priest, and I need rest, but we will be in the village in a short time. Now go. Run with the wind."

#

Mak Ut and Heregesob pushed their way through the waiting villagers. At the palace, Mak Ut climbed to the first terrace where Heregesob sat in the shade of nearby trees.

Mak Ut raised his arms to quiet the murmuring crowd. "People of Chalmuch, you know me as a village elder. I bring you truth about our destiny. The King of Dzibilchaltun cast a spell on Citu and our leaders. He convinced them to surrender our sovereignty to The Holy Center."

Many in the crowd stared questioningly at each other. Some were heard to say, "What?"

"We are no longer Chalmuchan," Mak Ut yelled. "We are people of Dzibilchaltun. Our heritage is lost. Our children will no longer know us as Chalmuchan. We cease to exist because of Citu's selfish ambition and a foreigner who rules through magic."

Pointing to the ex-priest, Mak Ut said, "This is the high priest of Dzibilchaltun who suffered because of his stand against the Most Holy One's desire to control our village. Hear his truth."

A man in the front of the crowd yelled, "How can a high priest be dressed in a loincloth—and a shabby one. He has no authority necklace or ear plugs!"

Heregesob stood, pulled himself to his full height, stepped forward, and stared first at the men up front then the rest of the crowd. He looked many of them in the eye then slowly raised his arms. He opened his mouth to speak but said nothing. Villagers stared at him as he stared at the sky. The priest unfolded his empty ear lobes that had been looped over his ears. "These lobes once held ear plugs given to me by the

Most Holy One." The priest paused as he displayed his empty lobes. "People of Chalmuch, Mak Ut has spoken truth. I refused to sanction the Most Holy One's domination of your village. I knew you worshipped different gods than those of The Center, so I refused to name a high priest to serve your village. I did this out of respect for our religious differences."

Someone in the crowd yelled, "The gods differ in name only!"

Mak Ut scanned the crowd to see who had yelled but failed.

Another man yelled, "We both have a rain god and other gods differing in name only. The home of the gods is the same for us as for Dzibilchaltun."

"That is somewhat true!" the priest yelled back, "but there are two gods which are very different."

"But they are minor gods—rarely called on," Mak Ut said. "Who can remember their names?"

The crowd was quiet.

"The great high priest of Chichen Itza should name our priests," Mak Ut said, "not Dzibilchaltun. This land is beyond its territory." Mak Ut paused to let the murmuring crowd quiet down. "The Most Holy One offered, and Citu accepted, a role equal to a servant of the distant king. In exchange for his servitude, Citu received the title Chieftain of Chalmuch, now a part of Dzibilchaltun. The Most Holy One and Citu sanctioned Dzibilchaltun's priests serving our village against any respect for our identity. In exchange for this sacrilege, we ceased to be Chalmuchans."

The crowd booed and shook their fists.

"We can be Chalmuchan and of The Center," someone yelled.

A few men, fists raised, moved toward the

palace steps ready to strike the priest, but Mak Ut shook his fist, and the men backed away.

The priest climbed to a higher terrace, obviously wondering why the villagers had threatened him.

Mak Ut stared at the crowd and raised his arms. "Don't fear us. We are the ones who bring truth. Don't be deceived by Citu or the foreign king. Declare your independence and distance yourselves from those who would rob you of our heritage. You know our so-called village leaders travel to Dzibilchaltun to support The Center's king, so Citu can retain his office and continue to surrender our identity. Do not listen to them when they return."

A man stepped forward. "Elder! I hunted in the jungle with Citu. I heard the words between the king and this Heregesob. This man struck at the king. I saw no magic. I heard no incantations, but I did hear the king speak about becoming our leader. Citu asked us hunters if we agreed. We did. This Heregesob made no mention of his disapproval of the king's concern for us or our gods. How could Citu, at that moment, know the Most Holy One would make him chieftain and village leader? All our leaders, but you, wanted the Most Holy One's leadership. Rumors say you want to be chieftain, but you failed to garner the council's support."

Mak Ut started to respond, but the hunter interrupted. "Mak Ut, I hear no truth from you or this priest man. You try to deceive our villagers for selfish reasons. If you lie about this matter, how can we trust you about anything? In my eyes, you are no longer a village leader. Be gone."

The crowd shouted insults and shook their fists at the speakers. Having verbally vented their wrath, the crowd broke up.

Mak Ut wondered why they treated him so. He stared at the priest. "I know of nothing more to do."

Someone in the crowd yelled, "Traitor!"

A stone struck the head of Mak Ut, knocking him to the terrace floor. Half-conscious, he rolled toward the palace steps.

Several more stones were thrown. The priest dropped to the terrace. He needed to protect himself—better yet—escape. He kicked the half-conscious Mak Ut down the steps like a sacrificed victim. Villagers, storming up the steps, moved aside to avoid Mak Ut's tumbling body.

The rest of the crowd stopped their exit to throw stones at Mak Ut. Feebly protecting his head with his arms, he watched the priest flee through the palace. Villagers pulled Mak Ut's arms away from his head as one man slammed a large rock against his head.

From a palace room, Heregesob watched as villagers gathered rocks from fire pits to stone Mak Ut. In a matter of minutes, his head had been crushed, making it impossible to identify his face. Several men dragged his body into the jungle and left it for animals. His existence would be lost from village memory.

Heregesob ran through the council room, down back palace steps then fled into the jungle, carrying the mental image of the villager's wrath. After running a great distance, his stone-heavy legs and aching lungs reached their limits of endurance. He ached for a drink of water. Gasping, he fell to the ground as if dying. *I knew I shouldn't rely on Mak Ut. I'd better hide until the time of the god's sleep.*

Rested, Heregesob wandered the jungle, seeking a path to Dzibilchaltun where he could find water. By morning, he had found the path. Stumbling along the dusty trail, he heard male voices in the distance and moving toward him. *They can't be warriors; they're too noisy. I hope they have water.*

Brushing dirt and debris from his body, the ex-priest stood tall to appear as threatening as possible without a weapon. *I know that dialect,* he thought*. It's Dzibilchaltunian.* When the men were closer, he confirmed their identity by their loincloths, their water tubes, and their back baskets.

The strangers looked at him in amazement.

"Water? Do you have water?" Heregesob asked.

"Yes. Of course," a man said, offering his water tube.

Heregesob grabbed the tube. Water dripped from his chin between gulps. Having quenched his thirst, he returned the almost empty tube, slumped to the ground, and leaned against a tree.

"Thank you, farmer," Heregesob said. "For two days, I've been lost. Nothing to drink."

"Who are you, stranger?" the water-tube owner asked. "I don't recognize your loincloth. Where are you from?"

Relieved the men didn't recognize him, Heregesob said, "I'm from Chalmuch. I was gathering fruits when a jaguar stalked me. I ran all night, hid, climbed trees, and lost my way, but I escaped its jaws. Where am I?"

"Near Dzibilchaltun," the second farmer said. "Chalmuch is in the opposite direction. Take my water tube for your trip."

Heregesob clutched the tube. "Thank you farm—"

"I'm Úcan," the farmer said.

"Thank you, Úcan. I'll rest then travel as you

pointed."

Heregesob rested until he thought the farmers could not see him then headed for Dzibilchaltun.

Úcan looked at his fellow farmers. "I suspect that man is from our center."

Úcan retreated toward Dzibilchaltun. "Why do we turn back?" a farmer asked.

"That man didn't wear a Chalmuchan loincloth," Úcan said. "In fact, he wore a skin tanned by someone from Dzibilchaltun." Úcan pointed to his loincloth. "His skin's marks were like mine. Even folded back, I could see his earlobes had holes for earplugs. Gatherers do not wear plugs. Only priests, nobles, and royalty wear such things. As for the jaguar, I know of no man who can outrun a hungry jaguar on land or in trees. I don't believe his story."

"Who do you think he is?" another farmer asked.

"The exiled high priest," Ucan said. "He's rumored to be in the area."

"Then we must tell the Most Holy One," the farmer said.

"That's why I'm returning," Úcan said, pointing toward The Center.

"Then let's run," a farmer said, breaking into a trot.

After a tiring half-day run, the farmers arrived at Dzibilchaltun's main plaza. They spoke to a passing guard who then yelled to Hakum pacing the king's terrace.

"Who calls me?" Hakum asked, placing his fists on his chest.

"These villagers have seen the exiled priest. They wish to tell the Most Holy One."

"Send them up," Hakum said. "I'll inform the Most Holy One."

Hakum entered the palace, while the guard escorted the farmers to the terrace.

In moments, Hakum reappeared. "The Most Holy One comes. Bow to our king."

The Most Holy One walked onto the terrace and approached the farmers who prostrated themselves. Their foreheads touched the terrace.

"Rise," the king said. "You have seen the exiled priest?"

"Most Holy One, we believe so," Úcan said, head bowed and eyes lowered. "At the far edge of The Center."

"Tell me more," The king said, sitting down on a pillow under a flapping awning.

Úcan informed the king about the stranger's story of the jaguar then described the man's ear lobes and his loincloth.

"Farmers, you have served your king well. Thank you. Hakum, call the guards. Have them follow these farmers to the spot where they saw the heretic. The guards are not to return without him."

Moments later, the farmers led guards to the area where they had encountered the ex-priest. From there, they went in different directions in search of the priest.

Chapter 19

At dawn, guards delivered Heregesob to the king's palace.

"The king has been expecting you," Hakum said, staring down at Heregesob from the king's upper terrace. "When he awakes, I will inform him you are returned. I will also ask the medicine man to treat your injuries. Guards, place him in a holding room."

Finishing a breakfast of berries, the king rose and paced. "Hakum, send for the heretic and send for The Center's priests and village leaders."

Confronting the ex-priest would not be pleasant for the king. His belly quivered as he stared at his shaking hands. *Gods help me control my anger for this heretic who would destroy me?*

A short time later, the assistant priests and leaders assembled in the council room.

"Choose a floor cushion," the king said, pacing. "Listen well. The former high priest has been captured." The king stopped pacing and took a deep breath. "Instead of death, I condemned him to exile. I spared his life, expecting him to obey my order but he hasn't." Sitting down on his throne, the king said, "He has attempted to create hate and distrust between the people of Chalmuch and Dzibilchaltun." The king stared toward the plaza for a moment and then paced again. "He spread lies about me, the royal family, and Citu, the Chieftain of Chalmuch." Staring into the eyes of each priest, the king said, "But fear not. The heretic has spent the night in a holding room." While the king spoke, his speed of pacing increased and his voice grew louder. "The traitor is being brought here now. I want your counsel in dealing with him."

"Most Holy One, we were shocked when we heard of his misdeeds," Priest Canche said as the other priests nodded agreement, "but we do what we must—"

"Forgive me, Most Holy One," Hakum said. "The leaders of Chalmuch have arrived."

The king continued pacing. "Give them drink then bring them here."

Moments later, Citu and the Chalmuchan leaders entered and bowed to the king and priests.

"Citu. Chalmuchans. We welcome you," the king said. "I sent for you to bear witness to my telling of your request that I become your king. I wanted you to repeat that invitation in the presence of Mak Ut, a traitor to you and me, but sadly, he escaped."

Citu reeled with shock. "This is the first I have heard of Mak Ut's disgrace, Most Holy One. I wondered why he could not be found when I and the other leaders left Chalmuch for this meeting. What has he done?"

"Our former high priest had Mak Ut come here to beguile my priests and leaders into believing I had committed a sacrilege against you, Dzibilchaltun, and Chalmuch. However, a short while ago, a runner brought word my former high priest and Mak Ut had been in Chalmuch spreading lies. Your villagers stoned Mak Ut and chased the fugitive priest into the jungle, but fear not. The heretic has been caught."

Citu rose and bowed. "Most Holy One, tell us of Mak Ut's disgrace."

The king stepped down from his throne, passed the priests, and stood before the Chalmuchans. "Mak Ut presented himself before my priests and spread lies sent by our former high priest. Mak Ut insulted my holy person. He said I used magic to beguile Citu and you into surrendering to this throne." The king walked to his throne and sat down. "I sent for you to speak the truth before my chiefs, priests, and Mak Ut, but he is dead. His flight spoke his guilt."

"Most Holy One," Citu said, "let us use our time to share the truth with all your people."

"Citu, you are wise. Tomorrow, I'll summon the villagers to hear the truth from you and your leaders. Afterwards, there will be no reason for ill rumors to be heard about our union."

The king clapped. Hakum entered and bowed.
"Make arrangements for the morning. I will address our people at the time of the high sun." Turning to the leaders of Dzibilchaltun's leaders, he said, "I seek your counsel on the fate of the heretic who defiantly returned to The Center."

"Where is he, Most Holy One?" an elder of The Center asked.

"He is being brought here now."

"Most Holy One, may we hear from you of the jungle incident that caused his exile?" the same elder asked.

"Citu is my witness," the king said. The former priest refused to value dreams sent to me and the queen. The god's message to me did not conform to our priest's interests. They told me to take the princess from the path to Chichen Itza. I need say no more."

Citu rose, bowed, and then faced the group. "Leaders of the Holy Center, I and my hunters heard of the king's dreams, and we saw the former high priest strike at him. We heard the Most Holy One order the priest not to return to The Center. The king had reason to strike the priest dead but did not because of his relationship with the one who threatened him."

Well said, the king thought.

"Thank you, Citu," a local leader said. "We didn't require your words in support of the Most Holy One, for he is held in high regard, but your words do weigh on our counsel."

A distant sounding commotion interrupted the group's discussions.

Hakum entered the throne room and bowed to the king and leaders. "Most Holy One, the prisoner is in the corridor."

"Bring him in," the king said, anger tingeing his voice. *I can't wait to hear what he has to say.*

Guards struggled to get the prisoner into the room. Despite evidence of recent trauma and multiple lacerations, the priest struggled to escape. The guards dragged him to the center of the room. There they forced him to his knees and pressed his head against the floor while pulling the leather tether binding his wrists behind his back.

The king walked around the prisoner, assessing his many injuries. The king, using his toe, raised the heretic's loincloth enough to note its origin. The king knelt then stared the priest in the eye. "Heregesob! You were ordered never to return to Dzibilchaltun. Why have you defied me?"

The priest said nothing.

The king stood then used his toe to raise the heretic's head and stared into his eyes. "Why do you wear this loincloth, and where did you get it?"

The ex-priest spat on the king's foot.

"You scum!" the king said.

"Defiler of men!" The priest shouted. "I came to tell our villagers of your sacrilege, your responsibility for the drought, and the queen's loss of faith in our gods. The gods didn't hear your supplications or receive your blood because you are faithless—filled with evil."

"No man could do more for the gods than me," the king said, letting the priest's head fall.

Hakum tried to clean the king's toe while he paced and the priest railed.

"You lie!" Heregesob yelled, "King of vile flesh, you know no truth!"

The word *truth* hadn't reached the end of its echo around the room when the group uttered a collective gasp on hearing the insult.

"How could I have trusted this son of a snake?"

Heregesob's face grew red and his voice shook "You refused to sacrifice the princess *after* you offered her."

The king walked around the prisoner. "You were my high priest, my friend, and my advisor, but you refused to hear the words of the Most Holy One to whom the gods had spoken through dreams. You hardened yourself to my views and raised your hand against me." The king kicked the priest. "It is you who committed sacrilege. Now, you must make whole what you have damaged—my holy honor."

The king returned to his throne. Hands shaking with anger, he gripped its jaguar heads.

"It is you who are broken, unholy king!" Heregesob yelled. "You and our center cannot be made whole until *your* heart beats in our cup of hearts. The gods await the hour."

"I don't fear you," the king said, his voice shaking.

"The temple is no longer yours, and the *gods* call for retribution. Your blood will make pure the dishonored images in our temples, the gods of the sky and underworld."

"Unworthy king, *you* cannot cause my blood to flow nor take my heart," the prisoner snarled. "Only the great high priest of Chichen Itza can draw my blood, and I will flee your bonds on any attempt to take me there."

The king walked to the priest then kicked him in the side.

"Neither I nor the village leaders fear your escape on a trip to Chichen Itza, for the great high priest will come *here* and oversee the Ceremony of Arrows."

The king smiled as Heregesob gasped then trembled on hearing the word *arrows*. He obviously had not thought the great high priest would come to The Center.

"No! No!" Heregesob yelled. He stared into the face of the king and became deadly quiet. His body stiffened then went limp, melting onto the floor where he whimpered and shook. He knew what the future held for him because he and the king had officiated at two Ceremonies of Arrows

"Take him away!" the king shouted to the guards. "Keep him until the great high priest arrives." The king returned to his throne and took a deep breath to quiet his spirit. Pointing to Priest Canche, he said,

"Hakum, help the priest collect materials to prepare blue paint for the ceremony. Much will be needed, for Heregesob is a big man."

On hearing the word paint, the ex-priest wailed. "No! No!"

"Hakum," the king said, "send a runner to Chichen Itza. Inform the great high priest he is needed here urgently."

The king addressed his leaders, "For the ritual, select twelve men with bows and arrows that are true. Prepare them for the ceremony within fourteen days." The king walked to Citu and said, "You and your leaders are also damaged by the lies of this heretic. You too need to see justice done. You and they are to witness the ceremony, and it is important for one of your men to carry a bow."

Heregesob's anxiety grew day-by-day. He had no appetite and ate little. He could not shake thoughts of his fate or find sleep. All day, he lay on the cell floor staring at the cell's low ceiling. Room heat became oppressive, causing him to often change positions to find a cooler stone on which to rest. *Oh to have one more water tube a day to quench this thirst. Just one.*

The guards were forbidden to give him more than three cups of water per day.

He reminisced about his wife, their early love making, the birth of his first daughter and how she mirrored her mother's beauty. Then the face of Calx, his male lover, came to mind. Heregesob remembered the young man's strong chest, strong arms, and his tender embrace. The faces of Heregesob's noble friends flashed across his mind, but he knew they could not help him.

His family would continue to live in their palace but on a lower level until his wife remarried the next high priest. This thought brought him some comfort.

Why should I think or worry about corporal things? Soon, this body will be no more, but I dread its mode of passing.

Daichi, a guard and admirer of the former priest, worried about his wellbeing. The priest had once cast a spell making it possible for Daichi's wife to conceive after many failed attempts. Finally, the guard had a son because of the intersession of this prisoner.

Out of gratitude, Daichi secretly brought him drink. "Take this. It's made with honey and will relieve your worry and help you rest."

"Thank you," Heregesob said, smiling for the first time in days. "Have the village men been invited to witness the ritual?"

"Yes. The king ordered all men to attend, along with your family and household."

"Please, ask the king, on my behalf, not to require my family's presence. Will you do this for me?"

"I will, in your honor, but you must empty the gourd. It can't be found here. I'm not to give you any drink."

The ex-priest paced his cell all night. He often peered out the slit window to see if the time of the god's awakening had arrived. Finally, dawn and Heregesob's spirit broke. He trembled so much he could barely stand. As much as he tried not to cry, a tear stole its way down his cheek. He watched the sky fill with dark purples and oranges. *Sacred colors. I don't deserve this fate, but the day has arrived. Strange, the morning colors are not in keeping with the day's mood. Have the gods forsaken me as they have the king?*

Heregesob heard the voices of village males gathering on the plaza. Women were not allowed. The buzz of the men's conversations sounded like bees. The men's presence was to emphasize the risk of defying the king.

Hearing voices outside his cell door, Heregesob stood, trembling. The guards, who would escort him to his death, had arrived. He backed against the wall opposite the door as the voices drew closer. The door opened, and he swallowed hard. He clenched his fists and held his breath as four guards entered. Two had their spears at the ready.

The first guard, Daichi, who had befriended him with drink, said, "Heregesob, we must take you to the plaza. Stand tall. Let no one see weakness in your demeanor."

Daichi, hands shaking, used a long strip of leather to tie Heregesob's wrists behind his back while another guard removed the prisoner's loincloth and threw it in a corner. Daichi held the tether as the second guard poked his spear in the prisoner's back saying, "Move."

Heregesob ducked his head under the stone lintel then entered a hall lighted by torches held by two guards. Silently, the men inched along the passageway leading to a lower terrace.

The priest closed his eyes as he stepped into the bright sunlight. *Gods, give me strength. Give me strength.*

The murmur of the crowd hushed on seeing the humiliated, naked priest standing on the terrace. He scanned the crowd. *It's bad enough I'm naked, but is there no one to help me?*

After a poke from a spear, Heregesob stepped sideways down the steep temple steps. Because his hands were tied behind his back, he could not use them to balance himself. Twice, he almost fell.

Once Heregesob stepped onto the hot plaza floor, he received another spear poke then inched through the parting throng and walked toward a nine-foot-tall narrow stone column at the foot of the Sacrificial Temple. He glanced at the stone then looked at the ground. *I can't look at that death stone.*

Not far ahead, twelve archers, local priests, local leaders, the great high priest of Chichen Itza, the Most Holy One, Chieftain Citu, and noblemen made their way to various viewing areas on the plaza based on rank and role in the ceremony.

Numerous incense burners, located around the Temple of Sacrifice, shared their sweet fragrance with the crowd and the prisoner.

Heregesob *thought, Sweetness. What a contrast to the bitterness of a ceremony of death.* He shuddered on seeing a freshly dug grave near the base of the temple. *That will soon be my eternal home with the earth gods.*

The solemn-looking entourage neared the killing stone.

The Most Holy One, the great high priest, and noblemen walked to their viewing area under an awning thirty paces away. Several villagers climbed nearby temples to better observe the ritual.

At the killing stone, the priest winced as leather ties were tightened around his ankles and the stone. He watched the leather thong, binding his wrists, being threaded through a hole high in the stone. The pain of his arms being almost stretched from their sockets caused him to moan. On his head, an assistant priest placed a conical hat made of blue-painted bark—the ultimate symbol of disgrace.

Two priests painted his body with the same blue paint as on his hat. The body paint felt cool, compared to the heat of the blazing sun. The assistant priests avoided eye contact with their former leader as they worked. His hands, feet, and head were not painted.

After the blue body paint had been applied, a third man painted a white circle, the size of a hand, on the priest's mid-chest, slightly left of his breast bone. The prisoner sucked air, for beneath the circle beat his heart. He knew the circle's purpose and prayed, *Gods, be swift in bringing me freedom, finishing this injustice, and ending this sacrilege to me—a holy priest.*

The sun, blistering hot, caused the ex-priest and villagers, without shade, to sweat profusely. Eyes closed, Heregesob tried to appear stoic as the assistant priests did their ritual work. His sweat caused the blue paint to run, requiring its reapplication to the most affected areas.

Heregesob forced himself to try looking eye-to-eye to known villagers, but they looked away. With each brief period of eye contact, he felt a growing fear engulf him.

The feather cloaks, capes, and crowns, along with the gold and silver worn by the king, priests, and nobles constituted a collection of wealth the likes of which had not been displayed in years.

The king kept shifting the position of his gold ornaments because they absorbed the sun's rays and heated the skin beneath. His heavy feather cloak added to his misery. He knew his guests were anxious to have the ceremony concluded, so they could retreat to cool interiors.

Leaning toward a nobleman, the king said, "This heretic's evil was avoidable. Too bad restitution like this must be made to cancel his debt of sacrilege and dishonor."

"He is more stoic than I expected," the nobleman said, swatting a fly and dabbing sweat.

"Faster," the king said to Hakum who used a suspended cotton cloth to fan the king and nobles.

The king spoke to another nobleman, "I wait for this prisoner's weakness. He will crumble like squeezed dirt becomes dust."

Watching the ex-priest scan the crowd, the king thought, *He's looking for his family, but he won't see them. I've honored his request, but he must have caught a glimpse of Calx, his male lover.* Heregesob nodded acknowledgement. Calx nodded then looked away, crying.

Having finished their work, the painters walked thirty paces to the nobles' area, bowed to the king, the great high priest and chieftains. "Most Holy One," the lead painter said, "the painting is done."

The Most Holy One walked to the temple then climbed four steps. He raised his arms to quiet the crowd. "I and the great high priest of Chichen Itza bless this day and this act to appease the gods of justice. Will the great high priest step forward?"

A hush fell over the crowd. Even the quetzal feathers in the nobles' crowns stopped fluttering as the great high priest faced the noble guests. His body glistened with holy oils. His gold and silver adornments, glistening sea shells, white jade ear plugs, and a loincloth and authority necklace laden with gold images conveyed his exalted position. He wore a crown made of tall, deep blue-green, quetzal feathers, which swayed as he moved. His leather sandals and straps gleamed with gold ornaments, and hand painted images of large-eyed gods.

The great high priest nodded to the Most Holy One then walked stiffly toward the center of the plaza as bamboo drums yielded hollow, mournful sounds in cadence with the steps of the striding elderly priest.

Walking backwards ahead of the great high priest, an assistant priest swept the plaza over which the priest would walk. Other priests carried the train of the elderly priest's multicolored feather cape.

The great high priest stopped in the center of the plaza and faced the prisoner twenty paces away. The great high priest then faced the crowd. First extending his arms overhead, he brought them inward and downward, inviting the crowd to take notice.

The king watched the prisoner's lower lip quiver, and his blanched fingers shake. *He's weakening as I expected.*

The prisoner apparently tried to swallow but couldn't. He looked at the king and yelled, "Unholy one. You will not see me die a whimpering coward."

"He is defiant to the end," the king muttered.

A nobleman, walking in step to the slow beat of drums, crossed the plaza and handed an arrow to the visiting priest.

"This arrow is true!" the great high priest shouted, holding it high for all to see. He sighted along its shaft, which he pointed toward the prisoner. "Its shaft is straight. It will serve well the holy act we make this day."

The great high priest returned the arrow to the nobleman who then handed him a bow. He examined it and tested the string's tension. Holding the bow in one hand and the arrow in the other, the priest held both toward the sky while turning full circle so the crowd could see them.

Heregesob took a deep breath and held it.

The great high priest moved a few paces back from the prisoner. A hush filled the plaza as the priest raised the bow and fitted the arrow's notch over the string. He sighted over the mid-portion of the bow then aimed at the target.

The king held his breath in anticipation of the loosening of the arrow.

Even the sun awning over the nobles' head ceased its noisy flapping.

"I will not cry out!" Heregesob yelled then took a deep breath.

The great high priest aimed then freed the arrow. The string twanged as the whizzing arrow sliced the air on its way to its target. The king gasped on seeing the arrow bury itself in the prisoner's genitals, mimicking ritual bloodletting from the penis of supplicants who voluntarily sacrificed their blood to the gods.

Heregesob's body stiffened. His head and shoulders arched backwards as he yelled, "Ahhh! Gods be my help!"

The king winced and closed his eyes in reaction to the ex-priest's wounding as if his own groin had been pierced.

With blood flowing, Heregesob prayed loudly. "Gods . . . bear me up this trial."

The great high priest's bracelets jangled as he motioned to twelve archers to come forward. Eleven were from Dzibilchaltun and one from Chalmuch.

The tempo of the drum beat quickened.

Heregesob yelled, shook, and moaned with the first three arrows striking just inside the white circle on his chest.

Archer after archer filed before the prisoner, aimed, and released an arrow into the circle. Eyes open, Heregesob's chin fell onto his chest. It appeared he watched his blood stream down his abdomen. His knees buckled and his weight strained against his wrists' bindings.

"Archers!" the great high priest yelled from the sidelines, "His *ik* is gone. Carry the body to the altar."

Four archers cut the prisoner's bindings then carried the body toward the temple. Mournful sounds of bamboo drums accompanied the bloody march across the plaza and up the temple steps. The remaining archers followed the entourage to the altar terrace.

The great high priest stood aside as the archers placed the body on the altar. He motioned for the Most Holy One and Chieftain from Chalmuch to come to the terrace for the completion of the ritual.

"Archers, reclaim your arrows," the great high priest said.

One-by-one, the archers extracted the arrow bearing the fletchings that identified its owner. Each arrowhead pulled free tore away lumps of flesh, which were knocked free over the sacrificial cup carved into the belly of the statue of Chaac. The great high priest removed his arrow last and handed it to an assistant priest to remove its barbed flesh.

The great high priest, with the assistance of

several assistant priests, shed his regalia then received the folded leaf containing a sacred obsidian knife. He murmured prayers, presented the broad blade to the sky gods, then the Most Holy One, and then the crowd. Using both hands, he raised the knife high then brought it down with the speed of lightning, stabbing the dead priest's abdomen. A collective gasp rose from the crowd as if the dead man felt pain.

The king looked away as the officiant cut his way to the dead man's heart. While removing it, the great high priest prayed, "Gods of the sky, earth, sea and waterholes accept this heart."

The great high priest held the extracted heart overhead. Assistant priests walked under its dripping blood while prayers were chanted for lifting the sacrilege against the Most Holy One and Citu. Blood covered, the great high priest placed the heart in the altar cup containing the flesh removed from the arrowheads. He said, "Priests of Dzibilchaltun assist me in removing the skin."

Assistant priests approached their former superior with obsidian knives at the ready.

This is the part I hate most, the king thought.

The king forced himself to watch the flaying, but many villagers looked away. They were bothered by this act committed on a man who had served them and the community.

Within minutes, the priests had flayed the body, sparing the head, hands, and feet which were severed and set aside. The four appendages would be roasted and later eaten by the male members of the royal family, leaders, and noblemen.

The ritual meal would prevent the hands from choking ritual members in their sleep or having the feet trip then trample them.

The head was placed in the cup beside the priest's heart. They would await birds and insects to devour them as gifts to the sky and the earth gods.

The assistants draped the flayed skin over the great high priest shoulders as a cloak of celebration, acknowledging the restoration of the honor of the Most Holy One and Citu.

In keeping with the Ceremony of Arrows, the assistant priests rolled the bloody body down the temple steps.

The twelve archers walked to the plaza floor and carried the torso to the nearby grave. The dead high priest had now risen to a new state of holiness, for he had paid for his sacrilege. He now had a place in The Center's pantheon.

Calling to the noblemen, the great high priest said, "All are to walk through the blood on this temple floor in keeping with other sacrifices. The blood is not to be washed until the awakening of the sun god. Do this to appease Etznab, the evil one who visits these rituals.

Citu, the Most Holy One, and noblemen did the priest's bidding.

After the ceremonial walk, the king said to Citu, "You are welcome to stay as my guest in the palace."

"Thank you Most Holy One, but I and my leaders ask to travel homeward while the sun god sleeps."

"Then go with my blessings. Take word to your—no, to *our*—people in Chalmuch. Tell them all is well with Ked, the god of justice."

Chapter 20

The queen paced the palace lounge, waiting for the king to return from the ceremony. As he entered, she rushed to his side and took his hand. "Did things go as you hoped?"

The king removed his crown and handed it to Hakum along with his feather cloak. He then held his arms out so Hakum could remove his bracelets and arm coverings.

Looking into the queen's face, the king said, "It went as it should. Justice has been done." Free of his ceremonial regalia, the king paced. "We are free of the blasphemy of the priest. However, I am without a high priest and advisor, but I did what I had to do to protect our interests."

"Most Holy One, I cannot remove your sandals if you don't stand still," Hakum said, following the pacing king.

The king paused, placed his hand on Hakum's shoulder and steadied himself while Hakum removed the king's bloody sandals.

Emotionally exhausted, the king sighed, slumped to a floor cushion then said to the queen. "Perhaps we should go to Chichen Itza to thank the gods for the blessing of this thing. We could accompany the great high priest on his return home, but we go without the princess."

"I'd like that," the queen said. "I'll start planning for the trip, but for now, you rest. The heat is too much to do otherwise."

At the hour of the sun god's sleep, the queen awakened the king.

"What?" he said. "What's wrong?"

"Nothing," The queen said. "The gods sent me a dream."

"It must have been a favorable one, for you look happy."

"It was. The gods said we are to rebuild the watering tubes."

"The gods sent me a similar dream." The king walked toward the door. "This is good."

"Where are you going?" the queen asked

The king yelled, "Hakum.

Hakum ran into the room. "What, My King? What is the danger?"

"When the sun god awakens, go to the builders. Tell them they are to rebuild the water tubes." The king rubbed both hands over his shaved head. "Make ready for two days from now. The queen and I will travel with the great high priest to Chichen Itza. We are going to pray in the great temple—thank the gods for our welfare."

The queen called, "Come to bed, Bulek. These matters can wait until morning."

At sunrise, the builders gathered in the throne room where the king presented his plan. "This request will challenge you little," he said, looking at the head builder, "It is similar to past experiences. Do this for your people. Make water flow while I pray in Chichen Itza."

The king stepped down from his throne and walked among the builders. "Ask the villagers to plant maize in the wet earth. It will give us food. The gods have ordained it in a new dream."

The king went back to his throne and sat down. "Hakum, have the fishermen gather fish to be delivered to Citu in exchange for gifts from the jungle—have the men fish day and night if they must. Inquire about any meat Citu can spare. Take salt for barter and some to prepare the meat for its journey here."

The builders had briefly talked among themselves when the chief builder said, "We have wanted to rebuild the tubes, but we feared the shaman's curse. We are heartened at seeing your excitement about the project.

Chapter 21

Bowing, Hakum entered the library where the king sat on a cushion reading a book. "Most Holy One, forgive my interruption, but the great high priest request we travel to Chichen Itza by way of X'Cambo."

X'Cambo, a small center near the sea, was a commercial center whose importance relied on its salt beds. It had few temples requiring only three priests.

Looking up from his book, the king asked, "Did he say why?" X'Cambo is out of the way. Going there will increase our travel time."

Hakum nodded then said, "Our honorable visitor said, 'Since X'Cambo is close to the sea, the shore route would be cooler than traveling through the jungle.' Besides, we might catch fish to eat as we travel."

"I too would like to avoid jungle heat," the king said, fanning himself, "but let's hope fishing is better in X'Cambo's sea than ours."

"The great high priest said, 'He would like to visit with X'Cambo's priests and take counsel with its king.'"

"I too would like to visit with their king. It has been many moons since we met. He is now elderly, and I have heard he is not well. Tell the great high priest we will do as he wishes. Inform the queen when she awakens."

Suddenly, the room resounded with giggles and the sounds of running bare feet. Prince Hiayalael and Princess Sac-Nicte ran into the room and hugged their father.

"My, you're growing . . . both of you. Sit here beside me," the king said, patting cushions Hakum had pushed close to the king.

"What are you reading?" the prince asked.

"A sacred book filled with ancient stories." The king showed his son the ancient text. "Here are stories describing a god who will come in a floating house to help our people."

"Who lives in the house?"

"A *white* god-man with white hair."

"The god is like a man but white?"

"Yes," the king said, pointing at his chest. "The god will be like me, but he will have skin the color of these walls."

"Sounds scary," the prince said, shaking his head and scrunching his lips.

The king laughed. "There's nothing to fear. He will be a good god. Now, go play with your sister. I want to finish reading."

Hakum stopped fluffing floor cushions, tucked his chin, and looked at the king. "Do I prepare the princess for the trip?"

"No. The gods have no need of her. Now go. Tell the priest we will visit X'Cambo."

Several days later, the king and the great high priest met to finalize the details of their journey.

Hakum gathered the bodyguards, servants,

priests, and king to begin the two night march to the sea.

The closer the group got to the shore, the more refreshing the sea breezes. "Perhaps we should live near the shore," the queen said, luxuriating in a long, cooling breeze that tousled her black ponytail. "Ahhh. If only it were possible to move The Center and its temples there."

"Yes," the king said, "the air is cooler, but the gods long ago dictated the Temple of the Six Dolls be built where it is. Come, let's not discuss moving temples. We have a great distance to travel."

By the second sunrise, the group had reached the shore. The expansive white beach had great depth. Here, the group would sleep until nightfall and then resume the trip.

While setting up camp, a local fisherman happened by. The darkly tanned man had twelve fish strung on a vine looped through their gills.

"Fisherman," Hakum said, pointing to the fish, "The Most Holy One of Dzibilchaltun and the great high priest of Chichen Itza would like to have some of your fish."

The man stepped back on hearing the nobles' titles in whose presence he stood. He bowed repeatedly toward each person wearing ear plugs.

"Welcome to our camp," the king said. "I am the Most Holy One and this is the Great High Priest."

The fisherman again bowed to each of the nobles and then fell to his knees. "I am Kexel, Most Holy One. Welcome holy ones."

"You may stand," the king said.

"One of your fish should feed three people," Hakum said. "May we have eight?"

"It would be my honor," the fisherman said in a quivering voice. He separated the fish, backed away, and then ran west along the beach.

Hakum cleaned and gutted the fish while a bodyguard gathered firewood. Hakum used the priest's smoke pot to ignite the wood over which he would cook the fish.

After eating, the king sought shade under the overhang of a long stretch of eroded beach held in place by millions of roots of a plant that grew overhead.

The king remained awake long enough to see Hakum, not adept at fishing, try to spear fish. The king offered a prayer to Chac-Uayeb-Xoc, the god of fishing, on behalf of Hakum and then lay on his left side and slept.

As the gods slept, Hakum woke the king then started a fire to warm some dried fish for the first meal of the day.

Hakum instructed a runner, "Travel east along the shore until you see smoke from X'Cambo. At that point, turn south and seek out King Cocom."

"What if I am assaulted by his villagers, thinking I'm a thief in the night?" the runner asked.

Hakum removed his authority necklace. "Take this," he said, pointing to the king's seal. "Tell the X'Cambo guards you represent the Most Holy One of Dzibilchaltun who travels with the great high priest of Chichen Itza. Ask for counsel with King Cocom."

Three times before sunrise, the king suggested a rest period for his entourage. As dawn broke, he asked to camp for another day's sleep.

Comfortably snuggled on ground covers pushed beneath leafy bushes, he had difficulty falling asleep because he daydreamed of a green jungle and maize growing in The Center. Finally, he fell asleep.

The king, awakened abruptly. "What is it?" he asked Hakum already moving about.

"Voices, Most Holy One."

The king sat up and shaded his eyes from the sun as he stared toward the east.

Hakum grabbed his spear and woke the bodyguards. The king woke the queen and the great high priest.

"What?" the queen asked, sitting upright, wide eyed.

"Not sure," the king said. "Voices. They're coming this way."

"We have no enemies here," the great high priest said, looking questioningly at the king while listening to the windborne sounds.

The frightened queen leaned against the king's back. "I hope they mean us no harm."

He squeezed her hand. "It's possible evil men from other tribes travel here. Hakum, scout inland. Find out who make these sounds."

The noises grew louder as Hakum moved inland.

"Whoever makes the noise is not trying to stalk us," the queen said, hugging the king's waist.

Soon the air filled with the whoops of what sounded like drunken celebrants at a festival.

Hakum, several hundred paces into the jungle, heard the whoops move quickly past his rear and move west. *I have gone too far south. The villains head for the king.*

With his heart beating like that of a victim readied for sacrifice, Hakum ran toward his campsite. Within moments, he heard even louder whoops, similar to hunters at a kill. *The king is in danger.*

Dodging low bushes and jagged stones, Hakum ran with all the energy he could muster. Suddenly, the binding of his left sandal broke, and he tumbled onto a thorny bush. At that moment, the distant whoops rose again. Picking himself up, Hakum said, "I pray the king still lives."

Without bothering to remove the thorns stuck in various parts of his body, Hakum ran, wearing one sandal. After what felt like a full day to reach the camp, he did—spear at the ready.

The king stared at the thorns in Hakum's chest, arms, and legs then smiled. "Hold your spear, Hakum. All is well. King Cocom sent food, water, and guards guided by our own runner." The Most Holy One pointed at the gifts. "The guards yelled because they were happy to meet the great high priest and me."

"My King, I worried for your life," Hakum said, picking plant needles from his legs.

"Thank you, but come. Let's enjoy the food from X'Cambo. These guards say the village is nearby. We can be there before the gods sleep."

Following breakfast, the king sent guards to notify King Cocom of the group's arrival by nightfall. X'Cambo guards remained with the Most Holy One to guide him to the village.

Shortly after nightfall, the king arrived at the outskirts of X'Cambo. Its torches of welcome flickered in gentle sea breezes.

The Most Holy One cupped his ear. "Listen. Conch blowing. We're being honored by King Cocom. Hakum, bring my crown."

The king adjusted his crown while the great high priest donned his.

"Let's hurry," the queen said. "I need water and rest."

"I'm sure King Cocom will have wonderful food and drink," the great high priest said, quickening his pace.

Nearing X'Cambo's plaza, the Most Holy One saw King Cocom and his high priest standing at the foot of the palace. King Cocom, an elderly, squat man with a large belly, stood erect. His bowed legs suggested a birth deformity.

King Cocom's young priest swung a fly wisp at pesky insects attracted by his sweet body oil whose scent wafted as far as the Most Holy One.

"Welcome honored guests," King Cocom said, opening his arms in a welcoming gesture.

He wore an icon-decorated loincloth, a gold bracelet, and a long authority necklace containing few gold icons. His leg coverings bore few jade decorations. His jade ear plugs and quetzal feathered crown were small.

The Most Holy One thought, *King Cocom's wealth is small otherwise he would wear more symbols of wealth.*

"Welcome in friendship," King Cocom said, removing his crown.

The kings greeted each other with a forearm grip. The local high priest touched his forehead to the nose of the great high priest.

"Welcome, Queen of Dzibilchaltun," King Cocom said bowing.

King Cocom asked, "Great High Priest, would you prefer to sleep in my palace or the priest's temple?"

"I should sleep in the temple. It will give me a chance to discuss your priests' needs."

"As you wish. High Priest Mulot will show you to temple quarters. You and he are invited to the evening meal."

King Cocom motioned for the Most Holy One to follow him up the palace steps.

"I am glad to see your trees are green," the Most Holy One said.

"They are, but many turn brown. Dead trees yield firewood to bake lime for making stucco, but we lose their fruits."

"We had to resort to artificial rain," the Most Holy One said. "Our builders use bamboo tubes to deliver drink from a waterhole to our fields."

"That is something we may have to consider," King Cocom said. "May I send my builder to examine your work?"

"Any time you wish."

Having reached the upper terrace of the palace, King Cocom walked to a doorway, held back a cloth door decorated with green and red images of the Mayan gods Chaac and Acantun. He motioned for everyone to enter. Flickering torches illuminated the room and burned floral incense, adding a sense of welcome.

"This is my wife, Queen Xal," the king said, bowing slightly toward her as she entered the room.

This queen is quite young for an old king, the Most Holy One thought. *Her loincloth has little gold and fewer bits of jade compared to Ix Tzutz's.*

Queen Ix Tztutz whispered to her husband, "Queen Xal's ear plugs are small for a royal woman."

"And her eyes are not crossed," the Most Holy One whispered, "and not as beautiful as yours." He then said, "This is my Queen, Ix Tzutz Nik."

Both queens bowed to each other.

"Please be seated," King Cocom said, gesturing toward floor cushions and then clapping.

Servants entered the dining room carrying a bowl of water and a cotton cloth. The Most Holy One cleaned his face and hands then passed the cloth to his queen. The second servant provided the same service for King Cocom.

"We have intruders off our shore," King Cocom said and dried his hands on his loincloth. "They travel in strange canoes."

"Strange canoes?" the Most Holy One asked. "Tell me more."

"The strangely tall canoe is said to be fifty times longer than ours."

"And its width?" the Most Holy One asked

"Two hundred times wider than our canoes, King Cocom said, using hand gestures to indicate its width.

"But there is no tree so tall or broad."

"It's not made of one tree. It's made of many trees trunks stacked one upon the other."

"And it floats?"

"Yes," King Cocom said, sniffing a dish of incense, "and it has large white cloths resembling our awnings."

"When did you see this canoe?"

"I didn't; our fishermen did—twice—one and a half moon cycles apart."

"Hmmm. What tribe or village owns such a canoe?" the Most Holy One asked, scratching his head.

"I can't say, but their skin shines like the sun and flashes when they move about."

"Has anyone seen their eyes?" Queen Ix Tzutz Nik asked as her gaze moved between King Cocom and his queen.

"No," King Cocom said, "the shine of their skin is total, including their heads. We've not been close enough to see if they have eyes."

The Most Holy One squirmed on his pillow then addressed King Cocom. "Any threatening acts?"

"I'm not sure."

"Not sure? What do you mean?"

"The canoe once belched fire and smoke and sent a loud noise from its side. Afterwards, a heavy black sphere landed on the beach." The King held his thumbs and forefingers together to indicate its size. "It was hot to touch when removed from the hole it created in the beach."

"What did you do with this . . . sphere?"

"We kept it," King Cocom said then smiled.

"May I see it?"

"Of course." King Cocom clapped to summon a servant. "Bring the strange sphere. Our guest wishes to see it."

"How have villagers reacted to this canoe?" the Most Holy One asked.

"Those who saw it were frightened." The king shook his hands to indicate the fear of the observers. "They shot arrows and threw spears at the canoe but none reached it."

"Maybe this is a *cisini* or devil in disguise," Queen Ix Tzutz Nik said, looking questioningly at her husband.

"My priests have never heard of such a devil," King Cocom said, "nor do we know if this strange canoe carries evil."

"It's good the great high priest is with us," the Most Holy One said. "We should consult with him. I would like to know if he thinks this canoe is mentioned in the prophetic texts."

At that moment, a servant retuned with the unusual black sphere and held it toward King Cocom.

"Give it to the Most Holy One," King Cocom said, waving the back of his hand toward the visiting king.

Nestled in the servant's hands, the object held the attention of the Most Holy One. At first, he did not want to touch it. His hands moved first one way and then another over the sphere. He wondered how he should take hold of it. Reluctantly, he gripped it just below the servant's grasp. As the servant released it, the Most Holy One's hands dropped under its weight.

Queen Xal stifled a chuckle, as she watched the king almost drop the orb.

"Hmmm!" he king said, surprised by its heft. "It's *very* heavy."

"I told you," King Cocom said.

"How did something so heavy fly? Someone or something very strong must have heaved it."

"Perhaps the smoke had something to do with its flight," King Cocom said.

The Most Holy One rapped the orb with his knuckle. "Hmmm. It makes no sound like I have ever heard. It has scratches on its surface. Maybe it's some kind of metal." He pointed to a hole in the object then looked at King Cocom. "This looks like a burned plant stem in this hole."

"I noticed that, but a stem that small could not have held such a heavy thing to any tree I know of."

While the Most Holy One examined the object,

High Priest Mulot and the great high priest entered the dining room. They bowed to the kings and queens.

"Come," King Cocom said, pointing to floor cushions. "Join us."

The great high priest noted the object held by the Most Holy One. "What is that?"

King Cocom shook his head. "We aren't sure; it might be a strange fruit."

"I have never seen such a fruit," the great high priest said. "May I see it?"

The Most Holy One nodded. King Cocom's servant bowed, took the object, and carried it to the great high priest.

"Careful," King Cocom said. "It's heavy."

The visiting priest took the object. With a startled look on his face, he said, "It is heavy. Where did you get it?"

"It came from a strange canoe that floated off our shore two days ago."

The visiting priest returned the object then he and the local priest settled onto their cushions.

The Most Holy One asked, "Great High Priest do you know anything about this strange canoe?"

"I just heard of it from the high priest," the great high priest said, squirming into his cushion. "I have never heard of such a canoe."

"Villagers saw the canoe twice," the Most Holy One said, "and maybe it will come again. King Cocom, perhaps one of your priests could camp at the beach for a few days, and hopefully, see this canoe and decide if it is evil."

"He must take care not to be bewitched," the great high priest said, shaking his head.

"Enough of this evil-canoe-talk," King Cocom

said then clapped. "It's time to eat."

Two servants entered with four shallow baskets and presented them to the visitors and then King Cocom. The baskets contained meat and fruits. A third servant poured fermented honey-mush and water into gourd cups.

Early the next morning, The Most Holy One watched a local priest and servant head for the beach to wait for the strange canoe. The Most Holy One hoped to learn if it carried a good spirit.

The Most Holy One joined the great high priest and other priests in performing a religious ritual asking for protection. At its conclusion, they stowed their ceremonial regalia and joined King Cocom and the queens for the morning meal.

"I trust you slept well," King Cocom said, addressing the king and his queen.

"We did, Most Gracious King," the Most Holy One said.

King Cocom smiled and clapped. Moments later, a servant entered the room carrying a gourd of honey-mush and filled a cup of the liquid for each guest.

King Cocom tasted the brew then said, "I hope you find this to your liking"

The Most Holy One sipped the brew then licked his lips. "I like its sweetness."

Suddenly, the servant from the shore rushed in and bowed before King Cocom. "My King, forgive my unannounced entry."

King Cocom continued to chew and nodded his permission for the sweating servant to speak.

Panting, the servant said, "Great King, the priest

sends news that the strange canoe is heading in our direction. He requests you and your guests join him."

At first, the Most Holy One was puzzled. He and the others glanced quickly at each other as if silently asking what they should do.

King Cocom leaned forward and addressed the great high priest. "Would you guide our path with prayers to protect us from evil spirits seeking to harm us while we observe this canoe?"

"I will. Have one of your priests bring a smoke pot."

While the Most Holy One and others waited for ritual items, the queens left to discuss domestic issues and check on Queen Xal's children.

When the ritual objects arrived, the two priests, the kings, Hakum, and two servants headed for the shore.

The well-worn path ran directly north and was easily crossed in a short time—if one ran. The first part of the path traversed areas of ground cover, but near the beach, the Most Holy One had to push his way through dense, leafy bushes to get to the beach.

To alert the encamped priest that King Cocom drew near, a servant blew a conch. The waiting priest blew his conch in acknowledgment.

The waiting priest wore a cloth over his sweating, shaved head to protect it from the sun. He bowed to each arrival. "Welcome great kings and Great High Priest."

"Where is this strange canoe?" King Cocom asked, looking north while shading his eyes with his hand.

"There," the encamped priest said, pointing toward the east, "It's a dot on the horizon."

Staring eastward, the Most Holy One squinted and scanned the horizon.

King Cocom shouted, "I see it and its awnings. It appears to move parallel to the shore and is headed this way."

"I'm glad I came," the Most Holy One said. "I want to see this thing up close."

"We all do," the great high priest said, dropping incense on the smoldering coals of his smoke pot. He and the local priests used their wands to draw holy symbols in the sand then drew a circle around the group who stood close together. The priests blessed the area, exchanged smoke pots, blessed each other, and then blessed each member of the group. In unison, the priests and kings recited a common prayer seeking a blessing for protection from any evil lurking in the sand, waiting to fall from the sky, or approaching from the sea.

After a short wait, the Most Holy One paced the beach while noting the progress of the oncoming canoe. The cooling breeze grew stronger, making the wait under the blazing sun more bearable but not comfortable.

"This wind will speed the canoe's arrival," the Most Holy One said.

"Maybe an early arrival is good," King Cocom said, his hands visibly shaking. "Then, maybe not."

The Most Holy One pointed toward his sandals. After Hakum removed them, the king waded near the shore, periodically plucking shells from tidal pools. "I wished we had time to swim," he said, looking out to sea. "The water is inviting." He soon tired of standing and sat down on the beach, watching the canoe's outline fill more of the eastern horizon.

One of King Cocom's servants broke leafy branches from bushes at the edge of the beach then gave them to the leaders. "Thank you," the Most Holy One said. "These will make shade to block the sun's heat."

"Such a strange thing," King Cocom said to the Most Holy One who stared at the approaching canoe. "I would never believe such a thing existed, but I am uneasy. I wonder if we should leave."

"This sight both compels and frightens me," the Most Holy One said, focusing his vision. "I think I see the logs you mentioned. They appear flattened."

The group discussed the openings in the sides of the canoe and the objects sticking through them

King Cocom said, "Their awnings provide no protection from the sun. They simply billow.

"It moves by evil," the great high priest said, incensing himself.

"Who knows," the Most Holy One said, as the awnings were rolled and lashed to supporting beams. "Maybe they are no longer needed for shade as we use awnings." Suddenly, he pointed to two moving shapes on the canoe. "Look! I see them. Their arms and chests reflect sun from silver coverings."

The local priest asked, "Should we be standing here—in the open?"

"I don't know," the Most Holy One said then gasped on seeing numerous shiny beings move toward the shore side of the canoe.

"Most Holy One, perhaps they are men who wear holy silver," King Cocom said, watching the beings mill about. "They are as numerous as ants."

"Most Holy Kings, what village has that much silver?" the great high priest asked. "Even Chichen

Itza's temples have less."

"Nor Dzibilchaltun," the Most Holy One said, "but they do gather like ants."

"They're gods from a world of silver," the local priest said. "Perhaps they bring us gifts of silver."

With palms to the sky, the Most Holy One said, "I know of no god who delivers silver for naught. It must be wrenched from distant land gods. It is not a gift." Shaking his head, he continued, "Perhaps we should move into the bushes until we know more about the shiny skins' intensions." As the Most Holy One entered the bushes, he said, "From here, we can watch in safety."

The Most Holy One watched the canoe move to within five hundred paces of the shore. The king's camouflaging leaves trembled in the shaking hand holding back the branch partially hiding him. "I wonder what that is?" the Most Holy One asked, watching a twiggy black object fall from the front of the canoe. "Its fall sounds like thunder and makes a large splash."

The great high priest recoiled in fear, bumping into the Most Holy One. "What a strange object. I hope they didn't put a curse in our sea." The great high priest walked to the water's edge, dipped his left hand in the sea, flicked drops of water in the air, and then blessed the droplets with his smoke pot.

"He's blessing the sea to ward off evil that might have caused that splash in the sea," the Most Holy One said. "He might also be concerned the shiny skins offered a sacrifice, like the ones he hurls into Chichen Itza's sacred well."

The Most Holy One waited to see if the silver-skins had reacted to the great high priest's blessing but saw nothing.

The great high priest returned to the Most Holy One, hiding in the bushes. "How should we respond to these beings?"

"If our gods are equal or better than theirs, we have nothing to fear," the Most Holy One said. "Maybe we should try welcoming them."

"I am unsure about that," the great high priest said, "but we certainly should not anger them." He stepped toward the sea then waved his arms over his head, beckoning to the canoe.

The Most Holy One left the bushes and walked to the water's edge. He and King Cocom waved leafy branches.

Moments later, the Most Holy One saw three silver-skins wave their silver arms. "They acknowledge us," he said and waved vigorously. "They wave many pieces of silver." The king waved again and then sat down on the beach. Puzzled, he stared at the canoe which had stopped its advance and bobbed on the waves. "All we can do now is wait."

The local priests, attempting to ease their fears, chanted prayers asking for protection from evil spirits.

"Look, King Cocom," the Most Holy One said. "Something comes over its side. It falls slowly as it nears the water."

The local priest's voice broke as he said, "Most Holy One, they lower a smaller canoe."

Standing, the Most Holy One said, "Even their smaller canoe is larger than ours." He watched the small canoe bounce about on the sea as it hovered near the larger one.

Moments later, the principal local priest pointed toward the top edge of the large canoe. "Most Holy One, they have dropped a net over the side, but it doesn't fall into the water. How can they catch fish like that?"

The great high priest placed his hand over his brow to block the sun and stared at the canoe. "I have never seen a net of such size."

"Maybe it's used to catch giant fish," King Cocom said. "What do you think, Most Holy One?"

"I know of no fish requiring a net that large," the Most Holy One said then counted the silver-skins climbing down the net into the smaller canoe. "One . . . two . . . three . . . It holds nine silver-skins. Ours hold two men, but look. Is that a whitehaired, white skinned man who wears no silver? He wears a long white cloth over his shoulders. See how it blows in the wind."

"Get ready to run," the local priest yelled. "They raise their spears."

"Strange," the Most Holy One said, "they dip their spears in the water."

"They poison the sea," the great high priest said, jumping back from the water's edge. "Stand back Most Holy One."

With the smoke pot, the great high priest blessed the land, sky, water and each member of the group. "I pray our magic is greater than theirs, but we should move away from the water. I'm unsure of what more to do or expect."

Chapter 22

"What's that?" the Most Holy One asked King Cocom while pointing to a small, flapping cloth tied to a pole held by the white-haired man.

"It looks like one of our cloth doors with a god painting," the Most Holy One said in a shaky voice. He walked to the edge of the water. "I've never seen this painted god they carry before them. Strange gods can be dangerous. Hand me the smoke pot. I must make *ahez,* magic."

With sweet smelling smoke rising from the pot, the Most Holy One, palms to the sky, invited everyone to pray, imploring the gods to protect them.

The Most Holy One's heartbeat, sounding like rhythmic drum beats in his head, grew faster the longer he watched and awaited the unknown.

The small canoe was now three hundred paces away.

King Cocom said, "The spears they put in the sea are not spears. They're oars—larger than ours, but oars. See how they use them to row."

The great high priest waved to the small canoe. The whitehaired man in its bow waved back.

Watching the white-clad man for a moment, King Cocom said, "Maybe that is a god-man and the silver-skins are his servants." He squinted then said, "I can now see the entire image on the white cloth. It's two crossed red lines. Red is our sacred color."

The encamped priest said, "Most Holy One, maybe it *is* a god-king with silver-skinned servants, but the closer it gets the more it looks like a man with white skin."

"White skin?" the Most Holy One asked. "Did you say *white*?"

"Yes. Look. It looks like a man with white hair and white skin." In disbelief, the local priest and King Cocom said, "*White* skin?"

The Most Holy One said, "Great High Priest, you know the prophecies in our sacred books about the benevolent god-man, Kukulcan. He will have white skin and white hair and will come from the east in a floating house?"

The great high priest squinted to get a better look at the standing god-man whose long white cloth flapped in the wind. "Yes," the priest said, "I've read those books, but let's hold our decision about his identity."

As the small canoe moved closer to shore, the Most Holy One backed from the water's edge.

"That *is* the face of a man," King Cocom said. "A face of white skin."

"The others' skin isn't silver but something silver covering it. Their skin is also white," the Most Holy One said. "See their hands. They are like ours—but white. Are they all gods?"

"Maybe gods or maybe men or maybe god-men," the great high priest said, pointing toward their heads. "They wear silver crowns."

The small canoe moved to within fifty paces of

the shore. The Most Holy One moved into the bushes at the edge of the beach. The others quickly joined him and watched in awe as the strangers came closer.

The whitehaired man called out, "Hello. We come in peace."

"Is the whitehaired man cursing us, Most Holy One?" the local priest asked.

"I don't know, but I want to flee this place. Yet, I want to know more about these strangers."

"So do I," the great high priest said, fear rattling his voice. "But I must stay. I am a priest who serves the gods. I must know if these are the gods I worship or need to worship."

The oarsmen maneuvered the canoe toward the shoreline until it ran aground. Its beaching created a scraping sound familiar to the Most Holy One. He visibly shook on hearing the sounds uttered by the stranger with the largest crown who then pointed toward two other silver-skins.

Two silver-skins jumped into the shallow water and pushed the canoe farther ashore. Their coverings made strange clanging sounds as they moved about.

The standing white god-man steadied himself by holding onto the shoulder of an oarsman then joined his first two right fingers and moved them from his forehead, to his chest, then to his left shoulder and then the right. His lips moved, but he made no sounds.

"Most Holy One," King Cocom said. "He swats at insects where there are none."

With the canoe firmly beached, the remainder of the god-men jumped from the canoe and waded ashore.

"I pray they come in peace," the great high priest said.

Two of the silver-skins stood at the front of the

canoe and lifted the whitehaired man onto their shoulders, carried him ashore, and then stood him on dry sand. The other silver-skins left the canoe and stood in a single line, parallel to the shore, on either side of the whitehaired man. The strangers pulled long, shiny stick-like things from a long, thin container tied to their waist. They then held the shiny things in front of their face.

"Those shiny sticks appear to have sharp edges," the Most Holy One said. "Are they weapons?" *Will they be used against us? Should we run or prepare to fight?*

"The standing whitehaired one is a god," King Cocom said. "You saw how the silver-skins carry and revere him with those shiny sticks."

The man wearing the white cloth knelt on the beach, made some marks in the sand then kissed them. Two silver-skins helped him to his feet. From under his white cloth, he removed a gold colored object shaped like two crossed sticks. He placed the long end of the object on the top of a wooden staff then plunged it into the sand. The white man repeated the finger motions he had made on his body, but this time they were made in the air.

"Look, he again swats at absent insects," King Cocom said. "I think he makes strange magic."

The Most Holy One thought, *I hope it is not against us.* He worried as he watched the whitehaired man hold his arms wide and utter strange sounds toward the sky. He then spoke strange words toward the silver-skins. They replaced their long shiny sticks in the thin containers tied to their waist.

"What do you think he said?" the local priest asked the Most Holy One

"I wish I knew."

The whitehaired man, arms held wide, walked toward the Most Holy One who trembled along with the others.

Hakum whispered, "He holds his arms as we do for embracing.

"Dare we welcome these strangers?" the Most Holy One asked and glanced at his group, seeking agreement.

"We should," the great high priest said, "but we have no gifts."

"We have a smoke pot," the Most Holy One said. "Let's make a blessing and present it to this god-man."

"Give me the pot," the great high priest said.

The stranger wearing the long white cloth stopped, looked into the eyes of the Most Holy One while dropping his arms to his side and tilting his head first right then left.

The Most Holy One dropped incense in the smoke pot and blew on its embers. A small flame arose and allowed to burn for a moment. The local priest blew out the flame, leaving only a sweet smelling trail of smoke. He then handed the pot to the great high priest.

"Come. Let's greet these strangers," the great high priest said, pushing through the bushes.

Reluctantly, the Most Holy One joined the great high priest who took short steps toward the whitehaired god-man. The Most Holy One stopped after taking a few steps from the bushes and watched the great high priest walk to within fifteen paces of the whitehaired stranger. The great high priest slowly lifted the smoke pot over his head.

The whitehaired man patted the air and spoke softly toward his men.

The Most Holy One watched the priest's every

step. He walked to within ten paces of the stranger and waited for the wind to die down. He made a large, vertical smoke circle and then stepped through it to stand within eight paces of the whitehaired god-man. With visibly shaking hands, the great high priest took half steps toward the stranger while presenting the smoke pot.

A silver-skin started to draw his shiny stick, but the whitehaired man raised his hand, stopping the action.

The great high priest stood tall but shook like a storm-blown leaf. "So far all is well," he said, speaking over his shoulder to the kings

Taking another step, the priest held his smoke pot in front of the whitehaired god-man. The Most Holy One watched the whitehaired stranger's lips become a smile, prompting the great high priest to offer the stranger the clay pot. The whitehaired man slowly extended his hand

Shaking, the Most Holy One heard the great high priest say, "Accept this gift. Take the smoke pot as a gift of friendship."

Priest and god-man appeared to stare eye-to-eye for a moment.

The whitehaired man smiled more broadly then turned his head toward one of his followers as if to ask, 'what do I do now?'

The silver-skin, with the largest crown, ambled to the side of the whitehaired god-man and spoke to him. The whitehaired man then smiled and extended both hands to accept the pot.

The great high priest placed the smoke pot in the stranger's hands. The Most Holy One was taken aback as he watched the great high priest use the back of his hand to stroke the back of the stranger's hand. Apparently feeling bolder, the great high priest placed the back of his hand next to the stranger's white hand, smiled, and then repeatedly pointed between his dark hand and the white hand

Holding the smoke pot in his left hand, the stranger extended his open right hand as he moved closer to the great high priest.

The Most Holy One thought, *I hope the stranger isn't going to attack our priest.*

Apparently not knowing what to do, the native priest stood silently with his hands at his side.

The whitehaired man used his left hand to slowly raise the great high priest's right hand then shook it with his right hand. At first, the great high priest seemed unsure how he should respond, but apparently thinking it to be a friendly act, he repeated the action.

The Most Holy One walked closer and watched the two envoys.

The whitehaired man pointed to himself and said, "Father Garcés. Father Garcés." He raised his eyebrows, tilted his head, and then pointed at the great high priest. The priest stared at the whitehaired man as if he had not understood the stranger's words, but then said, "Noh Halach Ahkin."

After a short time, the Most Holy One and others knew the whitehaired man as Father Garcés, and he knew the native envoy to be Noh Halach Ahkin.

The Most Holy One pointed to himself and said, "Maas Cilich Hun Ah Kinch."

Father Garcés smiled and stumbled over the words, "Ma…as Ci…lich Hun Ah Kin…ch."

The king nodded, smiled, and repeated, "Maas

Cilich Hun Ah Kinch."

The beach soon buzzed with the sounds of natives and visitors trying to pronounce the name of the other.

King Cocom whispered to the Most Holy One, "These strangers don't seem intent on harm. Should we extend the courtesy we would to visiting native people?"

"You mean invite them to your center?" the Most Holy One asked.

The great high priest must have overheard the discussion, because he backed toward the Most Holy One and King Cocom. "I want to know more about these strangers. We might learn from them. We can inquire about their gods, their village, their canoe, and culture."

King Cocom whispered to his guests. "We should welcome them in peace."

One-by-one, the Most Holy One and the others exchanged a Mayan forearm greeting with Father Garcés who then shook hands with each man.

Hakum whispered to the Most Holy One, "This god-man's white skin feels like ours."

Father Garcés motioned toward fellow travelers to exchange greetings with the natives.

The Most Holy One wanted to touch the silver coverings on the strangers' arms, but The great high priest stepped forward and touched the covering of the god-man with the most elaborate silver crown.

"The covering is hard and warm," the priest said to the Most Holy One, "and has a most unpleasant odor. Perhaps they use different body oils."

The local priest, last to examine the coverings on the god-man's arm, turned the arm over, examined it and then examined the broad silver chest cover. "The coverings feel the same," he said to the Most Holy One while trying to scratch it. "It's not soft like silver." He and the others were allowed to examine the body covers for as long as they wanted.

The Most Holy One wanted to touch a stranger's head covering but dared not touch another leader's crown. Instead, he joined King Cocom in approaching Father Garcés. They said, "Come with us."

Father Garcés apparently did not understand the invitation, but King Cocom pointed inland and then walked south. He waved to the Most Holy One and the strangers who obviously understood the hand signal.

Father Garcés spoke to the stranger with the large crown. He nodded, smiled, and then spoke to the other shiny skins. Most of them nodded. The stranger with the large crown pointed to Noh Halach Ahkin, the jungle, and then placed his hand on his thin shinny weapon and smiled.

I pray that was a friendly gesture, the Most Holy One thought then got behind King Cocom and waved to the strangers to follow.

The strangers took random positions between the natives and followed them off the beach. Each foreigner kept his hand on this shiny weapon.

The Most Holy One scanned the strangers. *The whitehaired god-man is not Mayan. He has no hair on the top of his head. We don't lose our hair. He wears his authority necklace of black spheres around his belly instead of around his neck, and it has a tail with a statue of a man on crossed sticks. Maybe it is a god icon like ours. I must be careful not to offend this stranger.*

Chapter 23

After walking south and out of the dense bush, Father Garcés stepped out of line. "Admiral, have you seen those buildings in the distance?"

"How could I miss them? They glow in the afternoon sun."

"Have you ever seen such gold or jade as on the native's necklaces and ear things?"

"A small fortune, wouldn't you say?"

Nearing the village, the padre noted not only its tall and multi-shaped buildings but their elaborate wall paintings, and strange three dimensional animal-like faces protruding from various building facades.

"One of these has to be a treasury, Padre," the admiral said.

"In due time, Admiral. In due time."

People in X'Cambo appeared shocked to see the whitehaired man enter their village. Wide-eyed and trembling, they touched their foreheads to the ground as he passed.

"These people seem to act more from reverence than respect," the admiral said.

"Maybe they think we're gods," Father Garcés said, looking at the bowing natives. "Do nothing to make them think otherwise."

They soon reached the tallest pyramid shaped building on the plaza. The padre stared at its top. "Admiral, this building is as tall as a cathedral."

"Yes, but no bell tower—just that rectangular structure at the top."

Standing on the pyramid's bottom step, King Cocom waved to the padre. He was to follow King Cocom to its upper terrace where two native men stood at attention. On cue, the two natives blew conch shells.

The padre jumped on hearing the mournful sounds.

Admiral Gonzales stifled a chuckle and asked, "Court trumpeters?"

"We are offered a royal welcome," the padre said.

"Then we must act royally."

On the top terrace, King Cocom motioned to the padre to follow him to a doorway. With hands on the hilt of their swords, Spanish guards followed the padre as the admiral stepped aside.

"Admiral, I'm glad your soldiers are vigilant," Father Garcés said.

"They're well trained."

King Cocom motioned for the padre to enter the building while he held back a door covering. Seconds later the padre came outside. "Admiral, there's no one inside. It's a large, cool, and safe room. It's painted like a chapel."

Inside, the padre studied the colorful murals depicting disfigured human images wearing elaborate costumes and headdresses. "Strange," Father Garcés said, scanning the murals. "I wonder if these are depictions of the essence of a god or the essence of many gods."

"Doesn't matter," the admiral said. "I just hope

they're not painted with blood."

"So do I, but they might contain clues about these heathens' religion *and* their gold."

"I prefer to simply demand their gold, Padre."

"Patience, Admiral. I think you want the gold *mine* not their trinkets."

"Don't forget, I'm here to claim territory for Spain, discover its riches, and that includes slaves. You want their souls for the church. I want their gold—trinkets *and* mines."

"Perhaps you should remember the adage about getting more with honey than vinegar."

King Cocom pointed to multicolored floor cushions then motioned for the padre to be seated.

The king sat down crossed legged on a cushion and watched the soldiers struggle with their armor as they sat down, scraping scabbards on the stucco floor.

"I hope we don't have to fight in here," the admiral said. "Getting up quickly could be difficult."

"Relax, Admiral. I don't think they have battle on their minds."

The admiral removed his helmet revealing a jagged scar that ran from the right corner of his mouth to his ear lobe. The admiral pushed his black, sweaty hair from his eyes then removed his metal hand covering, revealing an inflamed scar between his third and fourth fingers to the back of his wrist. Suddenly, rattling sounds masked conversation as the other soldiers place their hand coverings and helmets on the floor.

Clad in loincloths, two native men entered the room. One carried an olive-shaped jug the size of a barrel. Another carried a flat basket containing gourd cups. The men bowed to the native leader then gave each guest a cup. The servants filled each cup with foul smelling, foamy liquid from the jug.

"This stinks," Admiral Gonzales said sniffing his cup. "Corporal Juan, tell me how it tastes."

The corporal glanced at the admiral then reluctantly lifted his cup. He sniffed the brew, wrinkled his face, and said, "It smells awful."

"But how does it taste?" the admiral asked.

Corporal Juan took a sip, scrunched his face, and then shook his head. "Ugh. It has a harsh sweet-sour taste."

The admiral watched the corporal for a moment. "The corporal lives," the admiral said, then sipped the liquid. "Hmm. It taste like piss, but we shouldn't refuse it." He raised his cup in a toast-like fashion and said, "Drink.'

Glancing over his cup at the padre, King Cocom drank his liquid.

"*God*, what we do in the name of diplomacy," the admiral said.

"Watch the sacrilege, Admiral."

The padre asked the admiral what he thought about the murals and their drink while paying little attention to King Cocom or the natives. Suddenly, Father Garcés looked around. "Where are the natives?"

"I don't know," the admiral said, his sword scraping the floor as he stood. He walked to the low doorway and peered outside. "Padre, you've got to see this."

Father Garcés walked to the doorway, peered outside, and then crossed himself. "I have never seen such . . . Let's sit down and wait."

Moments later, the hosts reentered the room. The sounds of jaw-dropping gasps filled the space. The padre surveyed red, yellow, and blue-green feather covered garments, headdresses, and gold and jade jewelry worn by the hosts.

"Admiral, look at that gold," Father Garcés said. "Your prayers have been answered."

"Abundantly and I bet there's more."

The hosts sat down on their pillows.

From a distance, the sounds of giggling children grew louder. Two bare breasted females, along with a nude boy and a girl, entered the room. The women stared in apparent shock on seeing the whitehaired man. One of the women pulled the children behind her. The women, staring at the floor, bowed stiffly toward the strangers.

"Men," Father Garcés said, "don't stare at their breasts."

Stifling a snicker, the admiral said, "Father, how can we not look? It's been months since we have seen breasts. Besides, it would be an insult to ignore our hostesses."

Breasts touching the floor, the women prostrated themselves toward the native males then bowed toward the guests. One female coaxed the children to bow as she had.

"Saints bless us," Father Garcés said. "They have no shame in showing themselves."

"No, but do you see the lumpy gold and jade necklaces they wear, Padre? I guess you, as a God fearing man, can't see what beauty lies beneath the gold covering their breasts."

"Admiral," the padre said, "perhaps we should bow—a least at the waist."

The guests bowed as the women backed toward floor pillows then sat down, pulling the children to the floor beside them.

"Padre, I'm having a look at all that gold." The admiral said, walking toward Noh Halach Ahkin. "I've never seen so much gold on anyone." He pointed to the broad gold bracelet on the elderly man's left wrist. The native removed his bracelet and held it toward the admiral.

"Oh my. It's heavy," the admiral said. "It must be pure gold." He held it toward the padre. "It's worth a small fortune."

Father Garcés examined its engraved images. "The quality of workmanship is extraordinary. I wish I knew what these images mean." He looked at the ceiling. "They're similar to those up there." He bounced the bracelet in his hand and said, "It's worthy of a king."

"I'm keeping it," the admiral said, grabbing the bracelet then sliding it onto his right wrist. "We'll find another one for King Phillip."

The elderly bracelet owner bowed at the waist as the admiral admired the bracelet.

"The old man doesn't seem to mind you took his bracelet," Father Garcés said.

"Let's see what he does when I point at the other one."

The admiral returned to the elderly man and pointed at the man's right wrist. He removed his bracelet, handed it to the admiral, and then bowed at the waist.

"Unbelievable," the admiral said. "They surrender their gold unconcerned about it being returned."

"Don't get greedy," Father Garcés said, watching the admiral place the bracelet on his left wrist.

Servants interrupted the treasure hunt by placing a

tray of elliptical brown food in front of Father Garcés, each guest, and the natives.

King Cocom selected one of the objects from the basket then held it toward Father Garcés.

The padre stared at the lumpy gold rings worn on three of the king's fingers as he bit into the food. King Cocom spat out the covering of the strange looking food then chewed its orange colored meat.

Father Garcés bit into his food. "Hmmm. It's sweet. I could eat several of these."

"I agree," the admiral said, speaking with a full mouth. "Can't say I like its skin. It's tough and gritty. Wow! Careful of the seed. It's the largest I've ever seen."

The admiral looked at King Cocom, pointed to the food, and made questioning gestures."

King Cocom smiled then said, "Mamey."

"Mamey?" the admiral repeated.

The king nodded and said, "Mamey."

Meal completed, the native leaders walked toward the doorway. King Cocom motioned for Father Garcés to follow him. He followed King Cocom down steep steps toward a communal fire where village men sat on the ground in a semicircle. As the padre passed, villagers rose then knelt, noses to the ground, until he had passed. A waiting man, presumably a priest, dropped incense onto the open fire and said something sounding like a prayer.

"That's a welcoming fragrance," Father Garcés said to the admiral. Following King Cocom's lead, the padre took a seat on one of several stone seats. "Think this is in our honor, Admiral?"

"Padre, it's unfortunate King Phillip can't see this display of respect for us."

"Or the Pope."

King Cocom patted his butt, presumably trying to ascertain his guest sat comfortably on their stones. The soldiers then took a seat.

King Cocom clapped.

Startled Father Garcés jumped. "What the?"

Suddenly, drumming sounds arose nearby. Four males entered the plaza, beating on large bamboo tubes. The drummers danced, taking a step forward then backward, and then twirled, causing their loincloths to fly outward revealing bare flesh.

"I could do without the ass," the padre said.

Each drummer bowed when passing King Cocom. He nodded in recognition.

The dancers swayed and frolicked around the circle of natives and strangers. Their drumming pleased the padre who clapped to the rhythm of the beat and asked himself, *Why do the natives slap their thighs instead of clapping?* A servant approached him carrying a familiar looking jug. From it, another servant dipped its contents into a gourd cup then handed it to him.

"It's that sweet-sour brew," Father Garcés said to the admiral. "I have a feeling we'll be drinking a lot of this stuff. Better learn to like it."

"It reminds me of mead," the admiral said, taking a cup. "I don't care for it, but I'll drink it until we get something better."

The drumming continued for several minutes then the drummers sat quietly behind King Cocom. When he nodded, the drumming resumed but with a different tempo. From behind a nearby building, four flute players emerged playing a slow, mournful melody. They wore an array of body paints but were otherwise nude. When they neared the guests, the tempo morphed into a more rhythmical cadence. The padre clapped to the music and tried to hum its melody.

"I could get used to this feasting," the admiral said.

"Me too," a soldier said, "but where are the naked dancing girls?"

"Gentlemen," Father Garcés said, "if you had bothered to notice, there are bare breasted women beyond our circle. Guess it's a cultural thing."

"Why the hell don't they dance?" a soldier asked.

"I think this is a men-only event," the padre said.

Noh Halach Ahkin and the local high priest nodded to the padre then climbed the pyramid behind King Cocom.

"I wonder where they're going." Father Garcés asked the admiral.

"To get more gold, I hope."

The two natives reached the top most terrace then entered the small square building at the top of the pyramid. For a moment, they were silhouetted by flickering flames inside the small structure.

"I wonder why they chose this time to leave." The padre said.

A moment later, the natives walked back onto the pyramid's terrace, faced the padre below, and made strange hand movements as if blessing him.

"Look," the admiral said. "Look at that Noh Halach Ahkin. The one with the big ear things and all the crown feathers. He's wearing more bracelets. I wonder how much gold is in that room."

Noh Halach Ahkin had descended four of the pyramid's steps when the admiral hurried toward the building.

"Admiral, where are you going?" Father Garcés yelled.

"To see what's in that room."

"Careful. Don't do anything to wreck my mission. That may be a sacred place."

"You see to your mission, Padre; I'll see to mine."

Halfway up the steps, the admiral passed the descending natives. From the terrace, he waved to the padre then entered the small room. Noh Halach Ahkin followed him inside.

The admiral surveyed a myriad of gold objects stacked in niches. "Oh . . . my . . . God. The padre was right. This must be some kind of temple treasury." He picked up a three-hand-width long object shaped like a flat anchor. "Caramba! It's heavy . . . pure gold." One side had an engraved image of a man with a large ring through his nose. On its back was a black, glistening object, with sharp edges, two-hand-widths long. The admiral held the twelve inch anchor near a torch to examine the workmanship.

Still admiring the object, the admiral walked toward the doorway. Suddenly, the two older native priests blocked his way. They placed their hands on his shoulder armor and shook their heads. Gripping the anchor in his left hand, the admiral pushed the priests' hands off his shoulders, stared indignantly at them, and then snarled.

Noh Halach Ahkin said something while trying to take the anchor from the admiral's hand.

"I don't know what you're saying," the admiral muttered, moving the object away from the natives, "but I'm keeping it."

The other priest gasped as the admiral pushed Noh Halach Ahkin aside. A tussle ensued between him and the admiral. Noh Halach Ahkin continued trying to wrest the anchor from the admiral's grip. The admiral elbowed the other priest and tripped over Noh Halach Ahkin's foot. When the admiral hit the floor, his silvery coverings clattered like thunder.

"Admiral. What have you done?" Father Garcés yelled.

Standing, the admiral heard Father Garcés and his soldiers climbing up the steps to the room.

The admiral and Noh Halach Ahkin continued to scuffle. The golden anchor fell to the floor shattering the attached black obsidian object into glass-like shards that sparkled in the golden torchlight.

Noh Halach Ahkin gasped and clutched his chest on seeing the glistening fragments scattered on the floor. He gathered them then picked up the anchor. He scurried to the terrace, stood just outside the door, head bowed, holding the anchor at arm's length.

"What's going on?" the admiral asked, pushing the second priest to the floor.

Soldiers reached the terrace just as the admiral walked onto the terrace and faced Noh Halach Ahkin.

"Admiral, are you all right?" a soldier asked.

"Yeah," the admiral said, staring at the anchor in Noh Halach Ahkin hands. "I'm having that damn thing."

The admiral snatched the object from the priest's hand. The priest dropped his hands to his side and stood mute, head bowed.

"I don't know what's going on," the admiral said, clutching the anchor to his chest, "but this is mine.

Panting, Father Garcés lumbered onto the terrace with King Cocom and his guards following. "What in God's name have you done, Admiral?"

"Nothing," he said holding out the anchor. "I just took what I wanted."

"From the sound of things, I'd say you did some kind of sacrilege."

King Cocom arrived but did not step onto the terrace. Father Garcés motioned for the king to stand beside him, but he shook his head, said something, and then took a step down from the terrace.

"I don't know what Cocom said, but I think he is loath to walk here," Father Garcés said. "Maybe we shouldn't either." The padre took the admiral's arm. "Come. Let's leave this place."

The admiral waved the anchor. "I'll leave, but this goes with me."

The soldiers followed the admiral and padre to the festival fire and sat down on their stone seats. The admiral held the anchor so his men could admire its beauty.

"May I see that?" Father Garcés asked.

"Yes, but remember it's mine."

Father Garcés examined the object. "This has the shape of an anchor *and* cross. I wonder which shape is the most meaningful to these people." He wrinkled his brow, dropped his shoulders, and held the object toward Noh Halach Ahkin who stood nearby. "What is this thing?"

Noh Halach Ahkin tilted his head to the right and extended both hands as if to say 'may I have it?'

"I think he wants it back," Father Garcés said to the admiral.

"Don't give it to him. It's mine."

"Why not?" Father Garcés handed the anchor to Noh Halach Ahkin.

The elderly priest turned it over in his hand and

pointed to four hooks on its flat back. He then extended his hand to a native who handed him a shiny black object shaped like a knife blade.

"The blade fits onto the back," Father Garcés said, watching Noh Halach Ahkin demonstrate how the knife fitted under the hooks.

"Oh. I see," the admiral said. "It's made to hold a stone knife."

"Yes, but why such an elaborate knife holder?" Father Garcés asked and used hand gestures to ask about the knife's use.

Noh Halach Ahkin removed the knife from the hooks then grasped its widest end in his right hand. He held the knife over his head and then brought it swiftly toward his abdomen, stopping it just before it reached his skin.

Father Garcés gasped and almost fell off his seat. He crossed himself saying, "Oh, my God. The knife is for human sacrifice."

The admiral stared at Father Garcés in disbelief. He walked to Noh Halach Ahkin then snatched the anchor from his hand. "I don't care what it's used for. It's mine."

"No. You can't. For them it's a holy thing," Father Garcés said, crossing himself. "You can't keep it."

The admiral waved dismissively. "I don't care what these heathens do among themselves. Let them kill each other. There'll be fewer to fight when the time comes."

"Have you forgotten why I'm here?" Father Garcés asked. "These people are made in the image of God. They have souls. Christ and his church sent priests like me to save them—spread his word—and that's what I'm going to do."

"Fine. You spread the word. I'll spill their blood—all of it—if I need to. I'm after their gold!"

The admiral and padre argued. Father Garcés said, "Admiral, we and your drunken men should leave before someone does something regrettable."

The admiral agreed, tucked the anchor under his breastplate then beckoned his men to follow him to the beach.

King Cocom interrupted their exit to send a torchbearer to lead the strangers through the dark jungle.

Chapter 24

"Come aboard," the admiral said, taking the torchbearer's hand then motioning for him to step aboard the ship.

The awestruck native spent the early part of the night roaming the upper deck. He appeared fearful of touching anything as he stepped over sleeping soldiers sprawled on deck in order to escape the heat below deck. After midnight, he lay on the poop deck and fell asleep near the soldier standing night watch.

As dawn broke, the ship rocked gently, and the admiral roamed the deck. He watched two grey and black seabirds circle high overhead against a cloudless sky tinted a brilliant reddish orange. He called to Father Garcés who slept on the forward deck. "Sun's up, Padre. Take the villager to my cabin and show him our window glass. The morning light is bright enough for him to appreciate it."

The admiral escorted the padre and native into the admiral's cabin. The native fingered various pieces of paper scattered about the admiral's desk. He cautiously touched a map then ran his finger over its surface and along the outline of unknown shapes, smiling all the while. He picked it up, put his nose against it, and then licked it.

"No!" the admiral yelled. "For God's sake, take

that from him!"

Father Garcés smiled at the startled native and took the map.

"The ink is made of lamp black," the admiral said. "I don't want to be lost in this god forgotten place because some dumb native licked the ink off our only means of navigating."

As the priest turned, he held the map between himself and the window. Light shown through the mottled paper causing the native to drop to the floor and crawl away from the map.

"He must think the paper has magic," Father Garcés said.

The admiral examined the map. "Thank God there's no ink missing."

The priest took the native's hand then led him to an opening in the wall. At first the man ignored the window pane pushed out of the way. He put his head out the opening, peered down, and shrieked something unintelligible.

"Guess he's never been this far above the sea," the priest said. "Let's close the window and see how he reacts to glass."

Father Garcés tugged the man's shoulder to get him to withdraw his head from the opening. Pointing to the pane, the priest closed the window and knuckled the glass. Startled, the man stared at it in disbelief. The priest partially opened the window and put his hand behind the glass and wiggled his fingers.

The native tentatively touched the glass with a finger then instantly withdrew it. He looked at the end of his finger then looked at the priest.

"I think he is reacting to the coolness of the glass," the priest said, "or he's surprised his finger isn't wet because the wavy glass might look like water to him."

"Come," the admiral said taking the man's arm to give the native a tour of the deck. He allowed the man to touch, smell, and lick whatever he wanted.

A sudden thud behind the native caused him to spin around, eyes wide with fear. The admiral had dropped the lid of a water barrel while taking a drink from a wooden dipper. Watching the admiral's every move, the man approached the barrel and looked inside.

"Maybe he wants a drink," the priest said.

"Okay. Let's see how he likes our water." The admiral filled the dipper with water then indicated the man should drink.

The native took a sip, spewed it out, and made a strange face.

"Guess he didn't like it," the admiral said. "Hell, I wouldn't drink this piss if I had better. Hmmm . . . I wonder if he can lead us to freshwater?"

After much sign language, the admiral believed he had communicated well enough to get the native to lead him to a water source.

"Everyone out," the captain yelled as three longboats, carrying the native, eighteen blackened water barrels, the priest, and soldiers, scraped their way onto the beach. He pointed to two soldiers. "Carry the padre ashore."

With the priest on the beach, the remainder of the soldiers floated barrels ashore. The native hoisted one onto his shoulder then headed into the jungle.

"Let's follow him," the captain yelled, "but keep an eye out for danger."

Each soldier shouldered a barrel and followed the

native.

"Hope this isn't a trap," the captain confided to the priest.

"So do I, but I trust him."

After a long trek, the group reached a large hole. For a long time, the captain walked around its rim and stared into the darkness below.

The native guide kept saying, "*Dzonot*.

"Sounds like the native is saying *cenote*," the captain said. "I hope there's potable water here." He dropped a stone into the hole. Hearing a splash, he said, "We're in luck. There's water down there.

Using a ladder pointed out by the guide, the captain, priest, two soldiers and the native descended into the sinkhole. Standing on a gravel beach, the captain adapted his vision to the dark space.

"I like this coolness," the captain said, removing his helmet then pushing back sweaty hair.

He surveyed the three story tall cavern through which a slow-moving river stretched from end to end. A clear pool glistened in a narrow beam of sunlight that found its way to its pebbly bottom, highlighting several finger-length fish. The sight of the ceiling, partially hidden under thousands of dangling tree roots and sleeping bats, caused the captain's jaw to drop. Twelve or fifteen startled bats circled the room then flew out of the hole in the roof.

A wall, on the near side of the space, had a niche blackened by fire. On its ledge lay a collection of bones. The walls contained images similar to the ones in King Cocom's dining room.

Holding his scapular out of the way, the priest knelt on the gravel beach then cupped a handful of water. "Wonderful," he said, water dripping from his chin as he prepared to drink another handful.

The guide knelt at the edge of the pool, mumbled, and stirred the water with his hand before drinking.

"This must be a holy place," the priest said.

The captain yelled to the men above. "There are jugs here we can use to get water to the surface. Cut some vines to make ropes, so we can hoist them. I don't want to carry heavy loads up this rickety ladder."

Soon the eighteen barrels were filled, and the captain ordered their lids be secured.

"I'm worried about the men's hot armor," the priest said. "We don't want them drinking all the water before we get it to the ship. Let's raise a jug for the men to have a drink then have some men escort the guide to his village and have him bring natives to carry our barrels. The natives are accustomed to this heat."

Chapter 25

A platoon leader and two silver-skins followed the native guide into his village. He strutted like a victorious warrior with the silver-skins following. Villagers bowed, noses to the ground, until the silver skins had passed.

At the foot of the palace, the guide stopped and called to a guard on its terrace. Moments later the king walked onto the terrace and spoke to the guide. The guide motioned for the platoon leader to sit down on the steps.

Within a short time, thirty-six village men arrived with poles and vines.

"They must be our bearers," the platoon leader said.

As the guide, natives, and silver-skins left the village, the natives increased their pace. In no time, the guide and villagers had left the platoon leader behind.

"I hope this isn't about to become an ambush," the platoon leader said, scanning the area. "Stay alert, men."

The guide for the king's cadre stopped running and returned to the platoon leader, motioning he should catch up. The guide then ran ahead.

"I can't keep up," the platoon leader said.

"I can't either," a soldier said. "It's too hot, and

this armor is too heavy."

The platoon leader yelled to the guide a hundred paces ahead. "Hey! Stop!"

The guide and his cadre stopped and looked back.

Tired, the platoon leader walked to the guide's side. Using "walking" fingers on his palm, the stranger indicated the guide should walk slower.

The guide nodded then slowed his pace.

"I doubt these are god-men," the guide said to a villager. "I want to believe god-men could keep up."

"But you went to their canoe," the villager said, "What did you see?"

"Strange things. They have shallow hardened water with stilled ripples and hangs upright. You can put your hand behind it and see your fingers like in the sea. Move them and they look like little fish."

"Solid water. How strange."

"Yes. They have many strange things.

"So, they make magic?"

"Yes, but we must hurry; we have water to carry. Maybe you will see the things I saw."

While waiting for the barrel carriers, Father Garcés scanned the cavern as the captain and soldiers rested. Some removed their armor to cool off. One man waded into the river and sat down in a shallow pool.

An hour later, the platoon leader and carriers arrived.

"Glad you're back," the captain called up to the platoon leader who climbed down into the hole while his men and the carriers rested above.

"We have the needed help," the platoon leader reported.

"Good. Maybe we can get to the ship before dark," the captain said. "Do any of the natives have weapons?"

"No. Why do you ask?"

"Just want to be safe," the captain said, climbing the ladder. "I'll have the natives harness the barrels and then we'll head for the ship. You finish up down here."

The natives tied long vines between parallel bamboo logs then placed a barrel on the cradle of vines. Pairs of natives squatted, placed the end of a bamboo pole on each shoulder, stood, and then carried away their barrel, following the guide.

The captain followed the line of water bearers.

Father Garcés lagged behind. He looked back to see the last natives readying their barrel on the vine cradle. Suddenly, the man at the rear lost his footing, yelling and falling backwards toward the sinkhole. A soldier grabbed for the villager's ankle but the native's weight and the soldier's momentum caused both to fall into the hole.

A loud splash ensued as the native landed in the river. The soldier's armor created a loud clang.

"*Madre de Dios,*" Father Garcés said, crossing himself while running to the waterhole. He dropped to the ground and peered into the darkness. "Is everyone all right?"

The only sounds heard were coughs, moans, and the splashing of water.

Scurrying down the shaky ladder, Father Garcés yelled for two soldiers. "Come with me." Four rungs from the beach, the padre jumped to the ground. He rushed to the soldier lying on the beach, lifted his head, and removed his helmet. "Breathe man. Open your eyes."

The priest glimpsed a soldier wade into the river. He put his shoulder under the native's armpit and then helped him from the water. The limping native hugged his right side as if it hurt.

Father Garcés removed the fallen soldier's chest armor then his arm and leg coverings. The removal of his soggy clothing revealed cuts and multiple bruises.

"He's broken some ribs," the priest said to a gawking soldier. "He winces when I touch them."

"But he's not waking up," the soldier said.

Behind the priest the injured villager coughed and moaned.

"How's the native doing?" the padre asked.

"He broke some ribs and swallowed half the river," the soldier said, "but he's coughing it up."

"Good, but our man is in trouble." Father Garcés yelled to the soldiers and platoon leader who had returned to the rim of the waterhole. "Make a bamboo raft an arm's length wide. We'll use it to hoist our man. Have someone run to the convoy. Tell the captain to leave the barrels and return."

"Bring me a helmet of water," the priest said to a soldier. "Quick, man. Don't just stand there staring." The padre continued to examine the unconscious man as the soldier returned with the water-filled helmet. The padre dipped his scapular in the water then wiped sand from the man's face. "We'll need three men to get him onto the raft when it's finished."

"Don't worry. I'll get them," the soldier said.

The injured native, resting near the priest, stirred. Holding his side, he limped toward the ladder. Once there, he leaned on it and coughed. He placed one foot on the bottom rung, reached for a rung overhead, and then recoiled moaning. He grabbed his side then slumped against the ladder. He looked at the priest, shook his head, and slid to the ground.

"We'll have to hoist him too," the padre said, motioning for the native to stay put. "Platoon leader," the priest yelled, "make a second raft."

An hour later, the padre ordered a raft lowered.

Three soldiers climbed into the sinkhole and assisted Father Garcés lift the unconscious soldier onto the raft that had hoisting vines tied to each of the four raft ends.

"Careful," the padre said, pushing the soldier toward the center of the raft. "Make sure his weight is distributed." The padre checked alignment then yelled, "Start lifting!"

Soon, the raft neared the surface.

"Drop the foot end about fifteen degrees," the platoon leader said. "We need the tilt so we can slide the headend over the ledge."

The men pulling the foot ropes let the raft tilt downward five degrees.

The priest climbed to the surface to monitor the injured soldier.

"More tilt," the platoon leader ordered.

The raft was tilted to fifteen degrees.

"Uhmmm," the injured soldier moaned and moved his head left then right.

"He's waking up," the priest yelled.

The injured soldier opened his eyes, moaned, and then said, "Where am I?"

"Hold on, soldier," the priest yelled. "Rope pullers, get the raft on the ground."

"What?" the injured soldier asked, attempting to sit up.

"Stay down!" the priest yelled, crossing himself.

The injured soldier slid to his right, yelling, "Ahhhh!"

"Lie down! Lie down!" Father Garcés yelled.

Suddenly, uneven rope-pulling caused the head end of the raft to drop, and the injured soldier's shoulders slid off the makeshift stretcher.

"Idiots," the priest yelled, watching the injured soldier slide farther off the raft. The soldier's right ankle caught against a rope, stopping his fall but leaving him dangling in the air.

The priest yelled, "Lower him. Don't try getting him over the ledge."

In dazed horror, the injured soldier stared into the priest's eyes.

"Stay still!" the priest yelled. "We'll get you down, son. Hold still!"

The raft and soldier were safely lowered to the beach.

"Thank God he's safe," the priest said, crossing himself while scurrying down the ladder. He placed his hand on the soldier's head. "You're safe, son."

"What happened?"

"You fell," the priest said, pointing to the rim, "from there. You broke a rib."

"Feels like I broke them all."

The injured native moaned and squirmed his back against the wall. The padre nodded his recognition of the native's condition.

"Soldier, we're going to hoist you again," the priest said, "but you have to stay still."

With the soldier now tied to the raft, the surface men hoisted him to the surface without incident.

The priest yelled, "Send down the other raft for the injured native."

The native guide climbed into the waterhole and examined his fellow villager.

Using vines, other natives secured the injured villager to the stretcher and prepared to hoist him.

Father Garcés climbed to the surface, crossed himself, and prayed for a safe lift.

The natives at the foot of the ladder yelled what sounded like instructions to natives on the surface.

Suddenly, the padre yelled, startling the natives as he pointed to a knot at the right foot-end of the raft. "It's fraying!"

The natives seemed unsure where the priest pointed.

The padre yelled, "I'm coming!" As he descended the ladder, the village leader on the surface pointed to the shredding knot.

Another villager climbed halfway down the ladder and held the raft.

The king's guide scurried up the ladder to help steady the raft then motioned for two natives to climb down and help.

The padre yelled to the platoon leader on the surface, "Everything is under control."

Father Garcés paced the beach as King Cocom's guide monitored the hoisting. Hoisting and lifting was stopped so everyone could rest.

After resting, the natives on the ladder gave the raft a sharp upward lift a split second before the rested hoisters took up the slack in the vines. Suddenly, the weight of the raft, passenger, and men on the ladder created excess stress on the rung-supporting bamboo poles. They emitted a loud cracking sound.

The surface men accelerated their pulling, but the frayed knot ripped free of the raft, transferring more weight to the breaking ladder, hurling the yelling priest, a guide, and another native to the beach.

The man tied to the raft had managed to grab a hoisting vine as the foot end of the raft dropped. His weight strained against the rope around his chest, causing him to yell with pain and panic.

The raft swung back and forth while the upper crew struggled to pull it and its passenger to the surface.

The padre had landed face up on top of the plummeting natives, breaking his fall. Struggling, he got up.

One native had fallen, face first into the river. Another man had landed on top of him. The upper man got himself from the river, but the other remained motionless, face down in the water.

Father Garcés waded to the floating native, grabbed his arms, and then pulled him toward shore. A native assisted the priest in pulling the cyanotic man onto the beach.

Father Garcés' wet scapular hampered his movements so he threw it over his shoulder and pulled the motionless man semi-upright. The padre struck the native's back several times. *Please, Lord, don't let him die.*

The natives gasped when the priest pounded the unconscious man's back. They shook their heads as if to say, 'It's no use.'

A native limped to the wall niche, picked up some bones, and presumably muttered a prayer for the dead, but Father Garcés interrupted. He forced the praying native to kneel on all fours near the water. The padre dragged the drowned native to the kneeling man. The priest motioned for another native to help him position the unconscious man over the kneeling man's back.

Father Garcés pounded the drowned man's back. Periodically, small amounts of water trickled from his mouth. The padre made the sign of the cross then yelled, "Breathe!"

His yell obviously frightened the natives huddled nearby and visibly shaking.

"Breathe man! Breathe!" The padre yelled and made the sign of the cross. He walloped the man on the back, yelling, "Breathe!"

The man gasped then coughed. He coughed again and then took a deep breath.

"Thank you God!" the padre yelled, as the man took another breath.

The trembling natives mumbled and shook violently with apparent fear. The kneeling man fell flat on the ground weeping while the coughing native sat up.

The once kneeling man bowed at the padre's feet.

Despite their injuries, the other natives crawled to the priest.

"They think you're a god," a soldier said. "They want a miracle too."

"Get up," Father Garcés said to the natives. "On your feet."

The kneeling natives remained on their knees, faces to the ground. Father Garcés took a man's hand and pulled him upright, but the native refrained from looking at the padre's face. When he released the man's hand, the man stared at and rubbed the priest-touched spot on his hand.

Father Garcés dismissed his apparent elevation

to god status and examined the injured natives. Each seemed more interested in touching his hand than being examined. Nevertheless, he discovered one man had a broken arm.

The padre asked surface soldiers to sort through the remaining bamboo for pieces that could be used to construct a ladder that would allow the injured to climb out of the hole. He also wanted several short pieces to make a splint for the native's broken arm.

With completion of the ladder, each native had a rope tied around his chest to protect him in case he slipped or the quickly assembled ladder failed.

Fatigued, Father Garcés wiped sweat, flung it onto the sand, and then sat down on the beach to catch his breath. He wrung water from his clothing then prayed a portion of the rosary in thanksgiving.

"Padre," a soldier on the surface yelled. "You building a church down there or coming up?"

"I'm doing both. Drop me a rope and pray the ladder will hold a plump priest wearing wet, heavy clothing."

Chapter 26

Nightfall approached as Captain Rodriguez, his men, the padre, and natives prepared to leave the waterhole.

Using hand signals, the padre indicated to King Cocom's guide that he and the group needed to hurry to the ship.

The guide nodded his understanding, said something to the natives, waved the torch brought from the waterhole, and then set out for the ship. Waving goodbye to the injured being returned to the village, the water bearers hoisted their barrels and followed the guide.

During a rest stop, Father Garcés cupped his ear to better hear distant sounds.

"Sounds like jungle animals are voicing their displeasure at having to share their space," the captain said.

"No," the padre said, "Shhh! Captain, listen. I hear voices on our right flank."

"So do I. Who the hell is it?"

"The natives don't seem bothered," the priest said. "Maybe their king has sent more help."

"Then we'll wait and see," the captain said, drawing his sword.

Moments later, flickering torches were seen

through the underbrush. As torch bearers approached the captain's flank, the water bearers suddenly lined up, shoulder to shoulder, and bowed, foreheads to the ground.

"Must be someone important," Father Garcés said.

The voices and sounds of someone breaking underbrush grew louder. When the torches were a hundred paces away, the bowing natives shouted, "*Bat.*" Seconds later, the captain saw King Cocom and his entourage.

The king held his head high as he approached Father Garcés. For a moment, the two men stared at each other. Suddenly, the king dropped to his knees, touched his nose to the ground, and touched Father Garcés feet. The king muttered for several seconds while repeatedly touching the priest's feet.

"Padre, what's he's saying?" Captain Rodriguez asked.

"I don't know, but I'm guessing it has something to do with that drowned man."

"How did he know?"

"The returning villagers probably told him."

Shaking his head, Father Garcés pulled the king to his feet. "I'm a man. Only a man. A God-fearing man—I'm *not* a god."

The king removed his headdress and gold then placed all in the hands of the padre.

King Cocom bowed then said something to the villagers behind him. Four natives came forward carrying two large baskets.

"Padre, they're carrying something heavy," the captain said. "See how those handles strain."

The natives placed the baskets in front of the

priest, bowed, and then touched their noses to the ground. King Cocom motioned for the presumed god to remove the lids.

Father Garcés removed a lid then crossed himself. He took a shiny object from the basket and held it high. It gleamed in the torchlight. "Gold! These baskets are full of gold—lots of gold. This must be all the gold in the village."

Father Garcés handed a fist size gold statue to the captain. "Have you ever seen such treasure?"

"Now I understand why King Philip wanted this new world explored. There's gold here. I pray there's more."

"This will please the admiral," Father Garcés said, "but I'm afraid it will also spur his greed."

Father Garcés bowed at the waist then motioned for the men who brought the baskets to pick them up and follow him. The padre clapped and addressed the captain. "We should go."

The water bearers, and those carrying gold, hoisted their load and everyone resumed the trek.

Dawn broke as the group reached the beach. The sun appeared like a ball of fire as it rose, creating an avenue of sunlight across the still ocean.

"Padre, there are only two longboats here," the captain said.

"The other one was probably used to get our injured man to the ship last night," the priest said.

"Well, Padre," the captain said, "We'll put you and some barrels in a boat and get you to the ship. I'll have soldiers return with the third boat when we return in this one to get another load.

As the first longboat approached the ship, a

deckhand yelled, "Admiral, our men return!

The admiral walked to the railing and watched as the priest, natives, water barrels, and then baskets were hoisted on board. Several awe struck natives cautiously roamed the deck, touching various objects. The others remained in the longboats, apparently too afraid to leave them.

The admiral addressed Captain Rodriguez, the first soldier to step on board. "What took so long?"

"Sir, you'll never believe what happened. Let Father Garcés tell you, so there is no doubt about our tale."

The fatigued and panting priest took a drink of old water then sat down on a barrel to catch his breath. He related the water hole incidents and then the part about the gifts of gold.

For a moment, the admiral stared at the baskets then ripped the lid off the nearest one. "Oh my God." He picked up and admired two large gold bird-like statues. Suddenly, the natives stared in horror as he handled the objects, gleaming in the sunlight. Noting their behavior, he said, "Padre, what the hell's wrong with them?"

"Admiral, please put the objects back in the basket," Father Garcés said, taking the objects and placing them in the basket. "These are obviously religious objects. Things only priests are privileged to handle. I received this gold because King Cocom apparently thinks I'm a god. You don't want to be seen dishonoring these idols."

"I don't give a damn about dishonoring gold. It's mine." The admiral huffed then placed his hands on his hips and stood tall.

"Admiral, I suggest you treat these things

reverently while the natives are on board. When they're gone, you may do as you wish."

"Then get them the hell off my ship."

Father Garcés approached the king's guide and indicated he and the other natives should leave. The guide bowed then led his men to the boat that would take them ashore.

As the last native climbed over the rail, the admiral dumped the gold objects on the deck. "Padre, look at this. I have never seen so much gold outside a church."

Father Garcés and the admiral examined several of the gold objects.

"I wish I knew what these markings mean," Father Garcés said, handing a half-human image to the admiral. They might provide insight to native religious beliefs and suggest a way to present Christianity to these heathens."

"You worry about their souls, Padre. I want their gold."

"I can't imagine King Cocom giving me all his gold. If he had, he would seriously limit his priests' ability to worship their gods. No, there's got to be more."

"Then I want it," the admiral said, dropping an icon into a basket. "I want it all."

"Don't get greedy," the priest said, running his finger over an inscription.

"One must strike while the iron is hot, Padre. I say raid the village—tonight—take everything. Go house-to-house, temple-to-temple, and palace-to-palace. Take everything. Everything!"

"Are you crazy?" the priest asked, staring at the admiral. "It will soon be dark. How will you find your way?"

The admiral went to his cabin and returned with a covered shallow wooden sandbox. He removed the lid and then smoothed the sand. Looking at Father Garcés, he said, "We need worry only about the first part—through the underbrush." Using his finger, the admiral drew his plan in the sand. "Remember, there is a rough cut path here," he said, pointing to a freshly made line. "We'll burn the brush on either side of the path to light our way and leave an unobstructed path for our return with the booty."

"Oh my God. You're intent on total destruction aren't you?"

"No," the admiral said, pacing the deck, "I just want their gold." He stopped pacing. "All of it."

"I can't sanction such a raid," the priest said, following the pacing admiral. "In fact, I argue against it. It's ungodly."

The admiral stared at the padre. "I don't need your approval. I'm going to the village—tonight, and I'd like to have you with us."

"I want nothing to do with raiding." Father Garcés walked to the ship's railing, shook his head and looked toward heaven as he mumbled a prayer of protection.

"You should go, Padre." The admiral shouted, standing behind the priest. "In case a man needs last rites."

The priest stared at the admiral, then spoke thorough clenched teeth. "No one will need last rites if you stay here. Don't do this."

The admiral walked toward his cabin. "My mind is made up. We go tonight. Do as you wish, Padre."

The priest fell to his knees and prayed, "God,

forgive them."

As the three longboats and sputtering torches moved through the grey-blue night, the admiral watched two soldiers wave from the deck as the padre made the sign of the cross.

The boats landed, and the admiral waded ashore. Three torchbearers walked to the admiral's position near the bushes lining the beach. "Some of you have not traveled this trail," the admiral said, "so listen carefully." He pointed to the first torchbearer. "You follow me. You," he said, pointing to another torchbearer. "You'll be third in line. The third torchbearer will follow the second. The rest of you pay attention."

The men quieted as the admiral raised his hand.

"I and the three torchbearers will go first. We'll set fire to the brush to open a path." The admiral broke a stem from a bush. "This stuff is dry. It will burn quickly. Let the flames move away from our path so we can move safely through the burned areas. Any questions?" Hearing none, he said, "The first fifteen men will follow me to the temples, the second fifteen will follow Captain Rodriguez to the palaces, and the last fifteen will go hut-to-hut. Everyone . . . search for gold and silver—anything of value. Look in nooks, crannies, baskets, jugs—anywhere one might hide valuables. *Any* object that looks valuable, take it—necklaces, clothing—anything."

"Sir, what if owners resist?" a soldier asked

"Kill them. All matchlocks should be loaded, and don't forget you have swords. Any questions? Nothing? All right, let's go."

As soon as the bushes were ignited, flames grew into roaring columns of fire twenty feet high. The flames and heat quickly spread along the shore and inland.

"Admiral, we'll burn the whole jungle," a soldier said, shielding his face from the heat while watching westerly flames rapidly consume the brush a hundred paces away. "I'm glad the wind blows from the sea."

After the nearby westerly flames had died down, the admiral ordered the brush to the east be burned.

After a short while, the admiral stepped onto the hot path and yelled, "Forward, men! Captain, now I know what hell feels like," the admiral said. "I feel like I'm baking in this armor."

The admiral scanned the burned area. "No doubt about it. We've cleared a path. The natives have to know we're coming, but with no obstacles to contend with, we've shortened our marching time."

As dawn broke, a palace guard awoke King Cocom. "My King, there are flames in the distance, and they come this way."

"What?" King Cocom asked, shaking sleep from his head.

"My King, the jungle burns."

"From where?" the king asked.

"From the shore. Near the strange canoe."

"Stay here," the nude king said to his wife as he walked to the edge of the terrace. He stared at the distant flames, sniffed the smoke, and then shook his head. "This is an evil omen. There has been no fire in the sky. This is man's fire."

"What should I do, My King?"

"Alert the villagers. The flames must not reach the village. Blow the conchs."

With the conch's mournful sound lingering in his ears, King Cocom paced the terrace, waiting for his people to gather in the plaza. Shortly afterwards, the Most Holy One, his queen, and the great high priest walked onto the terrace.

"What is the disturbance?" the Most Holy One asked as a servant tied a loincloth on King Cocom.

King Cocom pointed toward the shore. "A fire. A bad one. An evil omen, I fear."

"Why do you think it's evil?" the great high priest asked.

King Cocom looked to the sky. "There is no sky fire to fall to the ground, and none of my people camp there. I fear this is man's work."

"Why would men burn the jungle?" the Most Holy One asked. "What is to be gained by such an act?"

"I don't know. Maybe it's an omen," King Cocom said.

Pacing, the king looked down on the growing crowd of his muttering villagers. He held up his arms to quiet the group. "Some of you may have already smelled smoke, for there is fire near the shore. The flames can be seen from this terrace. The fire is too large to extinguish, but we can keep it from the village. Go to the village edges and dig or gather anything that can burn. Move the debris away from the village then set a backfire."

King Cocom paced, collecting his thoughts. He stopped and walked to the center of the terrace where his guests waited. He called to the villagers. "We are fortunate to have two nearby bays and salt flats that will isolate the flames. I want twenty men to go to the south of each bay and start backfires. If we are lucky, we can save our food-bearing jungle. Now, see to it."

The crowd erupted in enthusiastic shouts of recognition of the task ahead then ran to fulfill the king's command. A lone bodyguard and two servants remained to serve their king. The other guards and servants joined the villagers who left to fight the fire.

The great high priest approached King Cocom. "Great King, I and your priests will go to the temple to implore the gods for protection against this fire and for the safety of your people."

"Thank you. We will all pray for protection. For now, there is nothing more to do. We wait word from our chiefs."

"Most Holy One," King Cocom said, "I'm sorry you must be bothered with such matters."

"Most gracious King, you are guilt free. We will pray for the gods' assistance."

Chapter 27

Approaching the village, the admiral watched locals hectically running about, yelling as they raked debris and extinguished small fires caused by flying embers. "They are too busy to bother with us," he said.

"They're starting a backfire," the captain said, taking his helmet off to wipe his brow. "That'll keep them out of our way, but this smoke is bothersome. We should move into the village as quickly as possible."

"I agree, but let's not tire the men so much they can't fight."

"Yes sir, but can we move a little faster?"

The admiral motioned for the soldiers to gather around. "Men, we need to take advantage of the situation and get to the village now." He slapped a soldier on the shoulder. "Let's move smartly."

The soldiers entered the village in three phalanxes, passing a few villagers who dug weeds and brush to create a firebreak.

The admiral headed to the largest temple. Making a thunderous sound, he ran up its steps and into what he believed to be a treasury. Inside, he encountered Noh Halach Ahkin and other priests performing a ritual. They were dressed in feathered regalia and wore a hoard of gold, jade, and silver. The priests noted the admiral's presence, but continued their ritual. However, the admiral's rummaging and looting gold-filled niches must have become too intrusive because the priests stopped their activities, stared at him with apparent disgust, and then left.

The priests were followed by the admiral. For a moment, he and Noh Halach Ahkin stared at each other. Abruptly, the admiral grabbed at the priest's gold bracelet. He blocked the admiral's hand, removed the bracelet, and handed it to him.

"Nice," the admiral said, admiring its brilliance. He pointed to the priest's other bracelet. He removed it and slammed it into the admiral's outstretched hand.

"The necklace too," the admiral said, reaching for the priest's necklace.

"Ma'!" the great high priest said, placing his hands over his necklace and shaking his head. The other priests stood silently as the elderly priest gripped his necklace as the admiral pried at the old priest's hands.

"Very well," the admiral said, drawing his sword.

Before Noh Halach Ahkin could react, the admiral plunged his sword into the priest's abdomen. He gasped and yelled as blood gushed from the wound. The other priests looked on in horror. As the dying priest fell backwards, the admiral withdrew his sword and yanked free the priest's necklace.

The observing soldiers apparently assumed the stabbing of Noh Halach Ahkin was a call to action. They stared at the remaining priests who shook with fear as they fell pleadingly to their knees. No longer questioning their duty, the soldiers stabbed them.

"Clear out the niches inside," the admiral said. "Put the gold in the basket in the corner."

"I can't, Admiral," a solider called from inside. "It's filled with gold."

"Then we've hit a gold mine. We're rich—very rich." The admiral scanned the room for another basket. "There isn't another basket here, but I saw some near the foot of this temple. Get them."

"What about the other priests?" a soldier asked, staring at the mayhem and blood pooling on the terrace.

"Kill them if you find them but take their gold and search every inch of this and the other pyramids for hidden treasures."

The admiral took a gold vessel from a niche. He smiled and fingered its images of cats and alligators as he climbed down to the plaza. Moments later, two men arrived with three baskets of gold from the temple.

"Take those to *my* cabin," the admiral ordered. Looking across the plaza, he saw the captain and his men scurrying up the steps of the building where he had dined with King Cocom. The admiral ran toward the palace. *I can't have those soldiers hiding any of my gold under their armor. I've got to protect it.* "Captain! Stop!" the admiral yelled, his armor clanging as he ran.

On hearing the order, the captain stopped on the palace steps.

The admiral rattled up the steps to the captain.

"Is there anything wrong, Admiral?"

"No. Everything is golden."

"Glad you could join us. I guess you found gold in that building."

"A gold mine," the admiral said, catching his breath. "All kinds of gold."

"I'm happy to hear that." The captain looked up the palace steps. "Bet we find some here too."

"I know we will. You search the far end. I'll

take the lieutenant with me."

King Cocom's bodyguard called to his ruler. "My King, we are invaded by the silver-skins."

"What? Why would they come now?"

"They take everything," the guard said. "All the valuables."

The king donned his authority necklace, loincloth, and gold bracelets. "There must be a mistake. I'll talk to them and their god-man."

"My King," the guard said, his torch shaking from fright, "the whitehaired god-man is not with them. Be careful."

"Surely, they mean us no harm.

A ripping sound emanated from the king's cloth door, startling him. In charged the admiral, sword in hand, accompanied by four silver-skins.

The king's bodyguard stepped forward. In one hand he held a torch; in the other, he held a club edged with obsidian blades.

One silver-skin drew his weapon as the king yelled to his bodyguard. "Stop!"

The admiral approached the astonished and shaking king and said something while pointing to the king's bracelets.

The king pointed at his bracelet and then to the admiral. The admiral nodded.

King Cocom handed over his right bracelet.

The admiral snatched the four inch wide bracelet then pointed to the king's left bracelet.

Reluctantly, the king handed over his second bracelet.

The admiral smirked and pointed to the king's authority necklace.

Shocked at the request, the king looked at his

bodyguard. "He can't be asking for my necklace?"

"He is, My King."

"No."

The admiral extended his hand, ready to snatch the necklace.

The bodyguard dropped his torch then swung his club at the admiral. Grazing the admiral's wrist, the club opened a small wound. The admiral stared at the bodyguard as the king retreated.

A drop of the admiral's blood fell on the floor. Without warning, he plunged his sword into the bodyguard. He dropped his club and grasped his abdomen as the admiral pulled his weapon from the slumping man.

King Cocom reeled with the dizziness of shock. His guard lay between him and the admiral, bleeding, moaning, and squirming.

The admiral stepped over the dying bodyguard and extended his hand toward the king's necklace.

"*Ma*," the king cried out, clutching his authority necklace. "I can't surrender this."

At that moment, Queen Xal, the Most Holy One, and Queen Ix Tzutz Nik entered the room. King Cocom glimpsed Hakum, club in hand, standing outside the doorway apparently on order of the Most Holy One. The arriving royals appeared shocked on seeing the bodyguard.

"What happened?" Queen Xal asked, taking a torch from a wall bracket. She knelt to evaluate the bleeding guard. A tear trailing down her cheek, she stared up at her husband. "He's dead," she said. "He served us many years and has died in your service. Who did this?"

"Greed," King Cocom said, pulling his wife to his side while staring at the admiral. "The silver-skins are after our treasures and this one wants my authority necklace."

Despite the queen's diminutive size, she approached the admiral while shaking her head and pointing at her husband's necklace. "You may not have his authority necklace. Our gold you may have but not his necklace."

"Quiet, Xal," King Cocom said, pulling her arm.

The admiral stared at her, looking puzzled. He hastily glanced at his soldiers and shrugged as if to ask, 'What did she say?'

The foreigners shook their heads

Xal held her torch toward her husband. He took it. His wife removed her bracelets then pulled the jade and gold figures from her skirt and breast cover. She removed her ear plugs then held everything toward the admiral. He smiled and took the loot, pushing it behind his breastplate.

A collective sigh of relief rose from the royals as the queen returned to her husband's side then took the torch from his hand.

King Cocom shook as the admiral spoke to his men then walked to the Most Holy One, grasped his unadorned wrist, pulled it to eye level, and pointed at it.

The Most Holy One, understanding the admiral's desire for gold, pointed toward the door. The admiral pushed the bare wrist so forcibly toward the doorway that the Most Holy One's body turned in that direction. The admiral then pushed him through the doorway.

As the admiral exited the relatively bright room, he did not see Hakum hugging the exterior wall to the right of the doorway. Barefooted, he crept up behind the admiral and struck his head with a club. Hakum swung with such force he lost his grip sending the club flying into the night.

The admiral's silver crown may have prevented a skull fracture, but the blow caused him to stumble, drop his weapon, and topple off the terrace. No Mayan had heard such sounds as those of the admiral rolling down ninety steps to his death.

Unceremoniously, the Most Holy One hugged Hakum. "You saved my life!"

They ended their embrace and looked in dismay toward the room the Most Holy One had just left. The other silver-skins walked onto the terrace, pushing King Cocom, Queen Xal, and Queen Ix Tzutz Nik ahead at sword point. Queen Xal and one foreigner carried a torch.

"What happened?" the lieutenant asked his comrade. He walked to the edge of the terrace, held his torch high, and peered at the admiral lying on the plaza. He lay in a twisted heap of metal that reflected the faint moonlight as his helmet could still be heard rolling away. "I can't see much in the dark, but he's not moving. I should go down and see if he's alive?"

"He couldn't survive that," the lieutenant said, peering over the terrace. "but, Juan, go down there. The admiral has a lot of gold tucked in his armor. We should take it. I'll take care of matters here. There's more gold to be had."

Brandishing his weapon, the lieutenant pushed his sword on the other presumed king's bare wrist and tilted his head questioningly to the left. "Where's your gold?"

The native pointed to a doorway thirty paces away.

The Most Holy One said, "Hakum, lead the way to my quarters. I'll follow. I'm sure the foreigner with the torch will follow us."

Hakum faced the soldier and pointed to the stranger's torch.

With his sword at the ready, the soldier handed Hakum the torch.

As Hakum led the way, the Most Holy One chanted, "When we get to my room, give me the torch." He hoped the foreigners thought he chanted a prayer. He continued chanting. "There is a club against the wall inside my door. Get it and hide it behind your back. I'll look for my gold and keep the torchlight in the silver-skin's eyes, so he is blinded. When I tell you, strike him, but we can't let him fall and alarm the guards. Cough if you understand."

Hakum coughed.

As the Most Holy One neared his door, he stopped chanting, tapped Hakum on the shoulder, and then took the torch. The silver-skin poked his sword in the Most Holy One's back. The king and Hakum entered the room with the soldier close behind. When the king bent over to get his bracelets, the soldier's greed surfaced. He pushed the king aside and gathered the gold. At that moment, Hakum struck the guard on the head, dropped his club on a pillow, and then helped the king keep the unconscious man upright.

"The gods are with us," the Most Holy One said.

"Now what?"

"Get his weapon." The Most Holy One said and adjusted his authority necklace so most of it hung down his back. "Put the enemy's weapon under the rear part of my necklace so the crosspiece will hold it against my back."

"That's good," the king said, settling the weapon between his shoulder blades. "Now, remove the man's metal sandals. I don't want them scraping the floor. After that, loosely retie the leather binding of his arm coverings, and then I'll be ready."

"For what?"

"You'll see."

The king pushed his forearms under the soldier's armpits then into his arm coverings so he could hold the foreigner upright. The Most Holy One's hands almost overlapped those of the soldier. The king held the torch in his right hand and had Hakum hang gold necklaces in the foreigner's extended left hand. The king hoped the torchlight would draw the waiting soldiers' eyes to the necklaces and ignore their unconscious comrade.

Hakum's jaw sagged on hearing the plan.

"Let's get him more upright," the king said, struggling with the man's weight. "I didn't realize how heavy he would be."

One of the soldiers on the terrace called out with unknown words.

Not knowing what had been said or how to reply, the Most Holy One mumbled loudly, and then he and Hakum got the soldier better supported on the king's forearms.

"Let's go," the king said. "I'll use my feet to carry his, but I'll need your help. Put your free hand between me and the stranger's back. Grip his cinch and help me hold him upright."

Side-by-side, Hakum and the Most Holy One squeezed through the doorway. Hakum mumbled something and appeared to hand his torch to the soldier while hiding a club behind his own back.

King Cocom, Queen Xal and Queen Ix Tzutz Nik waited on the terrace, quietly fearing pain of death. King Cocom watched the Most Holy One and the approaching soldier then chanted to the queens, "Something isn't right. I pray the Most Holy One has a plan."

"I'm sure he does," Queen Ix Tzutz Nik chanted. "My husband won't disappoint us, but the stranger's head moves strangely?"

"Hopefully he's dead and these foreigners only watch that dangling necklace," King Cocom chanted. "We should all chant, so the foreigners will watch us while the Most Holy One does what he wants." King Cocom nudged Queen Xal's arm and chanted, "Let me have your torch. I want to hold it, so its light blinds our guards."

"Good," Queen Ix Tzutz Nik chanted, "Let's all chant—confuse these silver-skins."

Despite the harshness of their voices, King Cocom and the queens chanted a common prayer of supplication for a good deed.

Hakum and the Most Holy One continued toward the royals and their guards.

The Most Holy One chanted, "Hakum, I can no longer hold the torch. Take it and hold it in front of us."

Hakum took the torch and chanted, "I'm sorry I can't help more with your burden, My King."

"Don't worry. We do what we can."

The Most Holy One chanted for the gods help while he, Hakum, and the unconscious foreigner moved within ten paces of the silver-skins guarding King Cocom. The two strangers guarding the royals shielded their eyes from the light of the torches.

The Most Holy One shook the guard's hand and gold, drawing the attention of the foreigners. As one man reached for a necklace, the Most Holy One pushed the unconscious man onto the foreigner, knocking him over. Weighed down by the unconscious man and his armor, the downed stranger tried to push the floppy man off his waist as the Most Holy One pulled the sword from behind his neck and plunged it into the struggling foreigner's left armpit and lung.

King Cocom watched with awe as the Most Holy One freed himself from the unconscious stranger's remaining arm covering.

Hakum swung his club at the head of a surprised foreigner but missed. King Cocom tripped the stranger who fell to the terrace. Hakum clubbed the tripped man's head, but he continued to move. Queen Xal, apparently overcome with fear, stood stone still. However, Queen Ix Tzutz Nik grabbed King Cocom's torch and struck the downed soldier's head.

Chapter 28

Captain Rodriguez and twelve soldiers searched the far end of King Cocom's palace but found nothing of value. Suddenly, they heard distant noises sounding like struck metal.

"I sense something bad has happened," the captain said. He had lead the search through a maze of rooms but did not remember which room connected to which. He now searched frantically for an exit. Finally, he reached the terrace. Fifty paces away, two burning torches lay on the terrace. "I don't like the looks of this," he said. "Men, ready your weapons."

The soldiers readied their matchlocks and slowly walked toward the five natives silhouetted by the fluttering torches. A female picked up a torch making it possible for the captain to see his fallen men and two natives waving soldiers' swords. A third native shook a club.

The captain stopped twelve paces from the natives and fired his matchlock at the male who had hosted his soldiers' dinner. Shot, the native dropped his weapon, clutched his abdomen, and crumbled to the terrace. The woman standing nearby grabbed at him as he fell onto the terrace, revealing a jagged hole in his back that bled profusely.

Approaching the other native male and his

presumed wife, the captain said, "You were at that dinner."

Oblivious to the captain's words, the natives stared at the fallen man whose blood pooled on the terrace.

The captain handed his rifle to one of his men and said, "Reload it."

The standing native leader trembled at seeing the smoking fire stick. He fell to his knees, pulling on his wife's arm to do the same. The other woman remained beside the shot man, wailing and cradling his head in her lap as blood pooled around her.

The captain nudged the shot native with the point of his armored shoe. "He's dead." He pulled the shot man's authority necklace from his neck then pulled the kneeling woman's necklace from her neck. She offered no resistance.

"Enough crying," the captain said, using his bloody foot to push the crying woman away from the dead man.

The remaining male leader spoke to his wife then both held their authority necklaces toward the foreign leader.

The captain snatched the lumpy necklaces then handed them to a soldier. "Keep these safe." He toe nudged a downed soldier to see if he was dead while telling a soldier to collect the gold scattered about the terrace. Kneeling beside the second motionless soldier, the captain said, "He's unconscious, but fortunately, his scalp has stopped bleeding. You," the captain said to a soldier, "take this man to the ship for treatment."

"Captain," a soldier yelled, pointing toward the base of the palace, "the admiral is down."

"See to him," the captain ordered.

Captain Rodriguez paced before the cowering natives, wondering who they were. He pushed his toe under the chin of the shot man and lifted his head. "He's dead."

Hakum apparently saw this act as an affront to the dead man and hurled himself and his torch at the captain. He jumped back, but the torch glazed his metal sleeve as the native's momentum caused him to fall to the terrace—the torch still in his hand. Hakum rose slowly to his knees.

Captain Rodriguez reached toward a soldier. "My matchlock!"

The soldier handed him the weapon.

Standing three paces from the kneeling man, the captain stared at the torch flames reflected from Hakum's fear-filled eyes. The native slumped in silent supplication and loosened his grip, letting his torch roll away as he held his breath and closed his eyes. The captain raised his matchlock waist high and shot the man in the chest. His death yell equaled the roar of the matchlock.

Queen Ix Tzutz Nik screamed and clasped her hands over her ringing ears as Hakum fell dead. The Most Holy One sprang to his feet to care for his servant, but the foreigner swung the butt of his fire stick, striking the Most Holy One's head. Stunned, he fell backwards.

Queen Ix Tzutz Nik reached to help her husband, but he said, "Stay there. They will kill you."

Crying, the queen crawled to her husband's side. "What is to become of us?"

The king rubbed his head. "I wish I knew." Looking skyward, he said, "Gods, leave us not in this moment."

"Fear not," the queen whispered, holding her husband's face. "You are the one who speaks to the gods for me and our people. We must trust them and ask for their help."

The queen sang a Mayan hymn of supplication. Queen Xal joined in the mournful plea as the Most Holy One rubbed his head.

"Quiet!" the captain yelled and kicked the women. He turned to a soldier. "Take these natives to the plaza and wait for me. I and the other men will search the remainder of the palace."

The captain found more gold, silver, and jade objects, which were dumped into a basket and carried to the plaza where the three prisoners waited.

"Give you any trouble?" the captain asked, nodding toward the natives.

"No, Captain," a soldier said. "Quiet as a ship's mouse."

The captain stood in front of one of the women and pondered her face. *She's the wife of the dead leader on the terrace. She attended that dinner.* He walked in front of the male prisoner. "Your clothes are different. I bet you're from a different village, aren't you?"

The cowering man glanced up at him but said nothing.

"Soldier, bring me a piece of gold," the captain called to the soldier guarding the plunder.

The soldier pulled a jaguar statue from a basket then handed it to the captain. He examined it then held it in front of the male prisoner who stared at it for a moment. The captain repeatedly pointed to the statue, the man, and then several directions.

The prisoner muttered something to his wife.

Visibly shaking, she whispered to her husband, nodded, and then looked at the ground.

The male captive said something in a quivering voice, nodded, and then sat quietly, shaking. He cleared his throat, looked at the foreign leader, and then said, "Dzibilchaltun."

The woman clutching the native man's wrist exhaled a sigh, shrugged, and said, "Ma'!" A tear ran down her cheek.

"Well, what is it, native?" the captain asked, tired of hearing the man and woman babble.

The male prisoner pointed at the statue then west. "Dzibilchaltun."

"Their gold must be in that direction," the captain said to his men.

The male prisoner touched the captain's leg and then used his fingers in a walking motion to indicate the group would have to travel a great distance. Next, he placed his hands under his tilted head, apparently indicating sleep, and then pointed to the ground.

The captain thought for a moment. "I think he wants to sleep the night here and travel a great distance tomorrow." Captain Rodriguez pointed at two soldiers then at the palace. "Make camp in there."

The captain looked around the plaza then said to Second Lieutenant Ortiz, "Have the trumpeter, sound assembly. I want to see what treasures the men have found. They can then rest for tomorrow's trek."

A short time later, all but three soldiers assembled on the plaza. The soldier, sent to check on the admiral, reported, "The admiral is dead."

The captain crossed himself. "Then, I'm in charge."

The soldiers snapped to attention and saluted Captain Rodriguez.

A newly arrived soldier pushed a red basket toward the captain. "Sir. You should see this." The soldier opened the container and held up a twelve inch long silver snake statue. "These things were taken from natives in that smaller stucco building."

"Good work," the captain said, examining the statue.

Manuel, the oldest soldier, dragged a tall basket before the captain. "I collected these weapons. We don't want the locals to have them. The wooden ones I threw on the natives' backfires."

"Good work," the captain said. "Men, we'll sleep the night in the palace. Lieutenant, find a room with one door and no windows for the prisoners then select two men to guard them."

Pushed and shoved, the prisoners walked up the palace steps and then into a room.

As the soldiers moved into the palace, the captain noted how quiet the village had become. *Hope everyone's fighting fire and unaware of our presence.*

Chapter 29

The Most Holy One and the two queens wiped sweat. The small hot room had no ventilation, no pillows to cushion the stone floor or cloth doors for privacy. No one slept well. Worry for the lives of his wife and Queen Xal filled the king's racing mind. *Gods, keep us safe . . . let us see Dzibilchaltun again.*

From the noise in the adjoining room, the king presumed the silver-skins were donning their metal coverings.

The queens, huddled together, asked, "What do you think they will do with us?"

"I wish I knew," the king said. "Just stay quiet."

A third foreigner rattled onto the terrace.

Looking between the legs of the guards outside the cell doorway, the king saw blue-grey smoke fill the sky, obscuring the fading stars as dawn broke. Off to the west, flames reached high into the sky.

"Too bad the natives haven't extinguished the fire," the captain said to a guard. "It burns where we need to travel."

"Captain, we could sail west and avoid the flames and more importantly the *natives*."

"Good idea." The captain looked around. "Has anyone found food?"

"I'll go see, Captain," the guard said.

Moments later, two soldiers presented a shallow reed basket to the captain. "Look at these," the guard said, taking a bite. "They're delicious."

"I know. I ate one," the captain said, grabbing the largest mamey. He took a bite and spat out the brown skin. "Strange, how quiet this place is."

Watching a dozen buzzards circling overhead, the captain knew they had spotted the native leader's body on the back terrace.

The captain walked into the cell and offered each native a mamey. The widow turned her head, refusing the fruit. The other woman and man, huddled together, took the mameys and ate them.

"Who knows how long it will be before you eat again," the captain said as he held a mamey toward the widow.

She shook her head, sneered, and looked away.

The other woman stopped eating and said something to the widow, but she shook her head and looked away.

Seeing the mamey rejected, the captain kept it and walked to the terrace where his soldiers ate in view of the prisoners. "Eat up, men. We're taking the prisoners to the ship and sailing west. That way we'll avoid land hazards and natives, but we should leave before the sun is much higher." He pointed to three soldiers. "Keep your swords at the natives' backs as we head for the ship."

The captain stared with disbelief at the fire damage just beyond the edge of the village. The jungle had been burned clear of any living thing. Plumes of grey smoke reached for the sky. Each man's footstep stirred ashes, creating low hanging clouds that made breathing difficult.

After walking for some time, everyone could see the ship in the distance. The women wore a look of shock as they saw it for the first time.

"Halt!" the captain ordered and pointed to the men nearest him.

The prisoners froze in place, perhaps expecting something horrible to happen.

"You six," the captain said, "carry the baskets of gold. The first carriers need a rest." The captain called to another soldier, "Let's have some of those fruits."

A soldier presented the basket of mameys. The captain removed three and took them to the prisoners. The male and his presumed wife accepted the fruits.

The other woman turned her head as the captain approached her. Holding a mamey in his left hand, he nudged her elbow. She took the mamey but threw it away then spat on the captain and threw herself on him like a bear attacking a deer. Startled, the captain pushed her to the ground, drew his sword, and rammed it into her abdomen. "Thankless wench." He withdrew his sword from her bleeding wound.

She panted and gripped her abdomen. Holding up a bloody hand, she stared at it and then extended it toward the male prisoner as if asking him to save her. Her arm suddenly fell and her jaw dropped in a silent scream.

A scream from the other woman startled the captain. He turned to see her hug her husband. She shook violently while her husband stroked her head and said, "Saaaa. Saaaa."

The captain pushed the male prisoner in the direction of the ship. "Let's go."

When the captain neared the beach, the female prisoner stared at the ship and stopped in her tracks. For much of the trek, she had stared at the ground. Now, she saw the ship close up and appeared awe struck.

"Move," the captain said, poking her in the back. "Keep moving."

The Most Holy One had been the first of the remaining royals to see the ship from the shore days earlier, but now he, and his wife, were prisoners on board. He trembled with each step he took on the flat-logged deck. Having never seen such boards, he took deliberate steps, watching where he placed his feet. Surrounded by unknown objects, odd noises, and strange shapes, he looked terrified.

"Captain, where do we put the prisoners?" a soldier asked.

"The brig."

"But Captain, the thief is in there."

"So? There's room for more."

"Aye, Captain."

Father Garcés stood by the rail counting each soldier who climbed aboard. "Captain, my count is two men short and where's the admiral?"

"Father, he and two men were lost."

"Then I must go to administer last rites."

Looking into a basket of gold, the captain said, "Padre, there's no time."

"But I must go. They must have last rites."

The captain glared at the priest. "No! Say a requiem for them on board."

Father Garcés crossed himself and huffed away. "And I'll pray for *your* soul as well."

The king almost fell down the steps leading

below deck. A guard pushed him and the queen toward a large cage. She covered her mouth to calm a scream as she glanced back and forth between her husband and a bound white man in the cage.

One guard unlocked the cell. Another poked the king with a sword.

Crying, the queen followed her husband into the cage. They cowered in a corner and exchanged glances with the white prisoner who wore smelly, tattered clothes. He had strange rattling bindings on his ankles and wrists and muttered strange sounds. "I wished I knew what he said," the queen muttered.

"So do I, but we must be concerned for ourselves."

A stranger locked the cage and left.

The king gripped the queen's arm. "This canoe is moving. Do nothing to alarm these devils. We must think of our children and how we can protect them and our people from these *hach k'as*." The king hugged her. "I wish I knew how to get out of here, but where would we go? We are too far at sea to swim to shore. If we escaped this cage and were found, we would be killed with no chance to save our children or people. No, we must be alert for other chances to escape." The king took a deep breath then said, "I'm concerned there might be a similar canoe with silver-skins already at Dzibilchaltun's shore, doing who knows what."

Shaking, the queen struggled to speak. "I would never have thought we would face such horrors as being caged. Gods bless us, for there is nothing we can do."

"We should pray for deliverance." The king said, examining several bars of the cage. "Strange. These are cold and unyielding—not like bamboo. They feel like that strange sphere King Cocom showed us."

The low top of the cage prevented the royals from standing. In order to exercise their legs, they hung from a bar and extended their legs forward and side-ways. As the king finished his exercises, a silver-skin unlocked the cage then motioned for the king to follow him.

The king thought, *Gods let this not be my day of execution.*

Shaking, the king hugged his crying wife. Glancing back at her with fear and uncertainty, he left the cage, wondering if he would return.

As the king stepped onto the top floor, the foreign leader smoothed sand in a shallow box that sat on top of something resembling a fat tree trunk.

The leader said something to the king then the guard poked him with his weapon.

Driven by sword point, the king walked toward the foreign leader. They stared at each other for a moment then the foreigner pointed to the sand. He drew the outline of a pyramid and then pointed to the building then the prisoner. The leader tilted his head left and placed his hands alongside his cheek, mimicking the sleeping position. "Where do you sleep?" he asked, pointing between the king and the drawing.

The king thought, *Does he want to know where I sleep?* With a trembling finger, he pointed to the center of the pyramid image.

"I'm glad you understand," the leader said and then smiled. He pointed between the shore and the prisoner several times, raised his palms to the sky, and then shrugged as if to ask 'where?'

The king shook his head.

The foreigner pointed farther west and then looked questioningly at the prisoner who shook his head. The leader pointed toward the far horizon and the figure in the sand. The prisoner nodded then shook when the leader yelled strange words.

"Prepare to sail a full day," the captain yelled. "Return this native to the hole."

Unharmed, the king returned to his wife, causing the cowering queen to cry with joy. "I'm so happy you're safe," she said. "What did they do to you? What did they want?"

"I think the leader wanted to know where I sleep."

"Why?"

"They want to go there to take our gold."

"May the gods bless us," the queen said. "Their need for that information suggests there is not another canoe in our waters."

Staring at the white prisoner, the king said "I wonder what this man has done to be here."

"Since he has no one to care for him, maybe he has done something horrible and is to starve to death."

"I hope that is not our fate," the king said and hugged the queen. "We must not upset the foreigners. They will kill us."

Night fell, but the king only dozed. He thought of death, pain, the white prisoner and their mutual suffering.

Suddenly someone yelled from above.

"What's that?" the queen asked, squeezing the king's arm with sweaty hands.

"I don't know, but we've stopped moving."

"I sense danger," the queen murmured in a quivering voice.

The king crawled to the end of the cage and peered out a square opening in the canoe. "I can see the shore. Perhaps we sleep the night here."

"I hope so. The canoe's motion sickens me."

"I felt the same sickness," the king said, "but now I'm hungry. I wonder if they'll feed us."

"Anything would do, but I need water."

Minutes later, the clang of a silver-skin's coverings rang out as two of them approached the cage. One carried a wide flattened log holding several wooden objects. Another silver-skin opened the cage. With his weapon drawn, the same stranger motioned for the prisoners to move to the back of the cage. The other foreigner placed the flattened log on the cage floor. It held three wooden cups of water and wooden discs with unknown foods. The guard pushed the objects toward the queen and then the foreigners locked the cage and left.

The queen quickly drank a cup of water.

Sniffing the food, the king said, "It looks bad, but it smells good."

"What if it's poison?" the queen asked.

"Better dead than starving in this cage."

"I wonder what our children are eating?" the queen asked, dipping her finger in the brownish, lumpy mush on the disc. She cautiously sniffed it then touched her finger to her tongue. "What a strange taste."

The king consumed his food then hand-fed the white prisoner and gave him water.

Chapter 30

As dawn broke, the king heard silver-skins moving overhead, apparently preparing for a new day. Someone yelled, and moments later the canoe's awnings flapped.

"Now what?" the queen asked, gripping the king's arm.

"I don't know, but we move. Perhaps the yelling was to ask their gods to move us."

As the king finished breakfast, the foreign leader approached the caged prisoners. A guard opened the cage and motioned for the king to follow him up the steps.

"Return to me safe," the queen said, letting her loosening grip slide down the king's arm.

The king and foreigner leader went through a series of sand drawings apparently to help the leader estimate the time needed to get to the native's home sea. Seemingly satisfied with the prisoner's input, the leader called to a man standing behind a large vertical wooden circle at the rear of the canoe. He turned the circle and yelled something to the leader. The white leader turned to his men and pointed toward the stairs leading below. "Take the native to his cage."

The heat of the day bore down hard on the

tossing, creaking canoe and the royals. Wind, which pushed the canoe westward, failed to enter the holes along its sides or reach the king. Even for him, accustomed to jungle heat, the temperature rose to unbearable levels. Odors from rotting food and excrement from slop buckets added to the misery.

Suddenly, the canoe shuddered, and a loud rumbling noise rose from the canoe's front left side.

"We've stopped," the king said, staring out a wall hole. "The silver-skins are lowering smaller canoes."

Moments later, a guard ran to the cage, unlocked it, yelled something, and pointed his weapon at the king.

What now? The king thought.

The queen hugged him, but he escaped her embrace. "Don't worry. I'll return soon."

"Yes, to save our children."

The guard forced the king to the upper floor and pushed him toward the leader who stood beside the sandbox. He said something, shrugged, and then drew the king's attention to the sketch drawn the day before.

The king stared at the drawing but said nothing.

The guard poked his back.

The leader pointed at the sketch then the shoreline. He waited for the king to react. The leader said something in the king's ear, shook the king's arm, and the guard poked his back.

The king pointed to the right of a clump of distant, low growing trees.

The captain directed the lieutenant's attention to the trees. "Alright men. Get into the longboats. We'll land to the right of those trees. Get to it. Take the prisoner with you."

Lieutenant Ortiz waved his men forward. "Be quick. Treasures await."

Thunder-like clatter of armor echoed around the ship as the soldiers climbed over the rail, down the net, and then loaded into longboats.

A stiff wind caused the longboats to bob like dead fish on the waves and bang against the ship as loading began. Slowly, the filled longboats headed for shore. The last boat waited for the captain and four soldiers, two of which guarded the prisoner. One man remained onboard to protect the gold.

Suddenly, Father Garcés waved from the deck. "Wait! I'm going with you." He climbed down the net. Almost falling, he stopped to free the toe of his sandal from a horizontal strand of netting.

"Faster, Padre," the captain yelled.

In his haste, the priest lost his footing and plunged into the sea. He yelled and flailed like a drowning man. A soldier grabbed the priest's scapular then pulled him toward the longboat. Inside, the priest sat down on a bench and crossed himself while buckets of water drained from his clothing. Panting, he said, "I must learn to swim."

"Saint Christopher must be your guardian," the captain said, sending sea water flying as he slapped the priest's shoulder. "Okay rowers we've fallen behind. Put your backs to it.

Exhausted, the rowers got their boats to shore. One soldier from each boat jumped into the water then pushed the longboats on shore.

"Help the padre ashore," the captain yelled, while scanning the narrow beach lined by dense scrub brush. "Listen, everyone. Hopefully, the prisoner will lead us to his village." The captain pointed to two soldiers. "Guard him. If he escapes, someone is going to get very wet. Know what I mean?"

One soldier mumbled, "Yeah. Keel hauling."

"I heard that," the captain said. "Go see if there is a path to get through those bushes. The rest of us will wait here."

Moments later the soldier returned. "Captain, the brush is too dense to cross in this area."

"Then we look farther to the west."

The group trudged through soft sand at a snail's pace.

We'll bake in this armor, the captain thought.

After walking for two hours, the captain saw a native man, seven hundred paces ahead.

"What should we do about him?" Lieutenant Ortiz asked the captain.

"Nothing. We don't want him alerting anyone of our presence."

The captain slowly approached the backside of the lithe, dark short man.

When the captain was four hundred paces from the man, he turned and gawked at the strangers. The man shook and dropped his fish-laden vine as if he had seen something supernatural. As the captain removed his helmet, the native dropped to the sand.

The native prisoner suddenly pulled away from his guards and ran past the captain to the cowering fisherman.

"Don't let him get away," the captain yelled.

The prisoner lifted the frightened fisherman's head and spoke to him.

The fisherman kissed the prisoner's hand then bowed his head.

A guard fired his matchlock into the air. Fearful,

the natives froze where they stood. With matchlocks at the ready, two soldiers grabbed each native by the arm. When the captain arrived, he slapped the prisoner, knocking him to the beach. The captain shouted to his lieutenant, "Guard these men as we continue."

The guard holding the arm of the fisherman repositioned his grip. This allowed the fisherman to escape then run west along the dense brush lining the beach.

The other prisoner remained in the grip of two guards.

Several soldiers chased the fisherman, but the weight of their armor made running impossible. Two guards fired their matchlocks, but the fisherman had run beyond their range.

"Padre, you're wearing nothing heavy," the captain said, "catch him. Don't let him get away."

The priest kicked off his sandals and ran while removing his scapular. After a short chase, the middle-age priest tired. Two minutes later, he stopped. Hands on his knees, he panted as he caught his breath.

"Padre, why did you stop," the captain called as he approached the priest.

"Sorry, Captain. This old body is no match for younger legs."

"Damn it, Padre, better pray we intercept him, or we may have a fight we don't want."

Captain Rodriguez waved for Lieutenant Ortiz. "Send the youngest soldier to follow the native's footprints. Find where he goes inland then have the soldier fire his matchlock to let us know. We'll catch up."

The selected soldier jogged along the beach then disappeared around a distant bend in the beach. A short time later, a shot rang out.

"Captain," a soldier yelled, "I see our man ahead. He's waving."

"Good. Let's hurry. I'm roasting in this armor."

The waiting soldier addressed the captain. "Look, Sir. There's an opening here with two exit paths. One goes south and the other southwest. Both reveal many footprints."

The captain divided the soldiers into two groups. One went south. The other traveled southwest.

The captain's group and prisoner trudged cautiously through the barren shrubs surrounding a large clearing while listening for unusual sounds.

A dust devil, twirling in the center of the clearing, attracted his interest.

Strange, the captain thought. *It's too quiet here.*

Three quarters around the clearing, a rustling sound arose from the captain's right. He put a finger to his lips, and pointed west. "Shhhh," he said. All eyes darted toward the sounds as the soldiers held their matchlocks at the ready. The captain's anxiety mounted as the sounds grew louder. "Hold your fire," he whispered, raising his matchlock to his shoulder and aiming toward the sounds.

Suddenly, the padre yelled, "Captain. It's our men."

A sigh of relief rose as the captain saw his comrades.

The lieutenant waved.

Father Garcés crossed himself.

"See anything, Lieutenant?" the captain asked.

"Nothing except a waterhole, sir."

"Good. We'll need water. Fall in with us." The captain pointed to the east. The village is nearby."

The captain arrived at the southern end of the

clearing and felt relieved about having no encounters with villagers.

"Should we move ahead or rest?" the lieutenant asked the captain.

"Keep moving," he said. "If there is an ambush, I want the safety of village buildings."

The captain offered his canteen to the prisoner, but he shook his head. "Can't say I didn't ask you," the captain said and then took a drink. He offered his canteen to the lieutenant and said, "At times, I think I'd feel better being as naked this prisoner. He doesn't contend with hot armor."

Chuckling, the lieutenant said, "Believe me, I've thought about it."

Forced at sword point, the prisoner moved ahead of the wary captain as everyone traversed the path connecting the clearing to the village.

Chapter 31

Arriving at the prisoner's presumed home village, the captain stepped onto its whitewashed plaza. He noted the prisoner appeared ill at ease.

Worried, the captain scanned the empty plaza. "Men, be alert." Only the rattle of armor echoed across the expansive space. "Perhaps the villagers have fled," the captain said, shielding his eyes from sunlight reflected off the plaza floor and whitewashed buildings. "This light rivals the shine of our armor."

"There's more to dazzle the eye here than in the last village," the lieutenant said.

"Captain," Father Garcés said, "look at the menacing faces staring at us from these walls. I'll bet they're some kind of pagan gods. They make me uneasy—especially their red eyes." Father Garcés walked to the nearest human-like bas relief, stared at its red face, and ran his fingers over its elephantine nose. "Look at the size of those ears. Huge. Definitely Pagan." Suddenly, he spat on the figure then struck it with the sole of his sandal.

The padre's actions must have infuriated the prisoner. He pulled free of his guards, lunged at Father Garcés, and struck him in the face several times before soldiers could intervene.

Without warning, a hail of arrows fell on the foreigners. Arrowheads striking their armor sounded like pelting rain.

The soldiers formed a protective circle around the padre then fired matchlocks at anything that moved. The plaza quickly filled with smoke as the sounds of shots rang out.

In the confusion, the captain watched helplessly as the prisoner fled into a nearby building.

"Take cover," the captain yelled. "One man is to stay with Father Garcés. The rest of you, don't fire again unless you can aim at the enemy."

"What about the prisoner?" the lieutenant asked.

"Forget him. Defend yourself."

In a short time, the soldiers had shot eleven natives divided over four buildings' terraces.

Spent arrows lay scattered about the plaza. Fortunately for the captain, the arrows did no damage except for one soldier who took a hit in the hand.

The king ran up the steps of the Temple of the Six Dolls where his spirit doll had stood since he left for Chichen Itza many moons before. He ducked into the room at the top of the temple from which several villagers shot arrows at the enemy.

"Why are you here?" the king yelled to villagers. "You should have fled to the jungle."

"Most Holy One, it's me, Citu. I could not leave you alone to fight the white devils. A man came to Chalmuch and told us of the horror in X'Cambo, so I came to help. Your order to flee to the jungle reached us, but we could not simply hide."

"Thank you," the king said, peeking around a corner to see what the foreigners were doing. Nodding to the men in the room, he said, "We have to leave. Arrows simply bounce off the silver-skin coverings, and we can't survive the enemy's fire sticks."

Several foreigners ran to the Temple of Chaac, the rain god, on the east side of the plaza. Their leader took five of his men to the Temple of the Sky god, Tzacol, yelling as he ran.

"What strange sounds this enemy speaks," Citu said.

"Yes. Too bad we can't decipher them."

Each time a foreigner stuck his head out a doorway or window to fire a shot, villagers shot arrows at him.

Most of the arrows came from the Temple of Ah Mun, the Corn God.

"Who hides there?" the king asked Citu.

"Priests, several villagers, and Prince Hiayalael, My King."

"No!" the king cried out. "The prince should not be here."

Citu shook his head. "The prince refused to leave, and the priests wouldn't counter his wish."

"He is brave but not wise—nor are the priests. I must get him then flee to the jungle."

"I'll go with you, as will these villagers," Citu said.

"We should go down these back steps," the king said, pointing to the south.

"We must flee like hawks," Citu said waving to the villagers.

"But I must get my spirit doll," the king said. "I dare not risk its damage."

The king ran to his doll. He grabbed it, stuffed it into its storage bag, and then pulled its strap over his head. He raced to join Citu and six villagers who fled down the temple's southern steps.

Sprinting from building to building, the king avoided detection. Once he reached the rear of the Temple of Ah Mun, the king and Citu ran up its steps and entered its holy of holies where the priests, Prince Hiayalael, and eight villagers hid. Shocked to see the king, villagers bowed as the prince ran into his father's arms.

"My son," the king said, hugging the prince. "Why did you disobey my order?"

"I couldn't leave you with the enemy," the prince said. "I had to defend The Center."

The king addressed his warriors. "You two protect the prince's escape. The others and priests follow me. I've seen villagers shooting arrows from the back of the Temple of the Sun. They will provide cover for our escape."

Two villagers, near the front doorway of the Temple of Ah Mun, struck their chest with their fists. "With honor, we defend the royal family."

"Gods bless you," the king said, grasping his son's wrist then heading for the rear doorway. As he reached the last step of the temple, the plaza echoed with shots. He looked ahead to see a priest yell and fall. "Run, son! Run!" he yelled, each gripping the other's wrist. Another round of shots echoed through the jungle. The king thought, *They're close.*

The prince stumbled. He fell face first into the dirt, kicking up dust. The gold icon used to hold his pony tail flew off, rolling across the ground. His loosened hair fanned out over his back as he landed with a thud. In falling, he pulled his father on top of him.

The king thought, *He's turned his ankle.*

The king jumped to his feet. Using his left hand to support the prince's back, he lifted his son in his arms and continued a stumbling run. "Don't worry, son. I'll get you to safety."

The king felt something wet in his left hand. He pulled his son against his chest and examined his wet hand.

"Blood!" the king yelled, turning his face to the sky and crying. He pressed his hand over the wound to stem the bleeding then noted the prince had stopped breathing. The king slowed his pace, threw his shaking head backward, and cried, "Noooooo!"

Startled, the men covering the king's escape stared in horror as blood fell from their grieving king's hand. Suddenly, the king stumbled, dropped his son and then fell on top of him. Tears flowing, the king struggled to upright himself and lift his son.

"No, My King!" a priest called out. "You can do nothing for the prince. You must get to safety."

Shaking his head and watching in horror as blood inched its way from under the prince, the king cried, "No! I can't leave him here."

"Most Holy One, you must leave him," Citu said. "He is with the gods. He needs us no more. We can't help him. You must think of your people who need your leadership."

Pulled forward, the king wailed as he looked back at his son's crumpled body. A villager closed the prince's eyelids then followed the king into the jungle.

After running at great speed for several minutes, the tiring king said, "I must rest."

Bursting into tears, the king struck his thighs and chest and cried out. "My son. My son."

Several villagers tried to console the king, but Citu stopped them. "Give him a moment."

Having composed himself, the king caught his breath. "Citu, where are the princesses and the young prince?"

Several priests and villagers took them to the jungle, Most Holy One. I believe they're safe, but where is our queen?"

"The enemy holds her prisoner in a cage in a strange house that floats like a canoe on the ocean."

"A cage?" Citu asked. "Our queen is in a cage?"

"Yes, a prisoner. I have to free her. Will you go with me?"

"We will, Most Holy One. Guide us."

"We must get to the beach, while the enemy is busy searching for gold. That should give us time to rescue her."

Citu waved to some villagers. "Follow me." To the king, he said, "I know a shortcut and a waterhole where we can rest."

The king led the rescue party onto the beach. "That's the floating house," he said, pointing at the large canoe three hundred paces away.

"Such a strange sight," Citu said, staring in awe. "Their smaller canoes are there. We can use one to get to their floating house."

The king ran to the beached canoes. He knew these boats, but his men were in awe of their size and construction. The villagers timidly touched them and examined their parts.

Citu seemed surprised to see they were not made from one hollowed log.

"Hurry," the king said.

Several of the natives had difficulty boarding the chosen canoe. Xulu, almost tipped it as he struggled to get in. Mukul moved to Xulu's side of the canoe and dragged him in.

The king instructed the men on how to use the oars. Despite high waves and difficulty rowing, the men reached the floating house.

"We must climb this net," the king said. "Careful, the footing is difficult."

The king asked Xulu to remain in the canoe and hold onto the net. "We don't want this canoe to float away." Waving to the other men, he said, "Follow me."

The king demonstrated how to climb the net. He helped Mukul and Citu aboard, while scanning the house of the enemy. "We're alone," he said.

The king pointed to a doorway. "We must go through there. The queen is in a cage at the bottom of the steps."

A snoring white skin slept behind coiled ropes near the doorway. Beside him sat a drinking cup with a strange smelling liquid. Despite the king's presence, the man did not move.

"Makul, watch him," the king said.

As the king reached the foot of the steps, the queen yelled, "You're safe!" She rushed to the cage door where she and the king hugged through the bars. "Thank the gods you are returned to me."

The king stared her in the eye. "And you to me."

"I feared I would die here."

"What a strange place," Citu said, looking about. "How do we free her?"

"See those long things hanging beside the steps," the king said. "One of them will open the cage.

Get them. I have seen how the white man used them."

Citu handed over the metal things. The king tried several keys before the cage opened.

The king embraced and kissed his wife then Citu bowed and kissed her hand.

"Free the white man," the king said while I take the queen to the small canoe.

Chapter 32

Standing on the beach, the king scanned the eastern horizon. "We shouldn't stay here. We need to go deep into the jungle and find the priests guarding the princesses and the young prince."

"And what of Prince Hiayalael?" the queen asked.

The king cleared his throat as a tear rolled down his cheek. He pulled her into a hug as he wailed.

She pulled back, staring wide-eyed into his eyes. "Why are you crying?" Shaking her head and pounding his chest, she yelled, "No! Tell me he lives! Tell me!"

After mustering his courage, the king said, "He is with us no more."

The queen stiffened and pushed herself away. Lip quivering, she gripped his arm and shook her head. "No!" she yelled. "No!" She crumpled to the beach crying, "Noooo!"

The sobbing king pulled her upright and embraced her. Their tears bathed the back of the other.

Whispering in broken speech, the king said, "Foreigner's fire sticks struck the prince as we ran."

The queen's gaping mouth filled with silent horror as she dropped her head on the king's shoulder.

Hugging her, he said, "We had no time for ceremony. Someday, we will return and perform our rituals, but now, we must go."

Almost dragging the weeping queen, the king entered the bush and headed south.

"We'll hide in the jungle," the king said to Citu. "The enemy will seek other villages to plunder and will kill anyone blocking their way. We can't risk being found."

"How long will we hide?"

"Perhaps . . . forever."

The king had ordered a rest at a waterhole when Citu said, "Smoke! It fills the western sky. I fear the enemy burns The Center."

"No. It can't be," the king said. "Citu, climb a tree to look for the source of the smoke."

Xulu and Mukul helped Citu scale the tallest tree. One limb broke under his weight almost sending him to the ground, but he grabbed another. Shielding his eyes from the sun, he looked westward.

"I think it's the Temple of Chaac," Citu called down. "I see smoke, but I can't be certain of its source." Citu shimmied to a lower limb then jumped to the ground and dusted himself off. "Most Holy One, I fear your palace and those of the noblemen also burn."

The queen, heartbroken over her son's death, wept. The king hugged her. Summoning all the empathy he could muster, he kissed her forehead. "In time, we will rebuild our home, but now, I pray our people are safe in the jungle, for without them, we lose our identity."

"Most Holy One, should we continue south?" Citu asked.

"Yes. We must hide far south in the jungle. We

know how to find water, but the enemy doesn't. Let's hope they die of thirst or return to their floating house and leave our seas."

The king stopped often to let the fatigued and depressed queen rest while others searched for food. After three days, the group reached a greener part of the jungle that provided shade, fruit, and small animals to hunt.

Midmorning of the seventh day, Citu paused, raised his hand, and put a finger to his lips. "Shhh. I smell smoke."

"What do you think it is?" the king whispered, adjusting his doll bag over his shoulder.

"I don't know. Maybe some of our villagers cook, or . . . it could be the enemy."

The king turned to Xulu. "Scout ahead. See what burns but move with care."

Citu cleared a resting space for the anxious king who awaited Xulu's return.

When Xulu returned, he looked dejected.

"What did you find?" the king asked.

"Evil things. Evil—"

"What do you mean?"

"I found two priests from The Center, seven villagers and . . . the young prince and princesses."

"And . . . ?" the king asked, holding his breath.

Xulu wiped a tear. "My King . . . all are dead."

For a moment, the king stopped breathing. The air was too thick with sorrow to inhale. He collapsed into the arms of the queen and grieved as though dying. He gripped her wrists as she said, "I have to go!" She stared in his eyes. "I have to see my daughters. My precious daughters. My son."

"Forgive me, My Queen," Xulu said, blocking her way with his outstretched arm. "You don't want to go there."

The king hugged her. "There is nothing we can do," he said between sobs. "Remember them as they were."

"I can't leave them," the queen cried. "They can't be found by scavengers. They are my flesh—our blood." She tried pulling away. "I must care for them. They're my children."

"Neither of us can do as we wish," the king mumbled through tears. He hugged her, washing her breast-covering with a flood of tears.

The sobbing king asked, "Xulu, how did they die?"

"They had fire stick holes," Xulu said in halting words while wiping a tear.

"We must leave this place," Citu said. "The enemy may be nearby."

"I agree," the king said, "but in which direction do we to travel?"

Suddenly, there were sounds of fire sticks far to the west.

"Those sounds mean more dead villagers," the king said, dropping his head.

"Now we know where we can't go," Citu said. "The enemy is to our right."

Lost in thought, the king rubbed his tear-wet face then glanced at the queen. "We should continue south. Hopefully, some of our people survive there."

Burdened with sorrow, the king trudged south, followed by the weeping queen who stopped often to look back.

"Remember them as they were," the king said.

"They are with the gods."

Each day started and ended with the king fearing he would encounter the enemy at any time. The smallest sound sent him into a state of heightened, and mentally exhausting, alertness. He had trouble sleeping and neared emotional collapse. Even though he had meat, he ate it raw for fear smoke might attract the enemy.

In the past, the king drank a shaman's brew, made from the Calea Zacatechichi plant. It's use was a normal part of a religious ritual in which he communed with the gods, but of late, he drank the brew for mental escape. As his sense of helplessness grew, he shared the brew with the queen to ease her anxiety. Its effects were long periods of sleep followed by drowsiness. While the drug may have reduced his anxiety, his long sleep created a problem for the men responsible for his safety.

Having finished a hot and humid day of hacking through dense underbrush, the king came upon an unusual waterhole. Its broad river flowed at ground level for a hundred paces then disappeared underground. Drinking animals had created an area of hard-packed earth near water's edge on which nothing grew. The king, like an animal, lay on his belly and drank the water. He then settled down for a short nap but he and the others unintentionally slept the night.

Citu stirred then sat up. He cocked his head, cupped his ear, and listened for what had awakened him. Hearing the sounds again, he shook the king's shoulder.

"Huh? What?" the king asked, sitting up and

rubbing his eyes.

"Shhh," Citu said, placing a finger over his lips.

"What is it?"

"I'm not sure, Most Holy One. There are rattling sounds in the west."

The king cupped his ear and listened. "I hear it. The sounds of foreigners' skin coverings."

"The underbrush is too dense for us to run," Citu said. "Running would alert them." Citu scratched his head then ran his fingers through his debris laden pony tail. "We have to hide in this waterhole. It's our only hope."

"What are you talking about?" the king asked, shaking his head.

Citu pointed to the edge of the riverbank. "That overhang was undercut by moving water. We can hide in the water—under the overhang."

Citu awakened the others and instructed them to hide their belongings away from the waterhole. The king covered his doll bag with leaves behind a small rock forty paces away.

With everything hidden, Citu, the king, queen, and villagers eased into the cool greenish blue water and bobbed near the overhang.

"We'll stay here until the foreigners are closer," Citu said, listening for the approaching silver-skins. "When they're closer, we'll hide under the overhang but don't make waves that would give us away."

As the foreigners drew closer, Citu took a deep breath then led his group under the ledge. They held onto roots of plants growing overhead and held their heads backwards, forcing their lips against the wet underside of the ledge. There, they sucked a breath from air trapped under the overhang. They repeated the act over and over. Moments later, Citu saw moving shadows on the surface of the water and heard foreign words. The foreigners knelt on the ledge and took handfuls of water. Their disturbance of the water created bubbles that augmented the air under the ledge.

Citu pulled the queen to his side, so she could share his larger air pocket.

The enemy had their fill of water then sat down near the edge of the river.

Citu wondered if they would ever leave. For him, time stopped.

The water burned his eyes, so he kept them closed as he moved from air pocket to air pocket. The queen bumped into him several times in rapid succession. He then bumped into someone else.

An eternity later, the sound of footsteps suggested the foreigners were leaving. Citu opened his eyes and saw nothing of the enemy. He swam to the edge of the overhang and quietly broke the surface. The enemy had left. He cleared his ears of water then listened for the enemy. Hearing nothing, he swam back under the ledge then tugged on the first arm he felt.

First, Xulu surfaced followed by Mukul and then the king.

Citu assisted the king onto the ground where he panted and coughed.

Citu dived beneath the ledge to extract the queen. He found and tugged on her hand, pulling her toward the edge of the overhang.

Citu and the queen surfaced.

Horrified, Citu noted the queen's blue-grey face and yelled, "She drowned!"

The king jumped into the water and swam to her side. "No!" he yelled, arching backwards and striking the water with his fists. "No. No." He hugged her limp body and shook her face. "She can't be dead. Nooo. She has given herself to save us."

"Get her on the bank," Citu said.

The king fell backwards and pulled the queen on top of himself. For a moment, both sank.

Rushing to their aid, Citu pulled both to the surface.

"We have to get her out of the water."

The weeping king nodded.

Citu pushed the queen to the river's edge where Xulu and Mukel pulled her from the water. The king swam to the spot where she lay. Wailing, he stumbled out of the water and knelt beside her. Rocking back and forth, he rubbed and kissed her blue hand.

"My King," Citu said, rubbing the king's back. "I share your sorrow, but we must be quiet. The silver-skins may hear us."

The king pulled the queen's head onto his lap. He tried to muffle his grief while his tears fell on the queen's face. He rubbed them away as sobs stole his breath, leaving him gasping. Staring at the sky, he cried in a loud whisper, "Why have the gods struck my family with such devastation? Why them and not me? Why? Why?"

Citu took Xulu and Mukel aside. "We must find a place to bury the queen. We can't risk returning her body to Dzibilchaltun, and we can't let the king take her."

Chapter 33

For three full-moon cycles, weariness and sadness filled Citu's days and nights. He had no place to go no task to complete except eat, sleep, serve the king, and avoid the enemy.

"Most Holy One," he said, "we roasted a deer and want to share it. It has been days since you ate."

"Thank you, Citu, but I have no appetite."

"You must eat, Most Holy One. You starve."

"Perhaps . . . I'll eat tomorrow."

Citu watched the king reach into his doll bag and remove several pinches of dried herbs used to make shaman's brew.

"Citu, boil some water. Will you?" the king asked. "I wish to visit the gods."

"As you wish, Most Holy One, but you know the brew steals your appetite."

"Don't worry. The gods protect me."

To prevent the wooden brew cup from burning, Citu soaked it in water while he gathered dry leaves and small twigs to make a fire.

After several attempts, his flint ignited the dry leaves. He then added twigs and wood. After filling the wet cup with water, he held it over the flame. As steam rose from the cup, the king dropped in a pinch of herbs then stared at the ground.

After a short time, Citu said, "My King, your drink is ready."

"Thank you," the king said dryly. "It must cool."

Citu, Xulu, and Mukul sat fifteen paces from the king and ate meat for the first time in six days.

"I'm worried for our king," Citu whispered to his friends.

"The king is strong," Mukul said. "Don't worry."

Citu watched the king drink his brew and then lay on the ground.

"We'll be here the rest of the day," Citu said. "Might as well rest while the king visits the gods. We'll move on tomorrow."

Citu awoke first. He rubbed his eyes and looked around. Slowly, the sun god spread his beneficence over the group. Fortunately, nothing had bothered the deer carcass stored high in a tree. Citu cut meat for breakfast then awakened the villagers.

"Do you want some deer?" Citu asked his friends.

"Yes," Xulu said, "and cut a piece for the king. Perhaps he'll eat today."

Suddenly, Citu heard strange sounds. "Silverskins," he said. "Let's go."

Citu shook the king's shoulder. "Get up."

The king stood, looking confused. "What? Where are we?"

"In danger, My King. We must leave—now!"

"Xulu. Mukul," Citu whispered. "Help the king. I'll cover our ashes and get the carcass. Get his doll bag, and collect our weapons."

Xulu and Mukul pulled the king's arms around their necks and left the campsite, almost dragging the king.

Citu followed. "Faster," he said. "We have to get away from here."

"We need to separate," the king mumbled. "Each goes in a different direction. Where is my club?"

"Most Holy One, we can't separate," Citu said. "Not now. You can't defend yourself. I'll stay with you while Mukul and Xulu spread out."

Citu placed his head under the king's right arm and told Mukul and Xulu to leave. Citu half-dragged the king eastward.

"We can't leave you two alone," Mukul said to Citu. "Not now."

"I agree," Xulu said.

The king forced his head upright. "Do as Citu ordered."

"My King, we ask permission to help defend you," Mukul said.

"Did you not hear Citu's order—my order?" The king spoke with a tinge of perturbance.

"Yes, Most Holy One," the men said, bowing and backing away. Leaving in opposite directions, Mukul and Xulu said, "Gods' luck."

"Gods be with you," Citu said.

The king stumbled forward. After he had traveled three hundred paces, he said, "Stop." He pushed Citu's arm from around his waist and stared him in the eye. "You need to go your way as well. We can't be caught together."

"My King, Don't ask me to leave you. I will defend you unto death."

"Citu, who knows how many of our people still live? It is my duty to see that a Mayan male survives to continue our culture. I've prayed to be able to return to a vibrant Dzibilchaltun and fulfill that dream, but the gods may deny my wish. The one to realize that goal may be you, Mukul, or Xulu—men who are young, fit, and able to defend our people . . . if any survive."

Citu dropped his head but said nothing.

The king extended his hand. "Give me my club. If you love your king, do as I ask. Travel east. I'll go south."

"But, Most Holy One—"

"Do my bidding and take my doll."

Citu handed the king a club.

The king pulled the strap of his doll bag from over his head then held it toward Citu.

"Travel east," the king said. "See to it that my spirit doll returns home if I don't. It and my spirit must rest with the other dolls so they may, together, watch over our people."

With the sound of rattling armor getting closer, Citu bowed to the king then ran east, pausing for a moment to watch the king stumble south. *Gods spare our king.*

Citu had traveled only a short distance when conscience gnawed at his pride for leaving the king. He backtracked toward the area where he had last seen the ruler. In the distance, he saw the king leaning against a tree. Two silver-skins approached him as he raised his club and yelled, "May I and the gods smite you."

Citu ran to aid the king but the silver-skins discharged their fire sticks. Citu stopped midstride. Through the smoke, he watched the king's club fall as he slumped to the ground. For a moment, Citu wanted to pummel the enemy, but he knew he could not save the king nor should he risk his life or the king's spirit doll. He retreated to dense undergrowth then broke leafy branches to create a hiding place.

Lying on his belly, Citu watched the silver-skins search the king for treasure. Finding none, they kicked him. Citu ached to attack the silver-skins but restrained himself. The enemy headed in his direction. Burdened by fear and sorrow, he checked his camouflage and held his breath as the foreigners passed ten paces away. He hid until the rattling sounds of the silver-skins' coverings had faded in the distance.

Fearing other silver-skins might be nearby, he cautiously emerged from his hiding place. His heart ached as he approached the king's body. A hole in his chest and one in his belly had left him covered in dried blood. Citu shook his head and sobbed as he closed the king's eyes.

Suddenly, Citu felt watched. Filled with fear, he turned. Mukul and Xulu stood nearby. "I thought you men would obey the king."

"We couldn't," Mukul said. "We heard the shots and knew we had to return."

Staring at the king, Citu said, "They put holes in his body then kicked him. Their sacrilege hurt me more than I could bear."

"What are we to do with his body?" Mukul asked.

"We must take him to Dzibilchaltun." Xulu said. "He so wanted to return."

"That would be a sacred act," Citu said, "but The Center is far away. Travel with his body would be too dangerous. We can't take him home." Citu stared at the sky as if looking for inspiration. "I'll do my best to keep my promise regarding his doll, but we must bury him here.

"Then we must waste no time," Mukul said.

Chapter 34

For the first time in many months, Citu, Xulu, and Makul stepped onto Dzibilchaltun's central plaza. The air was hot and still.

Citu scanned the area for signs of human activity. "It's deserted," he said. "Not even a weed grows here." His heart sank on seeing the burned temples and palaces.

The scavenged skeletons of villagers littered the plaza and palace terraces. Xulu tried to identify several of them by examining the simple necklaces they wore.

"We don't have time for that," Citu said. "I don't like those dark clouds to the north. I think God Hurakan is preparing a storm. We need to do our work then leave. This place is no longer our home."

Citu walked to the west side of the Temple of the Six Dolls. Halfway up its steps, he noted several stones with slightly different colors and chipped edges. He and Xulu pulled them aside revealing a walled up doorway.

"Watch for silver-skins," Citu said to Mukul who stood at the temple base with his bow at the ready.

"Remove your sandals," Citu said to Xulu. "This is a sacred place."

Citu removed part of the wall to open a hole large enough for the men to squirm through. The odor of mildew assaulted their noses as they coughed from stirred ancient dust.

"I'm not sure what we'll find in here," Citu said, "but be respectful. This is a place for priests. Since there aren't any, we do what we must. I pray the gods grant us their favor, for our mission is sacred and our intent pure."

Citu pushed the Most Holy One's doll bag through the opening then he and Xulu squeezed into the short hallway that led to an ancient, sacred room.

"I must stop for a moment," Citu said. "I need to let my eyes adjust to this dim light."

"Me too," Xulu said, rubbing his eyes.

"Ready to move on?" Citu asked.

"Ready."

Citu crept into a tall empty room that might hold twelve people. The room had an empty wall niche opposite the entrance. Below the niche were six faded brownish-red images of geometric figures.

"Wonder what those figures mean?" Xulu asked.

"I don't know," Citu said. "Hope they aren't a curse."

"So do I. This place makes me uncomfortable."

"I know what you mean, but we have a job to do."

Citu hand brushed dust from the center of the floor. "There's supposed to be a sacred well beneath this floor. If that's true, there has to be a moveable covering, and I'm guessing it's in the center."

Citu cleared dust toward his side of the room. Xulu did the same on his side.

Citu looked toward the hallway. "The sun sends us light. The gods are with us."

"I think I've found the cover," Xulu said.

Citu ran his fingers along the raised edge of a

floor stone. "Good," he said, brushing dust away. "Stand on your edge. Maybe your weight will raise mine."

After rocking and then pulling on the stone, it suddenly gave way, sending Citu and Xulu onto their backsides. Xulu stared at Citu with fear-filled eyes. "The gods are angry."

"No," Citu said, "that was not retribution. We simply fell."

Xulu remained where he fell, but Citu returned to the dislodged stone and noted its lighter colored underside. He moved it aside then stared at the subfloor.

"I see it," Citu said. "The well opening is circular."

"Be careful," Xulu said, rising on his knees.

"Hand me the stone," Citu said. "It can be used to reflect sunlight inside the well. It's not very deep."

"Do you see anything? Any water?"

"No water," Citu said, "but I think I see the leg of a doll and some cloth—maybe an old doll bag. Tilt the stone to reflect in more light."

"Maybe it's the sixth king's doll."

"You're probably right."

Reflected light flooded the interior of the well, revealing a sight, until now, seen only by high priests and kings. At the bottom of the well lay six clay dolls—one for each of the six past kings of the dynasty.

Citu shook his head. "We see what few men have seen. This well contains the spirit of each of The Center's six past holy ones. We should show them respect."

Bowing toward the well and touching his forehead to the floor, Citu chanted his acknowledgment of The Center's subjects in greeting a king. Reverently, Citu removed the Most Holy One's spirit doll from its bag. He laid the bag in the well then nestled the doll on top of it. The men, foreheads to the floor, repeated their acknowledgement of the kings' spiritual presence then replaced the well cover.

"Our king is home," Citu said, smiling. "He rests in the Temple of the *Seven* Dolls. My promise has been kept. May the gods bless our work."

"Come," Citu said, "our task is finished." He left the room then crawled through the opening he had created in the wall that had blocked the hallway.

"What did you find?" Mukul asked excitedly, climbing up the steps.

"Wondrous things," Citu said, brushing dust from his body. "Help us replace these stones so all is safe."

The men replaced the step stones then threw dust and debris on them to camouflage their recent removal.

"I'm glad we're finished," Mukul said, pointing to the north. "The sky grows darker."

Suddenly, a terrifying flash of lightning struck a nearby tree, splitting it to the ground. The ear splitting thunder rattled Citu's nerve.

"Have we angered the gods?" Xulu asked, fear filling his voice as he scanned the sky.

"I don't know," Citu replied, "but let's get more debris on these stones."

Just as he finished the work, the sky gods cried. For the first time in years, rain pelted Dzibilchaltun.

Citu turned his wet face to the sky and then his friends. "The Most Holy One is home, and the sky gods send their tears. We have served them well."

The three men walked toward the dry jungle. Citu said, "You are now free to live your life as you wish. I pray we never again encounter the silver-skins."

"I pray some of our villagers survive deep in the jungle," Xulu said. "If they do, we will need a leader, and I think the king chose you, Citu, when he entrusted you with his doll."

Citu smiled. "Thank you, but only time and the gods will reveal our future. While we as a people may disperse, we will never disappear."

The End

Frank Barham has published: *Saving the World One Dog at a Time; The Religious Right is Wrong – the Ethics of Religion; Why Republicans Are the Way They Are; Puppy Love; Men Who Loved,* and *The Milk Murders.*

www.ingramcontent.com/pod-product-compliance
Lightning Source LLC
LaVergne TN
LVHW051540070426
835507LV00021B/2346